THE RULE OF LAW IN CENTRAL EUROPE

The Rule of Law in Central Europe

The Reconstruction of Legality, Constitutionalism and Civil Society in the Post-Communist Countries

Edited by

JIŘÍ PŘIBÁŇ
Faculty of Law, Charles University, Prague
Cardiff Law School, University of Wales, Cardiff

JAMES YOUNG
Cardiff Law School, University of Wales, Cardiff

Routledge
Taylor & Francis Group

First published 1999 by Dartmouth and Ashgate Publishing

Reissued 2018 by Routledge
4 Park Square, Milton Park, Abingdon, Oxon OX14 4RN

and by Routledge
605 Third Avenue, New York, NY 10158

Routledge is an imprint of the Taylor & Francis Group, an informa business

A Library of Congress record exists under LC control number: 99022607

ISBN 13: 978-1-138-36425-7 (hbk)
ISBN 13: 978-0-429-43144-9 (ebk)

Contents

PART III: HUNGARY

PART IV: POLAND

PART V: RUSSIA

List of Contributors

Bill Bowring, School of Law, University of Essex

Agata Fijalkowski, T.M.C. Asser Institute, The Hague

Malgorzata Fuszara, Institute of Applied Sciences, University of Warsaw

Mark Gillis, Constitutional Court, Czech Republic

Dušan Hendrych, Faculty of Law, Charles University, Prague

Jacek Kurczewski, Chair of Sociology of Custom and Law, University of Warsaw

Miroslav Kusý, Department of Political Science, Comenius University, Bratislava

Istvan Pogany, School of Law, University of Warwick

Jiří Přibáň, Faculty of Law, Charles University, Prague and Cardiff Law School, University of Wales, Cardiff

Andras Sajo, Central European University, Budapest

Grażyna Skąpska, Jagiellonian University, Poland

Vladimír Sládeček, Faculty of Law, Charles University, Prague

Soňa Szomolányi, Department of Political Science, Comenius University, Bratislava, Slovakia

James Young, Cardiff Law School, University of Wales, Cardiff

1 Central Europe in Transition: An Introduction

JIŘÍ PŘIBÁŇ and JAMES YOUNG

"There's no way around it; the rule of law is back."[1]

Introduction

This collection of papers explores the constitutional transition in Central Europe since 1989. The period of transition following the dramatic collapse of communism has breathed new life into the idea of the rule of law and the closely related concepts of constitutionalism, pluralism and civil society in the Czech Republic, Hungary, Poland and Slovakia since 1989. These papers are part of that debate and included, as a revealing comparison, is chapter on the Russian Constitutional Court.

The Concept of Central Europe

The term "Central Europe" is used, rather than Eastern Europe to emphasise that the four countries of the former Soviet Block have a shared political and cultural history which both distinguishes them from the countries of Eastern Europe and unites them. The territory of Central Europe is identified mainly with the dual monarchy of the Habsburgs, but also sometimes with at least some of the German lands. The area of the monarchy was dominated by a German-speaking culture, but was ethnically diverse. The economic conditions and political status of the nations inhabiting the territory differed radically. Only Austrian-Germans and Hungarians realised their political ambitions and occupied positions of political power at the expense of other ethnic groups, mainly Slav nations within the region.

The use of the term Central Europe should not be turned into romantic nostalgia for a non-existent ideal past. The Habsburg monarchy was full of

1 V. Havel, *Summer Meditations*, New York, Vintage Books, 1993.

modern economic and industrial tensions and nationalist political tensions. Indeed Central Europe is typified by a diversity and plurality of national cultures and histories.[2] Central Europe is thus a concept born of this political history which also finds an aesthetic and cultural expression in the work of such artists and thinkers as Klimt and Kafka, Musil and Mahler, Hašek and von Hayek, Schiele and Szymanowski, Bruckner and Bartók, Freud. During the post-war communist domination of the region, the idea of Central Europe was submerged, at least politically, in the simple opposition of East and West.

1989 transformed this. There can be no doubt about the historical and political importance of the year in which the main political, geographical and strategic borders between the Soviet East and the liberal democratic west disappeared. The Soviet Union ceased to be the dominating military, economic, cultural and ideological power to the east. Some of the hopes for the dawn of a New World Order of co-operation and mutual trust espoused by politicians proved unrealistically optimistic. The talk of the end of history in an age of globalisation was premature and unrealistic. However, the destruction of the Soviet union revived the popularity of the term "Central Europe". From the political viewpoint of Western Europe, two clubs were formed out of those European states emerging from the dominance of the Soviet Union – those regarded as early candidates for membership of NATO and the European Union and those who, even if they aspired to membership, would not qualify in "the first wave". Those countries in the first wave were primarily defined by belonging to the historic territory of Central Europe. The demotion of Slovakia from this club may seem to gainsay this, but this is to a considerable extent a product of the Slovaks history within Central Europe.

We have preferred the term Central Europe to refer to the Czech and Slovak Republics, Hungary and Poland. "Central Europe" seems less cumbersome and in this context evidently refers to that part of the historic Central Europe which, with East Germany, had the distinctive characteristics of being satellites of, but not absorbed into, the Soviet Union. This is not to ignore the historical value of the concept of "East Central Europe". Over a longer span of European history there is evidently a strong argument for dividing up West Central and East Central Europe and this latter term has become common among historians to describe the

2 R.A. Kann, *A History of the Habsburg Empire, 1526-1918*, Berkeley, University of California Press, 1974.

land now comprising the Czech Republic, Slovakia, Hungary and Poland.[3] In the contemporary context Austria and East Germany have become assimilated in ordinary usage into the West, while these four states are seen as a distinct part of Europe, since while they may "look west" culturally and in more recent history, their distinctive history owes much to their borders with what is unequivocally the eastern part of Europe. In the second half of the twentieth century they share an emergence from satellite statehood since 1989, a transformation which in legal and constitutional terms is different from those of nations achieving statehood, or of East Germany being re-united with the Federal Republic within the Federal Republic's constitutional and legal framework.

Political Sovereignty and Nation States

One of the most obvious characteristics of post-1989 Central Europe is the renewal of the political independence and international sovereignty of each nation state. Nation states in Central Europe emerged relatively late in modern European history, after the collapse of the Austro-Hungarian Monarchy in 1918. The inter-war period was troubled and not straightforward and countries like Poland, Hungary or Austria were threatened by the politics of authoritarian nationalist, populist and autocratic regimes. The only exception was Czechoslovakia which, was nevertheless confronted with national conflicts between Czechs and Germans, and which also faced ever-increasing Slovak self-confidence and political demands for Slovakian autonomy. The achievement of political sovereignty by Czechs, Hungarians, Poles and Austrians, after 1918, was bound to usher in a complicated period, but was in any event all too brief. In spite of some shared history and common features, the concept of Central Europe does not have a single political and constitutional significance, since, between the two world wars, each of the countries developed in its own way with differing internal political dynamics. While they shared some common cultural features and history, there were some fundamental political differences between them.[4]

3 The historians use is obviously defensible, especially in a long historical perspective, see O. Halecki, *The Limits and Divisions of European History* London, Sheed & Ward, 1950, pp. 125-141 and P. Wandycz, *The Price of Freedom : A History of East Central Europe from the Middle Ages to the Present*, London, Routledge, 1992, chapter 1. See also K. Dawisha & B. Parrott (eds), *The Consolidation of Democracy in East-Central Europe*, Cambridge, Cambridge University Press, 1997 and I. Pogany, chapter 9, *infra*.

4 E.g. P. Crabitès, *Beneš: Statesman of Central Europe*, London, Routledge, 1935.

Before the second World War Czechoslovakia had a brief history as an independent state.[5] It was the only one to have been a western-style democracy with a liberal constitution from the end of the First World War until the German invasion. The Czechs and Slovaks were brought together as one State, if not one nation, in the dismemberment of the Austro-Hungarian Empire after the First World War. Forging a single state for the Czechs and the Slovaks was never without its opponents, especially among Slovaks. The democratic state of Czechoslovakia initially steered by the commanding presence of Tomáš Masaryk and then by Eduard Beneš existed effectively until the German invasion in 1938, as France and Britain washed their hands of their ally. During the War, Slovakia was set up as a puppet State of Germany, while the Czech Lands were under direct German occupation and rule. Following the War, the Government in exile returned under the presidency of Beneš with the one state of Czechoslovakia reunited under the pre-war constitution, until in 1948 the Communists seized power.

In Poland the history of democratic constitutional government was different again. Threatened from its rebirth by war with Soviet Russia, the democratic constitution established in 1921 was overthrown by General Piłsudski in 1926. In Poland too nationalism brought its tensions, making the position of non-Polish minorities uncomfortable. Under the "Sanajca Regime" independence and nationalism expressed through the consolidation of an independent Polish state had priority over democracy and the strict adherence to principles of legality. Piłsudski's death did not lead to the restoration of democracy and the Second Republic was strangled by Nazi invasion in 1939. The brief restoration of the 1921 Constitution after the second World War soon gave way to communist rule and subordination to Moscow.[6]

Hungary was of course a different case since under the dual monarchy its nationhood had been recognised. Whereas the inter-war period was a period of opportunity for the new states of Czechoslovakia and Poland, for Hungary, as for Austria, it was a period in which the nation found its international status diminished. Moreover, its nationality problem was as much that of the many Hungarians left living outside its borders after the peace settlement as it was non-Hungarians living within the new boundaries. For a brief period, a repressive soviet regime was established. This was violently overthrown in 1919 and in 1920 Horthy became regent,

5 The constitutional history is traced by Hendrych in chapter 2, *infra*.

6 N. Davies, *God's Playground: a History of Poland*. Oxford, Clarendon Press, 1981, vol. 2, chapter 3.

remaining head of state for twenty four years. From a constitutional viewpoint this period left little legacy for re-building after 1989. Participation in politics was confined to a small property-owning elite and the government was authoritarian. During the Second World War successive governments tried to coexist with all sides in the conflict. However, as war progressed Hungary became more closely associated with Germany and towards the end of the war Jews in Hungary were persecuted and murdered.[7]

After the war, instead of Central European diversity and plurality, Stalinist Russia set up and controlled the region, usually then referred to as Eastern Europe. Together with countries like the German Democratic Republic, Czechoslovakia, Hungary and Poland, it included the Balkan states (with the exception of Yugoslavia, Greece and later Albania) and the Baltic states occupied by the Soviet Union from the beginning of the Second World War. The concept of Eastern Europe was a political concept, deriving its meaning purely from the fact of Soviet occupation and the domination of communist ideology in the region from 1945 to 1989. Soon after Stalin's death in 1953, it became evident that the countries under Soviet domination, and especially those in Central Europe, aspired to autonomous policies.[8]

Post-1989 Constitutional Reconstruction

With the collapse of the communist regimes, new-born democracies and political elites in Central Europe had to formulate new political goals. The political ideals and principles of western liberal regimes have been adopted and, in spite of some political traditionalism and nationalist conservatism supported by some political parties in each country, have become a part of everyday political life in Hungary, Poland and the Czech Republic. In Slovakia these political goals have yet to be achieved in the political struggle. Even traditionalist and nationalist politicians have, with the exception of some extremists, emphasised their interest in reconstructing the rule of law, the principles of a civil society and the protection of human rights. The main political goals to be achieved by the process of transition can be summarised as follows: the rule of law (*Rechtsstaat*) and

7 J. K. Hoensch, *A Modern History of Hungary*, London, Longman, 1988, chapter 3. See I. Pogany, chapter 9 *infra*.

8 F.A. Fejto, *A History of the People's Democracies: Eastern Europe since Stalin,* New York, Penguin Books, 1974.

constitutionalism, human rights protection, market economy reforms, integration with NATO and the EU, and the principles of civil society and individual autonomy

Very soon after the re-establishment of national sovereignty the political rhetoric in Central Europe included the need for integration with European Union structures. All the countries of the region looked for the constitutional and legal expression of their intentions to be tied to and bound by existing European and international institutions.[9] From what has been said, it seems important to point to this double process of the renewal of national sovereignty and independence going hand-in-hand with integration into the EU and NATO.

One of the main political tasks in Poland, Czechoslovakia and Hungary was the adoption of new constitutions expressing and codifying liberal and democratic values. This struggle for new constitutions must be understood in the context of the symbolic value of constitutions and their cultural and integrative functions. Constitutions codify the system of authority in society and help to give it legal legitimacy, but they also "construct" communities.[10] This collection of essays points to the symbolic importance of the new constitutional order and the values enshrined within them: the rule of law, entrenched protection for human rights, the underlying idea of constitutionalism.

One of the most striking legal facts in post-1989 legal and constitutional development was, however, the continuing existence of socialist constitutions. New legislators only abolished provisions constituting the system of one party rule and the communist regime, and supplementing old texts with new democratic and liberal provisions.[11] New Czech and Slovak Constitutions replacing the amended communist constitutions were drafted much more rapidly than in other countries, coming into force when the separation took effect in 1993. The situation in Slovakia was singular in these terms, because the split of Czechoslovakia and the establishment of an independent Slovak state required the "construction" of new nation state - probably the last nation state to be created in the region. In Hungary the new constitution took, and still takes, the legal form of amendments to the 1949 Constitution rather than reviving the 1946 Constitution or creating a

9 See e.g. Czech Constitution, Art. 10, Hungarian Constitution, Art. 7, Polish Constitution, Arts. 9 & 87, Slovakian Constitution, Art. 11.

10 R. Cotterrell, "Some Aspects of the Communication of Constitutional Authority", in Nelken D (ed), *Law as Communication*, Aldershot, Dartmouth, 1996.

11 J. Kurczewski, *The Resurrection of Rights in Poland*, Oxford, Clarendon Press, 1993, I. Pogany *Human Rights in Eastern Europe*, Aldershot, Elgar, 1995.

new one. In Poland, the existing socialist constitution was retained amended. In addition an important constitutional law redefined the relations between legislature and executive and became commonly known as the "Little Constitution". In Poland after protracted parliamentary deliberations it was not until 1997 that a completely new Constitution was put to a popular vote.

Nationalism and Civil Society

The principles of a civil society must be understood as the necessary supplement and counterweight to the market economy and as a social, and possibly moral aspect, of the whole process of transformation.[12] Civil autonomy and individual and group independence of political power structures were formulated in order to "limit" the formerly omnipotent state power, in which all organised activities of citizens needed the State's seal of approval. This political vision also sees civic virtues and values as worthy ideals in the new political condition. It supports individual responsibility together with civil collective actions and aims to be a kind of alternative to nationalistic barbarism.

Many scholars think that the region's stability is threatened by new nationalisms emerging after 1989. In fact, this is a typical prejudice among social scientists and jurists, trying to distinguish the "savage" nationalism of the countries in transition in the East and "civil" patriotic virtue, characterising the western rule of law countries. In fact, nationalism did not make its appearance after 1989 and cannot be treated as a spectre suppressed by communists and reawakening after the collapse of the communist regimes. It was actually promulgated by the communists and communist societies were filled with traditional prejudices.[13]

We cannot escape from the question of who is to be sovereign in the state, whether it is to be "the people" understood as individual citizens, or the people understood as an ethnic collectively. The right of any nation to political self-determination is considered as something "natural", recognised in international law. In fact every modern European state combines civil and national principles, but culturally it is conceptualised as a national institution. This brings, however, great instability into the multi-

12 E. Gellner, *Conditions of Liberty: Civil Society and its Rivals*, London, Hamish Hamilton, 1994.

13 On the role of nationalism not only under Stalin but also in the Party struggle in each country during the Second World War, see F.Fejto, *op. cit*, n.8 *supra*.

national and multi-ethnic region of Central Europe and its political and international life. The symbolic importance of constitutions lies partly in how liberal principles are expressed in a state's constitution.

Every multi-national society produces a seeming paradox and incommensurability between majority and minority. The respect demanded of the majority for the rights and interests of minorities is limited by the demand for loyalty from those minority members as citizens of the state – a state which is primarily the state of majority, which may well actually define its national identity as against the nationality of the minority. There is also a distinction between the nationalism of rulers and those who are governed by them, that is, between the nation constituting the majority and the minority nationality which may have limited access to public life, political participation and public administration. Of central importance is that ethnic minorities are always subject to the jurisdiction, authority and power of a state legislative body constituted under free general elections in accordance with the majority-will principle. This leads to tensions – on one hand, integration, leading to loss of identity, on the other, isolation leading to marginalisation; secession involving potential conflict and bloodshed against loyalty to a state perceived as belonging to somebody else.[14]

Conclusion

All the chapters in this book are concerned with some aspect of the themes raised in this chapter in the context of a particular country. A number of the chapters are concerned with the process of constitution-making since 1989. Hendrych and Přibáň trace the origins of and the influences on constitution-making in the Czech Republic, while Kurczewski discusses this process in Poland. Skąpska places the task of constitution-making in the context of contemporary social theoretical debates to constitution-making in Poland.

If constitutions are symbolic, embodying aspirations and values, their concrete realisation is not straightforward. The realisation of the rule of law, whichever definition we take, is never perfect or complete. The communist legacy is one recurring motif. Gillis and Fijalkowski are concerned with the difficulty of ensuring that new constitutional forms of government are not subverted by office-holders who consciously or otherwise are committed to ways of thinking conditioned by a totalitarian

14 W. Kymlicka, *Multicultural Citizenship: A Liberal Theory of Minority Rights*, Oxford, Clarendon Press, 1995.

system in which the distribution of State power between different institutions operating as a check on each other was an anathema. Fuszara argues that communist–created myths about equality of the sexes inhibit progress. Pogany is also concerned with the damaging effect of political myths in the suggestion that there was a pre-communist rule of law state in Hungary, protecting human rights, or that 1989 has introduced the benefits of constitutionalism and the rule of law to ethnic minorities. In contrast, Přibáň and Kurczewski consider the legacy of the dissidents in the constitution-making after 1989 in the Czech Republic and Poland. In Slovakia, Kusý and Szomolányi consider the failure of this influence on post 1989 politics.

Some authors are concerned at the way in which the constitutions are being, or are not being, implemented. Hendrych expresses concern about the failure to implement parts of the Constitution. Fuszara, Kurczewski and Sládeček focus on the difficulty of creating institutions which give effective human rights protection and the problems of constitutional adjudication. Kusý and Szomolányi consider the evident breaches of the Constitution in Slovakia and the weakness of the Slovak Constitutional Court when faced with a Government which simply ignores its rulings. Sajo highlights the difficulties of transition from a communist economy to a market economy in the context of welfare reform in the context of constitutional adjudication in Hungary. This is an interesting variation on the familiar theme of the proper limitations of judicial adjudication and the place of social rights in a constitution. Bowring provides an interesting counterpoint from the Constitutional Court of the old imperial master, Russia.

A number of the authors seek to analyse the struggle to establish the principles of a civil society. This is an important theme in the papers of Kurczewski, Fuszara and Skąpska in Poland, while Kusý and Szomolányi seek to explain the special circumstances in Slovakia which has led to an authoritarian government, using nationalism and anti-minority rhetoric and action as a political tool. Pogany questions the extent to which ideas of constitutionalism and the rule of law have ever operated effectively in Hungary to protect ethnic minorities, a sensitive topic in all the countries of Central Europe.

These papers by social and political scientists and jurists provide stimulating insights into the Central European experience since 1989. They give some impression of the shared themes within the region, together with the uniqueness of the working out of those themes in each nation. The political and constitutional structures are still new, in some cases yet to be created, and in all cases young. We believe that these papers will be of value in understanding past and future events.

Postscript

Since the text of this volume was prepared for publication, there have been developments in all the countries in the region. The most significant of these merits a short postscript. Both chapters on Slovakia refer to the elections in September 1998 and their importance in determining the future of the rule of law in Slovakia. In the elections with 82.4% of the electorate casting their votes, the opposition coalition won a parliamentary majority. Significantly, they obtained a "constitutional majority", i.e. a majority sufficient to amend the Constitution and to pass constitutional laws. Fears that the defeated Prime Minister, Mečiar, might not accept the results have not materialised. The new four-party coalition government, including representatives of the Hungarian minority, have taken steps to restore constitutional regularity. The Constitution has been amended to allow the direct elections of the President, an office left vacant by constitutional deadlock since March 1998, with elections in May 1999. Policies discriminating against the Hungarian minority have been reversed and the Government has made conciliatory gestures towards gypsies. In foreign policy the Government is mending its fences with the Czech Republic and with the European Union, receiving encouraging responses from some European Governments and a cautious, but positive, response from the European Commission. If the coalition Government continues to hold together, the election results of September may prove to be highly significant to the construction of the rule of law in Slovakia and for the region.

PART I

THE CZECH REPUBLIC

2 Constitutionalism in the Czech Republic

DUŠAN HENDRYCH

Constitutionalism

Most of the constitutional changes which have taken place in Central European countries since 1989 were introduced with the idea that one of the most meaningful principles that must be introduced is the enshrining of the democratic law-based state. In addition, in view of past developments, this transformation process represented an entirely new experience for many states, having little or even no basis in the former governmental structure, pre-communist included. Naturally, this led to various euphoric assertions that it sufficed to designate in the constitution that the state is democratic and law-based and, by this, to succeed in achieving the desired changes in the totalitarian framework. At this juncture, it is instructive to recall the words of Karl Popper: "Everything can and must be tied to legislation, the main instrument for conscious changes in modern society. To draft and adopt a good law is an immensely difficult task calling for a high degree of responsibility. It is a far more difficult task, however, to bring into existence a law-based state".[1]

Developments in the post-communist states up to now have for the most part confirmed the truth of his words. A genuinely functioning law-based state, however defined, does not come into existence merely by declaring it to be so in the constitution, rather a whole host of further factors are involved, only some of which are of a purely juridical nature. Nonetheless, it is necessary to assert that the law-based state and the Rule of Law, are concepts that represent for a society and its government a standard that is achieved only by an unceasing struggle between the dominion of law and of might. It is not the purpose of this chapter to analyse the general characteristics of "constitutionalism", nor to study this phenomenon in a European, much less a world, context, but to deal solely with

1 K.R. Popper, *Die öffene Gesellschaft und ihre Feinde*, 7th German edition, Tübingen, 1992., Foreword.

constitutionalism in the Czech Republic, which, while a new state, is one with a rich and often conflict-filled tradition of statehood.

Nevertheless, I consider it necessary to make a few general comments on constitutionalism. I take the principle of constitutionalism to mean that the use of any sort of state power must be controlled by law. In general, it is typically expressed negatively as a system of government in which power is limited by law. It expresses the opposite of that form of government in which power is wielded arbitrarily or despotically or is otherwise exercised without restraint. Special significance is attached to liberal constitutionalism, which, on a theoretical level, is associated with Hobbes, Montesquieu, and Locke in particular, as well as with the birth and great longevity of the U.S. Constitution, with its emphasis on the sovereignty of the people, the rights of man, and the autonomy of human reason.[2] In view of the dissimilar historical foundation for the realisation of this idea in American and continental European life and its projection into constitutional principle, it is certainly reasonable to think that American conceptions of constitutionalism differ from the usual European conceptions.[3] This does not mean that the American concept of constitutionalism cannot be implanted into the European context, even though quite often indirectly through constitutional texts from the period of the French revolution, primarily concerning the separation of powers and the rights of man and citizens. But, as Jellinek aptly observed, France gave the world a Declaration ". . . which in the course of later revolutionary events and restorations remained more a wish than the law. Without American, it is possible that we would have a philosophy of freedom, but by no means legislation which would guarantee that freedom".[4] His words remain vibrant and thought-provoking on the significance of the American conception of constitutionalism for continental Europe.

2 D.P. Kommers and W. Thomson, "Fundamentals in the Liberal Constitutional Tradition", in J.J. Hesse and N. Johnson (eds), *Constitutional Policy and Change in Europe*, Oxford, Oxford University Press, 1995.

3 This point refers, in particular, to the fact that the wording of principles in the U.S. Constitution results first and foremost from its experience of relative self-government on the local level and from natural law thought on the sovereignty of the people and the people's right to self-determination and to separate from the mother country. These were also reasons given in the Declaration of Independence. In continental Europe, it was more a problem of binding already existing state power, or power in the process of forming, by law in force.

4 Jellinek G., *Allgemeine Staatslehre,* Berlin, O. Häring, 1905.

If the concept of the law-based state is generally conceived of in Europe today as meaning the democratic law-based state, this linking of terms is an expression of the idea that, while constitutionalism in the sense of the delimitation of political power through law can gain ground without liberalism (ancient Athens, German *Rechtsstaat* in the 19th Century), liberal democracy, in the sense in which I am using it, cannot gain ground without constitutionalism.[5] The democratic law-based state presupposes an active civil society[6] which fully respects the basic rights and freedoms of citizens. The concept of the democratic law-based state closely resembles the contemporary concept of constitutionalism, which is usually characterised precisely by the fact that it is only conceivable in a civil society founded on the primacy of the individual over the state and the equality of all citizens.[7] The existence of a democratic, law-based state is connected with the state's natural-law foundations. Such a state becomes the guarantor of the fundamental rights and basic freedoms, which are, as a rule, either enshrined in one section of the constitution or contained in a separate charter which constitutes a component of the constitutional order. As a consequence of this guarantee, the democratic, law-based state undertakes the responsibility of protecting minorities and that, in such a state, the sovereignty of the people cannot be asserted as an unbounded power, dictated solely by the will of the majority. One of the basic hallmarks of the democratic, law-based state, and a criteria for the evaluation of it as such, would, therefore, be the instruments it offers to guarantee the effective legal protection of equal rights and freedoms, including the protection of the interests of minorities.

The Czech Constitutional Tradition

With the political changes following 1989 and the drafting of a new Czechoslovak Constitution, there was much discussion of the return to constitutional traditions. Events demonstrated, however, that it was not easy for the Czech and Slovak representatives to find a common denominator. This difficulty was not due merely to differing views on the future organisation of the state, but also to the divergent historical

5 D.P. Kommers and W. Thomson, *loc. cit.*, n. 2 *supra*.
6 A. Broestl, *Právny štát*, Košice, 1995.
7 V. Klokočka, *Ústavní systémy evropských států*, Prague, 1995.

experiences of the Czech and Slovaks, the two main partners in the creation of the new constitutional framework. The Czechoslovak Republic was in existence for a total of 74 years, and for six of them (1939-45), its actual existence was cast into serious doubt. During that period, one major portion of it (Bohemia and Moravia) became a German protectorate and the other (Slovakia) became an independent state, albeit entirely dependent on Germany.

The Czechoslovak constitutional tradition was relatively short and filled with conflict. The conflicts resulted especially from the fact that the representatives of the various political forces, quite often motivated by divergent national interests, never managed to come to agreement on the basic issue of whether they would favour a state organised primarily on the basis of civil society, meaning a group of free and independent individuals endowed with certain rights, or on the basis of nationality, that is, in accordance with the citizens' membership in a particular nation, in the sense of an ethnic group. In particular, a portion of the Slovak representatives, and an even greater portion of those representing the large German minority, took up the banner of the latter position. During the communist era, following World War II, a divergent conception of the constitutional tradition arose according to which the idea that it was a unique constitutional tradition was rejected as a bourgeois notion that had been superseded.

On the basis of the foregoing, one is led to inquire what significance constitutionalism has for the Czech Republic, to what values does it declare allegiance, and what are the source of these values?

It can generally be stated that the Czech Republic declares allegiance to all the positive values represented by humanity and democracy and to the good traditions of its long-existing statehood. The Preamble to the Constitution of the Czech Republic expresses them in the following words:

> We, the citizens of the Czech Republic in Bohemia, in Moravia, and in Silesia, at the time of the restoration of an independent Czech state, faithful to all good traditions of the long-existing statehood of the lands of the Czech Crown, as well as of Czechoslovak statehood, resolved to build, safeguard, and develop the Czech Republic in the spirit of the sanctity of human dignity and liberty, as the homeland of free citizens enjoying equal rights, conscious of their duties towards others and their responsibility towards the community, as a free and democratic state founded on respect for human rights and on the principles of civic society, as a part of the family of democracies in Europe and around the world, resolved to guard and develop together the natural and cultural, material and spiritual wealth handed down to us, resolved to abide by all proven principles of a state governed by the rule of law, through our

> freely-elected representatives, do adopt this Constitution of the Czech Republic.

Nevertheless, it will prove instructive to recall in some detail the basic historical features of the modern era, in order to shed light on the influence they have had on the constitutional development of Czech society. In the years 1848 to 1867, constitutional developments in Austria were characterised by the adoption of a number of constitutions, mostly "octroi" constitutions, that is they were almost all proclaimed by decision of the Emperor without having been adopted by a legislative body. Their contents reflected the political situation of the moment.[8]

The Austro-Hungarian Compromise (Ausgleich), which was agreed upon in 1867, was of fundamental significance for modern constitutional developments in the whole of Central Europe. As a consequence of this Compromise between the Austrian and Hungarian parts of the monarchy, while the Czechs, Slovaks, Austrian Germans, Hungarians, Slovenians, Croatians, a portion of the Polish people, and the other nations continued to live in a common state, the state was organised on a federal basis. Hungary assumed the dominant position in one part of the monarchy (called Transleithania), and the Austrians retained their dominant position in the remaining part (called Cisleithania). The Kingdom of Bohemia, the March of Moravia, and the Duchy of Silesia (the territories of which approximately coincide with the current territory of the Czech Republic) fell within the Austrian sphere.

In order properly to understand constitutional developments after 1918, it must be remembered that the territory of the present Slovak Republic did not at that time form an independent autonomous or even administrative unit of any kind, rather it belonged to the unitary state of the Hungarian crown. The differences between the two parts of the monarchy can also be seen on the constitutional level and in the concept of law and the legal order. In contrast to the situation in the Hungarian Crown lands at that time, an ever stronger growth in democracy in public life was exhibited in Cisleithania, which in this half of the Monarchy appeared in the guise of relatively strong regional self-government, guaranteed regional constitutions, and judicial review of administration. In addition, it was during this period that the Czech nation gradually became emancipated and experienced, in a European context, its own national revival. On a

8 K. Malý et al., *Dějiny českého a československého práva*, Prague, 1997.

constitutional level, its revival was linked in part to the historical right to the restoration of the Czech state[9] and in part to the natural right to self-determination and to a separate existence as a state (at the beginning, however, not one separate from the Austrian state system). Support for liberal democracy, influenced by western European political thought, was quite strong at the time.

The most significant period for modern Czech constitutional tradition is the period from the birth of the Czechoslovak State in 1918. There are two overriding features of this period. First and of greater significance, Austrian and Hungarian law were received into the legal order of the newly formed state, and in the interest of maintaining legal certainty, this reception was effected on October 28th 1918, the first day of the new State's existence. This reception was effected by a statute which provided that "all provincial and imperial laws presently in force shall remain in force for the time being". Since Austria-Hungary did not have a unitary legal order, it was a dual legal order which was received: in the Czech lands, its own regional law and Austrian imperial law were received; in Slovakia and Ruthenia, the Hungarian Crown's legal order applied. Founded as it was on diverse legal cultures and cultural traditions, this legal dualism was only expunged with great difficulty, and this was not finally achieved until the Communist era, when an insensitive unification was effected in the context of the establishment of "socialist" law.

The second feature was the adoption of the first Czechoslovak Constitution in 1920, in place of the "provisional" constitution from November, 1918, which, in actual fact, merely played the role of a kind of framework act. While the Constitution of the Czechoslovak Republic was not a markedly creative conception (in contrast, for example, to the Austrian Constitution, the creative spirit and drafting of which is ascribed to Kelsen), it was, nonetheless, a democratic constitution of legal values which provided sufficient guarantees to human rights and freedoms, as well as to the state's democratic and legal regime. It was primarily inspired by the constitutions of the European democratic states of that period, the French Constitution in particular. Other models were carefully studied as well: the U.S. Constitution, the Swiss Constitution, and even the British Westminster model. While based on the traditional conception of the separation of state powers, the chosen system was of a parliamentary democratic republic, featuring a two-chamber parliament, a weak president,

9 The Czech State is commonly recognised to have been founded in the first half of the 9th Century.

and a cabinet responsible to the parliament. The constitutional provisions for the judicial system were especially highly praised for guaranteeing the independence of courts in relation to the legislative and executive powers.[10]

The period referred to as the Second Republic (1938-39), while admittedly quite brief, was witness to a number of significant events. Among them was the Munich Agreement, by the terms of which a portion of the territory of Bohemia and Moravia was annexed by Germany. As far as the other parts of the Republic were concerned, a separatist movement in Slovakia took full advantage of the political weakening of the Czechoslovak Republic brought on by the Munich Agreement to force the granting to it of wide-ranging autonomy.[11] Autonomy was also granted to Ruthenia. The continuing critical situation resulted in further assaults on the integrity of the 1920 Constitution: a constitutional act granted the President of the Republic the right to amend the Constitutional Charter by decree and granted the government extraordinary powers to issue regulations. From the perspective of constitutionality, this period can be characterised as one in which the constitution's original democratic and liberal principles, as well as the principle that state power is bound by law, were seriously eroded.

In my opinion, the events of this period marked the overthrow of constitutionalism. This unhappy situation persisted in our land, under various ideological pretexts, for the better part of the next 50 years. The opportunity to remedy this condition only became a realistic possibility after the events of 1989. In March, 1939 Czechoslovakia ceased to exist. Slovakia became an independent state, the Czech lands, bearing the title, "Protektorat Böhmen und Mähren", were incorporated into the German Reich and were for the most part directly occupied by the German army. Ruthenia and a part of Slovakia were annexed by Hungary. There are two points of interest from a constitutional perspective: the Slovak State and the Provisional State Order of the Czechoslovak Republic were conceived and declared abroad.

According to its constitutive documents, the Slovak state was founded on Christian, national, and estates principles. Only three political parties were permitted, on the nationality principle and not even on an equal basis. The Hlinka party, organised on the basis of the Führer principle, was

10 L. Adamovich, *Grundriss der tschechoslowakischen Staatsrechtes*, Vienna, Österr. Staatsdruckerei, 1929.

11 Constitutional Act No. 299/1938 Sb.z.a n.

granted the leading role; citizens were required to organise themselves in accordance with their status, etc. The similarities it bore to the prototype totalitarian, fascist state were obvious.

At this point in time, the Provisional State Order of the Czechoslovak Republic was promulgated abroad, and it explicitly declared its constitutional and legal continuity with the Czechoslovak Republic of 1918-38. This Provisional Order was declared by means of the Constitutional Decree of the President of the Republic of 15 October 1940, concerning the Provisional Exercise of Legislative Power.[12] This empowered the President of the Republic to exercise legislative power by decree for the duration of the period in which the legislative body constituted for that purpose by the 1920 Constitution was unable to exercise its legislative power. Despite the fact that, soon after the war in 1946, the Provisional National Assembly ratified this constitutional decree and declared it to be a constitutional act from its very inception, it was not unequivocally decided whether this constitutional decree, issued as it was in a state of constitutional urgency, was nothing more than a simple declaration of the ongoing validity of the legal order of the First Czechoslovak Republic or whether it was an act that constituted a new state order which received the legal order of the First Republic.[13] Later political developments suggest that the latter was more likely correct.

Following World War II, a restored Czechoslovakia, in contrast to other states coming within the Soviet Union's sphere of influence, briefly, from 1945-48, enjoyed a relatively high degree of democracy and constitutionalism. That period was also distinguished by the restoration of the legal order, consisting of two measures: a declaration of continuity with the legal order of pre-war Czechoslovakia, and the exclusion from the legal order of all legal enactments issued by bodies operating within the state territory during the era of non-freedom, 30 September 1938 - 4 May 1945. From the point of view of constitutionalism, this period was also characterised by the fact that constitutional decrees of the President of the Republic and other constitutional acts fundamentally modified the 1920 Constitution in a number of respects. A one-chamber Parliament was introduced in place of the two-chamber Parliament, Slovak autonomous

12 The assertion of constitutional and legal continuity, resting on the argument that Czechoslovakia never ceased to exist as a subject of international law, gradually became the basis upon which Czechoslovakia won international recognition.

13 J. Budník, *Prozatímní státní zřízení československé republiky*, (English summary) Prague, Československý Kompas, 1947.

bodies were established or confirmed (which marked a change in the state's original unitary conception), the number of political parties was restricted, and one of the basic constitutional demands made by the returning Moscow government in exile was granted when national committees were formed at the regional, county, and municipal level in place of the original dual-track system of public administration (central state and local autonomous).[14]

During the period from 1948 until 1989 the constitutional situation was effected by three relevant constitutional documents: the Constitution of 1948 (the May 9th Constitution), the Constitution of the Czechoslovak Socialist Republic of 1960, and Constitutional Act No. 143/1968 Sb., on the Czechoslovak Federation, which fundamentally amended and supplemented the 1960 Constitution. During this period in Czech history, constitutionality was resolutely suppressed in all its forms and aspects. A distinctive feature of the era was the contempt shown for rights and human freedoms, values respected and universally recognised in a whole host of international documents, as well as former Czechoslovak law. In addition, the principle of a unitary state was definitively rejected at this time, since the adoption of the Constitutional Act on the Czechoslovak Federation marked the start of a new constitutional tradition which continued until the dissolution of the common state in 1992. The nationality problem of the Slovaks was not, however, resolved in this way, it was merely shifted to another level. The Constitution of 1948, adopted shortly after the communist coup, still displayed some features of constitutionalism. Very soon thereafter, however, the communist regime ceased to respect it and the political processes going on at that time bear witness to the rejection of constitutionalism and legality in favour of the expedient adoption of law as an instrument of the class struggle.

In contrast, the Constitution of 1960 displayed a number of characteristics that are entirely incompatible with genuine constitutionalism. As with all "socialist" constitutions it had one fundamental defect: it was a proclamation that formally met the general requirements for a document traditionally designated as a constitution; it did not, however, constitute a complex of legal norms immediately in force and directly applicable. Thus, no criteria even existed for determining whether something was or was not constitutional, only "criteria" for socialist legality. This same constitution confirmed the leading role of the

14 D. Hendrych, "Transforming Czechoslovakian Public Administration: Survey of Reform Steps Taken", [1993] *Public Administration*, 71-2.

Communist Party in society and the state and Marxism-Leninism as the state's world view.[15] By these means, in actual fact it rejected the principle of constitutionalism at its very core. The federalisation of Czechoslovakia in 1968 was carried out primarily in accordance with the model of the Soviet nationalities policy. Even today it seems ironic that the introduction into the constitution of the equal rights of nations and the expression of the right to self-determination, including the right to break away from the state, was enacted into law at the cost of the suppression of human rights and fundamental freedoms. A federation created in this manner, together with blunt centralisation in political leadership and economic management (the leading role of the Communist Party!) was in blatant conflict with the notion of federalism as co-operation, the uniting and balancing of limited sovereignty of the member subjects, and their participation in the exercise of power by the common state. A socialist federation could never be a true federation, due to the simple fact that it lacks a pluralistic political system.

The changes in November, 1989 led to a whole host of measures on the constitutional level which were intended gradually to do away with the deformities in the constitutional documents then in force and, at the same time, to deal, in particular, with the separation of powers, human rights and basic freedoms, and their effective protection, especially judicial protection. The introduction of the new political and economic system required an extensive transformation of the legal order. Even the federal set-up of the state became an object of criticism, so that the drafting of a new Czechoslovak constitution became the acid test of Czechoslovakia's continued existence.

The causes which led, during the course of 1992, to the end of Czechoslovakia and to the birth of two independent successor states, the Czech Republic and the Slovak Republic, can be traced to a whole series of events. They had their origins in the period of the Czechoslovak Republic after 1918 when no resolution was found to the nationalities problem within the framework of the civil society anticipated in the constitution. The Slovak nation's right to self-determination was supported by the Constitutional Act on the Czechoslovak Federation, particularly the text prior to the amendment in 1970. Several proponents of Slovak independence even referred to the Slovak State that had existed during World War II, when the Slovak nation founded an independent state for the

15 Arts. 4 & 16.

very first time in its history. Naturally there were other causes as well, including economic and contemporary political factors.[16]

The Constitutional Solution to the Dissolution of the Czech and Slovak Federal Republic

The principal political agreement on the break-up of Czechoslovakia was concluded between the representatives of the strongest political parties in each of the Czech and Slovak Republics, the Civic Democratic Party and the Movement for a Democratic Slovakia. This agreement, as well as the secession measures adopted by the Slovak Parliament (National Council), represented the definitive decision on the fate of Czechoslovakia. All subsequent measures were aimed as much at making the separation peaceful, as well as politically and economically acceptable for both parties. It was also necessary to agree upon the continuing functions of all federal authorities, on the one hand, as guarantors of Czechoslovak statehood and, on the other hand, as authorities competent to effect the dissolution of the Czechoslovak state in a constitutional manner. The fact that these objectives were attained does not mean that it was an easy task.

As a constitutional matter, the dissolution of the Czechoslovak state on 31 December 1992 was effected by means of Constitutional Act No. 542/1992 Sb., on the Dissolution of the Czech and Slovak Federal Republic, adopted on 25 November 1992 after complex and repeated negotiations, reconciliation procedures, and voting by the Federal Assembly. A full analysis of the significance of this Act is beyond the scope of this chapter. Nevertheless, its contents should be briefly outlined. First, the Act stated the date of the Federation's dissolution. Secondly, it declared that the successor states to the Czech and Slovak Federal Republic (CSFR) would be the Czech Republic and the Slovak Republic, to which would pass all powers previously exercised by the CSFR on the basis of constitutional and other acts. Thirdly, it provided that, on the date of dissolution of the CSFR, all bodies and authorities of the federation, all federal state organisations (profit making and non-profit-making), and the army and the federal armed security corps should be dissolved. Fourthly, it contained a problematic provision, which, in the end, neither successor

16 D. Hendrych, "Constitutionalism in Czechoslovakia", in J.J. Hesse and N. Johnson (eds), *op. cit.*, n. 2 *supra*.

state respected. Beginning on 1 January 1993, legislative power in both successor states was to be exercised by legislative bodies composed of deputies elected in the 1992 elections both to the federal representative bodies and to the representative bodies of the Republics. In this way, the Act was meant to bind the existing legislative bodies of both member Republics to respect the legitimate election of their colleagues in the Federal Assembly, by making room for them in the legislative bodies of the successor states. Further, the Act provided for the transfer of powers of federal judicial bodies to the judiciary of the successor states. Finally, the Act contained two significant provisions enabling a continuous transition to the new constitutional state of affairs. First, it established the power of both member states' parliaments to adopt, even prior to the actual dissolution of the CSFR, constitutional and other acts that would ensure the proper exercise of powers by each successor state from 1 January 1993 at the earliest. Secondly, it authorised the Czech Republic and the Slovak Republic to conclude, on their own behalf, treaties with third parties even before the dissolution of the CSFR, with the proviso that they would enter into force only after the dissolution.

The above-mentioned Constitutional Act is closely related to Constitutional Act No. 541/1992 Sb., on the Division of Property between the Member States and its Transfer to the Czech Republic and Slovak Republic. As a number of Deputies demanded that this problem be solved as a necessary precondition to the adoption of the Constitutional Act on the dissolution, it was put to a vote first. With its adoption the process of the constitutionally effected dissolution of the CSFR was finally brought to a close.[17]

The Constitutional Foundation of the Czech Republic

The Constitution of the Slovak Republic was adopted on 1 September 1992, and despite the fact that the CSFR was still in existence, it proclaimed the Slovak Republic as an independent, sovereign state and declared the supremacy of Slovak law over federal law in certain cases. After its adoption, there was no longer any doubt that it would be necessary to speed up the drafting of the Constitution of the Czech Republic, also making it an independent, sovereign state. Up to that time, on the Czech side all work on drafting the constitution was devoted primarily to the

17 *Ibid.*

expected new federal constitution and only secondarily to one for the Czech Republic, reflecting the fact that it would be a subordinate constitution for one of the CSFR member states. All experts' drafts of a Czech constitution, as well as draft constitutions proposed by Czech political parties, proceeded on this basic assumption.

Therefore there was insufficient time to prepare the Czech Constitution, a fact which undoubtedly influenced the drafting, and even the formulation itself. The possibility of attaining in Parliament the consensus required for the adoption of a constitution was certainly also a not insignificant consideration. For this reason, the Czech Constitution contained, in principle, only the fundamental and undisputed solutions, which were demanded by the situation at the time of the re-birth of the Czech State. In view of the need to gain consensus in the Parliament, the Constitution was not drafted as a single and comprehensive constitutional document. In this regard, Art. 112 of the Constitution defines the constitutional order in the following manner:

> The constitutional order of the Czech Republic is made up of this Constitution, the Charter of Fundamental Rights and Basic Freedoms, constitutional acts adopted pursuant to this Constitution, and those constitutional acts of the National Assembly of the Czechoslovak Republic, the Federal Assembly of the Czechoslovak Socialist Republic, and the Czech National Council defining the state borders of the Czech Republic, as well as constitutional acts of the Czech National Council adopted after the sixth of June 1992.

In the process of drafting of the Czech Constitution, it was agreed that the fundamental law of the Czech Republic would neither deal with the detailed consequences connected with the dissolution of the CSFR nor regulate related measures. That decision was correct in my view, even though it was not possible entirely to exclude the possibility of a constitutional settlement of the problems of the past directly in the constitutional order of the Czech Republic itself, and such an approach was presupposed and made possible by the above-cited Article 112 of the Constitution.

In relation to the Constitutional Act on the Dissolution of the CSFR, the Czech National Council's reaction thereto should be noted, in particular, the adoption of the Constitutional Act of the Czech National Council, No. 4/1993 Sb., on Measures Connected with the Dissolution of the Czech and Slovak Federal Republic. This Act is significant especially in that it maintained legal continuity with the legal order of the former CSFR and acknowledged the resulting international status of the Czech Republic as a successor to the CSFR's rights and obligation. At the same time, however, the Czech National Council called into question the federal constitutional act on the dissolution of the CSFR in respect of the future exercise of legislative power in the Czech Republic. From the position of a sovereign, the Czech National Council declared its position thereon in its resolution, No. 5/1993 Sb., to the effect that it is the legislative body with the exclusive right to modify constitutional conditions in the Czech Republic, thus, admitting of no doubt as to the continuity of its legislative power. This declaration naturally aroused numerous discussions, even among political representatives, concerning the Council's authority to take such a step. No conclusion was reached on the issue even though the two-chamber parliament offered a viable solution. Disputes arose concerning whether the Czech National Council was authorised to continue exercising legislative power in the renewed Czech State, or whether it should rather have been exercised by a new legislative body composed of both the duly-elected deputies of the Czech National Council and the duly-elected Czech deputies of both chambers of the dissolved Federal Assembly. The issue was never actually resolved and ceased to be relevant only after the Czech parliamentary elections in 1996.

The Constitution of the Czech Republic

In drafting the Czech Constitution, consideration was given not only to the progressive Czechoslovak constitutional tradition from the period of the First Republic (1918-38), but also to contemporary constitutionalism in both Europe and America as enshrined in modern constitutions which could serve as a model for the future Czech Constitution. While, due to this method of proceeding, the Constitution was not finally perfect, it certainly met the standards of modern constitutions. It has all the basic attributes of modern European constitutions, which have succeeded in coming to terms with mankind's long experience (of struggling) with political power, expanding in this very century into the monstrous dimensions of various forms of totalitarianism, of government not constrained by law, rather using law as an obliging instrument of power.[18] Therefore, during the

18 It also appears that, despite some criticisms, in the context of the constitutional development of Central and East European states, the Czech Constitution has been

drafting of the Czech Constitution much depended as well upon ensuring that the Constitution would be directly effective law, that it would not be a mere program or celebratory declaration, as was typically the case with the constitutions of states in the former communist bloc.

A highly significant characteristic of the Czech Constitution, in comparison with the Czechoslovak Constitution of 1920, consists in the fact that it is not neutral as to values. This conclusion may be inferred from a number of the Constitution's provisions as well as from provisions of the Charter of Fundamental Rights and Basic Freedoms. Its value orientation can be inferred from Article 9 of the Constitution concerning additions or amendments to the Constitution.[19] Also, the Constitutional Court's very first judgment, handed down on 21 December 1993,[20] is of fundamental significance for the continued development of our legal order, as well as for the interpretation and application of its law.

This judgment became a subject of debate among experts, and it appears that it has not been fully accepted even today. The view that the Czech Constitution is founded upon natural law principles predominates among

judged favourably abroad: P. Bohata, "Die Verfassung der Tschechischen Republik" (1994) XXXV *Jahrbuch für Ostrecht* ; Häfelin, U. (1996), "Zur verfassungsrechtlichen Entwicklung in den osteuropäischen Staaten", in *De la constitution, Études en l'honneur de Jean-Francois Aubert*, Bâle and Frankfurt am Main.

19 Article 9 provides:

(1) The Constitution may be amended or altered solely by constitutional laws.

(2) Any change of fundamental attributes of the democratic law-observing state is inadmissible.

(3) Legal norms cannot be interpreted as warranting the removal or threatening of the foundations of the democratic state.

20 "The Constitution of the Czech Republic is not founded on neutrality with regard to values, it is not simply a mere demarcation of institutions and processes, rather it incorporates into its text also certain governing ideas, expressing the fundamental, inviolable values of a democratic society. The Constitution accepts and respects the principle of legality as a part of the overall basic outline of a law-based state; positive law does not, however, bind it merely to formal legality, rather the interpretation and application of legal norms are subordinated to their content and substantive purpose, law is qualified by respect for the basic enacted values of a democratic society and also measures the application of legal norms by these values. This means that even while there is continuity of 'old laws' there is a discontinuity in values from the 'old regime'. This conception of the constitutional state rejects the formal-rational legitimacy of a regime and the formal law-based state. Whatever the laws of a state may be, in a state which is designated as democratic and which proclaims the principle of the sovereignty of the people, no regime other than a democratic regime may be considered legitimate." Collection of Judgments and Resolutions of the Constitutional Court, Vol. 1, No. 1.

Czech legal theoreticians. Interpretative practice, however, is still dominated by a positivist perspective and quite often burdened by a lack of appreciation for the fact that the Constitution is the foundation of the constitutional state, to which citizens and institutions may refer in specific disputes and on the basis of which demand protection of their basic rights and freedoms directly.

The variety of these positions is shown in full force when the issue concerns the binding nature of Constitutional Court judgments, which is the guardian of constitutionality not only in matters concerning the conformity with the Constitution of legal acts of a lower force, but also in regard to constitutional complaints by private individuals alleging the violation of their fundamental rights and basic freedoms. It is as if the arguments on this very issue divide lawyers in the Czech Republic between legal positivists and advocates of natural law (super-positivists). This is understandable since, in democratic states, constitutional court review and its effects are among the meaningful criteria for the credibility of constitutionalism itself and the creation of a law-based state.

To sum up the interpretations to date, we can say that the Czech Constitution fulfils in principle the requirements of modern constitutionalism and provides sufficient guarantees that the Czech Republic be a genuinely democratic, law-based state founded on respect for the rights and freedoms of man and of citizens, as Art. 1 of the Constitution declares. Some criticism must, however, be directed at the fact that, in certain respects, the Constitution of the Czech Republic has not as yet been implemented by legislation. In effect, this failure concerns two specific issues, the creation of territorial administration and the establishment of the Supreme Administrative Court. The first issue primarily involves the implementation of the self-government principle, not just in regard to municipalities, but also for larger territorial units (regions). The second issue concerns the crowning of the administrative law jurisdiction with its highest judicial forum, which in administrative matters is competent to take decisions and exercise judicial review over public administration.

Naturally, the road to satisfying all constitutional principles is one that is unduly difficult and long-term. The fact that the road to constitutionalism has never been simple or brief can be garnered from a reading of the history of every democratic state. I believe that this truth holds as well for the nations so burdened by various forms of totalitarianism as are the states of Central and Eastern Europe.

3 Legitimacy and Legality after the Velvet Revolution

JIŘÍ PŘIBÁŇ

Introductory Notes

This chapter does not pretend to answer all questions about the character, causes, consequences and possible outcomes of the 1989 revolutionary changes and later political developments in Czechoslovakia and the Czech Republic. It only seeks to show that these changes, usually referred to as the Velvet Revolution, had its own specific character and historically original nature, when compared with other modern revolutions, and that they raised some of the most important legal philosophical and general political issues, among them the relation between legality and legitimacy or legitimation.

Socialist Legality and its Legitimacy

The Velvet Revolution is usually understood as an event of discontinuity which destroyed the communist system and restored a liberal democratic political system. The events of 1989 November and the subsequent political development also, however, had their own continuity with the struggle of Czechoslovak dissident initiatives, foremost Charter 77, against the communist power in the late 70s and 80s. Dissidents and human rights activists always argued that the communist system was illegitimate and the platform of Charter 77 developed an original strategy involving different kinds of legal, philosophical and ethical arguments. Topics and issues of this "legitimation battle" between dissidents and the ruling communist ideology significantly influenced the whole constitutional, legal and political transformation of Czech society after 1989 and they still sometimes dominate current public life debates and disputes.

Hannah Arendt, one of the most outstanding critics and analysts of totalitarian regimes, suggests that they are to be conceived as the rule of instability and uncertainty, which enables the population to be controlled much more effectively by terror and violence. Both Nazi and Bolshevik political systems are characterized by the lack of legal, constitutional and political order and predictability. Distinctions between Party and State are blurred, legal institutions are overshadowed and dominated by Party decisions. Law becomes a facade of political voluntarism.[1] This characteristic also corresponds to Lenin's concept of a dictatorship, as a rule not requiring law, because law just blurres the violent nature of every govenment.[2]

Lenin's revolutionary concepts, when later confronted with the political reality and problems of the soviet system, had to be re-shaped or abandoned by the official ideology. The developing communist totalitarian state had to find its legal and constitutional representation, so as to build an image of stability and legality for the repressive party policy. New legal doctrines emerged which attempted to explain the nature of the new political system in legal terms. Vyshinsky's theory, in particular, backing Stalin's own unpredictable repressive policy, produced the concept of socialist legality.[3] The communist totalitarian system, such as that developed under Stalin during the 30s and surviving in the Soviet Union and other countries under its domination until his death in 1953, declared itself to have its own "higher degree" legality and to act constitutionally. Stalin even adopted the Soviet constitution in 1936, containing liberal principles, which would have meant decent social and political conditions, if ever enacted and obeyed. In fact, it was just a rhetorical veil for terror and arbitrariness. Isaac Deutscher described this Stalin's legislative attempt as a political tactic enabling him to execute opponents and innocent citizens under the mask of constitutionalism and liberal provisions.[4] In reality, no constitutional provisions, which as such incorporated the highest humanist ideals and principles of the enlightened free and democratic society, were obeyed by the ruling political elite, especially the secret police. Under this constitutional and legal surface, political crimes and atrocities going beyond the limits of human imagination were a part of everyday social life. Socialist legality became synonymous with sheer

1 H. Arendt. *The Origins of Totalitarianism*. New York, 1956, chapter XII/1.
2 V.I. Lenin. "The Proletariat Revolution and the Renegade Kautsky", in *Selected Works* VII, New York, 1936, p.123.
3 A.J. Vyshinskij, *Voprosy teorii gosudarstva i prava*, Moscow, 1949, chapter 3.
4 I. Deutscher, *Stalin: A Political Biography*, London, Penguin, 1949, p.381ff.

political terror, as practised by the totalitarian political power[5] and the role of communist constitutions was always more ideological than legal.[6]

The character of totalitarian communist regimes, however, underwent significant changes and the open political terror, common in the early 50s, disappeared after Stalin's death and the XXth Party Congress. As for the particular Czechoslovak political environment, it is important to realise that the repressions following the invasion of the Warsaw Pact armies in 1968, never had the character and intensity of repressions in the early 50s. Communist repressions affected hundreds of thousands of people and created new "second class" citizens, but the regime did not resort to mass imprisonments and executions.[7] It preferred to introduce a policy of "normalisation", which discriminated and persecuted mainly by mechanisms of social and economic sanctions.[8]

Reflecting political, cultural and social changes in Czechoslovakia in the 70s, Václav Havel and other dissidents started to speak about a "post-totalitarian" political system.[9] Havel did not mean by this term that the totalitarian nature of the communist system would disappear, but that it was, in a way fundamentally different from classical dictatorships, different from totalitarianism in its usual meaning. It was not founded on open political terror or violence, but on the ritualization of the public life and a kind of "blind automatism which drives the system".[10] The overwhelming majority of the population was not exposed to an open confrontation with the regime and only had regularly to express loyalty to the existing political system.

Another Czechoslovak dissident, Milan Šimečka, brilliantly described this state of the petrified inner stability of the communist regime as a special kind of social contract between the ruling Party elite and population

5 H.G. Skilling, *The Governments of the Communist East Europe,* New York, Crowell, 1966, p.172.

6 *Ibid.*, p.50ff.

7 A. Oxley et al., *Czechoslovakia*, London, Penguin, 1973.

8 For an analysis of political "normalisation" in Czechoslovakia during the 70s, see V. Kusin. From *Dubcek to Charter 77*, Edinburgh, Q Press, 1978, or J. Pelikan, *Socialist Opposition in Eastern Europe*, London, Allison & Beesby1976, p.25ff., 61ff.

9 V. Havel. "The Power of the Powerless", in J. Keane (ed). *The Power of the Powerless: Citizens against the State in Central-Eastern Europe*, London, Hutchinson Press, 1985, p.27.

10 *Ibid.*, p.30.

subjected to its government.[11] The population was provided with some guarantees of its material existence only and required not to interfere in political affairs. Furthermore, they were guaranteed a certain autonomy in the private sphere which was limited to material wealth. Lewis, for example, calls this unique political and social condition a "consumer-based conservatism".[12] The distinction between the political and the private may be formulated as a distinction between an official enthusiasm and private cynicism. Ritualized accomodation to the regime was to some extent compensated by an improvement in economic standards of living which, nevertheless, subsequently appeared to be only temporary.

Constitutional laws and the legal system represented a part of the political sphere characterized by manifestations of such official enthusiasm. Under the surface, the Communist Party continued to control the whole social body. Political terror did not vanish, but was limited and exercised only against a tiny minority of dissident groups and human rights activists. This "limited use of terror", limited in its intensity and social targets, nevertheless had a significant symbolic political function, because it required the population to approve the system ritually and, at the same time, reminded the population that all the instruments of political violence and open repression were still alert.

What was then the nature of the social and political role, goals and strategy of Czechoslovak dissidents? Trying to answer this question, the concept of socialist legality seems to have a crucial importance. Charter 77 and other dissident organizations tried to point out all the time that the whole nature of the regime, which claimed to be a socialist, legal and constitutional state, was in fact bluntly discriminatory, kept its repressive character, broke all international standards of human rights and civil freedoms, and therefore was illegitimate. The dissident struggle in 70s and 80s, I believe, was a struggle to show and witness the illegitimacy of the Czechoslovak communist post-totalitarian system.[13]

11 M. Šimečka, *Obnovení pořádku* (Order Restored). Brno, Atlantis, 1990. Quoted also in H.G. Skilling. *Charter 77 and Human Rights in Czechoslovakia*, London, Allen & Unwin, p.53.

12 P.G. Lewis, *Central Europe since 1945*, London, Longman, 1994, p.178f.

13 A Czech historian and journalist Jan Urban says, in the context of differences between 1968 and 1989 Czechoslovak political events, similarly that: "... while twenty years ago it was predominately a matter of a crisis of legitimacy within the governing Communist elite in one country of the Communist bloc, in 1989 it concerned a phenomenon of a greater degree. It was the Czechoslovak variant of the crisis of legitimacy of the whole Communist system. ...." See: J. Urban, "Czechoslovakia: the power and politics of

Charter 77 originated in an attempt by persecuted dissidents to support artists from the musical underground threatened by criminal proceedings and prosecuted for their artistic activity. The trial of the "Plastic People of the Universe" rock group musicians in autuum 1976 initiated a wider response from dissident circles and led to the Charter 77 document in January 1977. From the very beginning, the Charter 77 strategy was to operate within the discourse of legality and the need for respect for the law and to point out the "double-speak" nature of principles of socialist legality and the communist regime.[14] The drafters of the Charter 77 document appealed to the International Covenant on Civil and Political Rights, the International Covenant on Economic, Social and Cultural Rights and to the Helsinki Final Act.[15] It was argued that, as the Czechoslovak Socialist Republic signed these legal documents they were now incorporated into its legal and constitutional order.

Political science books usually define political domination by the Party as being backed by three coercive enforcement agencies - the secret police, the army and paramilitary organizations, the courts and prosecutors. It is typical of the post-totalitarian regime that it diminishes and blurs the role of paramilitary organizations and the army and transposes its coercion and force to the system of judicial power, which can serve as an illusion of general obedience to laws. Instead of the Party militia, it is courts and prosecutors who become the real "iron fist" of the Party. To show the discriminatory and repressive nature of the system therefore requires the unmasking of the machinery of justice and socialist legality and show its real political function. This legal approach of the Charter 77 movement appeared to be a very effective strategy, which clearly showed that the language of law meant absolutely nothing within the communist system of justice and that decisions of the judiciry were made outside judicial institutions.

The Charter 77 declaration was not a political programme, but a list of human rights and civil liberties violations by the communist regime. It emphasized the well-known fact that the political and legal actions of the regime were inconsistent with international human rights conventions. Although very mild and careful in its criticism and demands, the Charter 77

humiliation", in G. Prins (ed), *Spring in Winter: The 1989 Revolutions*, Manchester, Manchester University Press, 1990, p. 108.

14 See, for example, G.H. Skilling, *op. cit., supra*, n.11, p. 125.

15 *Ibid.*, pp. 209-212.

declaration caused a hysterical reaction from the regime and its media and the whole anti-Charter campaign recalled the state of ideological emergency, so typical of the Stalinist totalitarian system.

From a legal and political philosophical viewpoint, the Charter 77 movement and other dissident groups raised a fundamental question of the legitimation of the political system and its law. The issue of the nature of legality had to be addressed because the communist system had a paradoxical double structure - it was based on a widespread and arbitrary abuse of power, but also declared its acceptance of the principle of legality.[16] The dissident movements used this doublespeak of a declared respect of communists for the principle of legality because it was the most vulnerable part of the system. Because communist law was never only a set of regulations for human behaviour, but also played a symbolic ideological function, in order to disclose the nature of the system it was necessary to operate within legal discourse. Havel even called such a dissident approach "legalistic" and found its greatest value in the possibility of demonstrating the ideological nature of socialist legality, its inconsistency with the liberal rule of law and also the absurdity of the excuse that communist officials have all observed the law and therefore could not commit any crime.[17] The dilemma of Nazi and Stalinist political crimes was still present in the post-totalitarian political system. According to Havel, legality was so important for the system, because it established its legitimacy as a whole before its own citizens, before the international public and before history.[18] It established the illusion of legal justice. To show the paradoxical adherence to the legality rhetoric and its constant abuse by the communist power meant to show the illegitimacy of the communist system and its law.

On the surface of this "legitimation battlefield" between the communist regime and its dissidents, it may seem that the dissident strategy is really legal or even "legalistic". Looking more carefully at the whole issue, it is nevertheless possible to unveil a more fundamental strategy. Dissidents never demanded that the communist system of justice and administration should obey its law. The legitimation question was, in fact: "What content should the rule of law and legality have?" They argued that not everything that was commanded by the sovereign political power had automatically the character of law. From a more general point of view, this struggle puts in question Bentham's or Austin's definitions of law or the early Kelsenian

16 V. Havel, *op. cit. supra* n.9, p.69ff.
17 *Ibid.*, p.74.
18 *Ibid.*, p.75.

definition of the *Rechtsstaat* (the legal state/the rule of law) which states that every state, in fact, is the legal state because the category of state is subsumed into a more embracing category of law.[19] According to the dissidents, on the other hand, no legal procedures, nor any legal rules fitted within the principle of legality and the rule of law. So far as the principle of legality and the rule of law is concerned, legal rules and procedures must represent certain values, political principles and procedures supporting the division and separation of political power.

The legitimation strategy chosen by Czechoslovak dissidents in the late 70s and 80s was in fact deeply influenced and "infected" by existential ethical discourse, when talking about the universal character of human rights and their inviolability and independence of any political power structure. It has almost a symbolic value that one of the first Charter 77 spokesmen was a Czech philosopher, Jan Patočka, who always emphasized the ethical dimension of dissident opposition to communist power and who had such an enormous impact on Václav Havel, and other dissidents. Patočka, who collapsed and died after two days of police interrogation in March 1977, was influenced in his philosophical works, besides other philosophical schools, by the existentialist philosophy of Martin Heidegger. The intellectual background of the Czechoslovak dissident movement thus, among many other things, bears a unique witness to possible implications of Heidegger's philosophy, so often identified with conservative political thinking in western political and legal philosophy. Similarly like Heidegger, Patočka criticized the western concept of technique and was convinced that the communist state was an implication of the technical hopes in politics.[20] According to him, the concept of human rights is:

> ... nothing but the conviction that states and society as a whole also consider themselves to be subject to the sovereignty of moral sentiment, that they recognise something unqualified above them, something that is bindingly sacred and inviolable even for them, and that they intend to contribute to this end with the power by which they create and ensure legal norms ...[21]

Czechoslovakia was a country with a political dictatorship founded on a universal lie and ideological mystification and it was, therefore, a crucial

19 See, for example, H. Kelsen, *Der soziologische und der juristische Staatsbegriff*, Tübingen, J.C.B. Mohr, 1922.

20 J. Patočka, "What Charter 77 Is and What It Is Not", in G.H. Skilling *op. cit., supra* n.11, p.217ff.

21 *Ibid.*, p.218.

task to show its inconsistency with human nature. It is obvious that the legal legitimation strategy here goes beyond any legalistic discourse and is entrenched in the moral and existential vocabulary - vocabulary which does not perceive morality as some sphere of rules, prescriptions and governance, but as that sphere which opens a possibility to experience human authenticity and independence. This call for authenticity and independence is also contained, for example, in the dissident project of a "parallel polis", worked out by Václav Benda, suggesting the creation of parallel structures of intellectual, cultural and spiritual life, which would ignore the official structures of social life colonized by the communist party, its coercive power and aggresive ideology.[22]

This foundation of the legitimation discourse and strategy in morality is also typical of Havel, who, in spite of his comments on the importance of using a legalistic approach against the communist regime, talked of a "higher responsibility" and a decent "human order" that must stand behind any critique and civil action aimed againt the repressive power. Havel's famous concept of "living in truth"[23] is very close to Patočka's own philosophical and ethical perspective. The dissident movement thus can hardly be taken only as a legal struggle against a political power. It also has to be taken as an attempt better to understand humanity itself. Havel and others talked of an "existential revolution"[24] which would overcome the crisis of western technical civilization and rely on the independence of human life, citizens' initiatives and which would respect every human being in its uniqueness, individuality and free will.

The aspirations of the Czechoslovak dissident discourse were therefore much wider than just a critique of existing post-totalitarian communist practices, because one of its fundamental topics was the call for a fundamental existential shift. Although the concept of natural rights was not commonly used in the dissident literature and political texts in the late 70s and 80s, the ethical universalistic vocabulary, standing behind a legal critique of the communist power, included the same implications as the natural rights and natural law criticism of positive law and legality. I believe that, against the background of all that has already been mentioned here, it is possible to speak about a "weak version"of natural rights and natural law discourse within the Czechoslovak dissident movement and especially within the Charter 77 initiatives. Under the surface of a legal

22 *Ibid.*, p.183f.
23 V. Havel, *op. cit., supra* n.9, p.95.
24 *Ibid.*, p.90.

battlefield and legalistic language, it was possible to unveil the true reasons for the dissident struggle against communism growing from the ethical commitment to "the will to truth".[25] Pragmatically speaking, it would be hard to imagine someone who would risk so much of his/her life and comfort, so as only to prove that the communist law did not fit within the positive principles of formal legality.

The Will and Absence of the People in the Velvet Revolution, or "How much is the ferry to England?"

Although the 1989 revolutionary changes in Eastern Europe are often discussed as one big historical event, it is a plain fact that each country, in spite of many features common to all former Soviet bloc countries, had its own development and socio-political and legal dynamics. Changes in Hungary were dominated by political decisions of the communist party and political opposition groups were integrated into the whole process of political transformation.[26] In Poland, Solidarnosc and the Catholic Church represented a strong popular force and political opposition, which had to be respected by the communist system and which, in a better international constellation in the late 80s, could apply strong pressure for the transformation of the one party political regime.[27] Unlike these two countries, Czechoslovakia, the German Democratic Republic, Romania and other Soviet bloc countries remained inflexible and the ruling party elites were unwilling to make any political changes. Revolutionary changes in those countries were concentrated into shorter time intervals. The fall of the Berlin wall remains probably the biggest and most popular symbol of all 1989 changes in the European Soviet Bloc countries.[28]

Speaking from a socio-legal or legal philosophical perspective, the events of November 1989 in Czechoslovakia are hard to compare with any stereotypical images of modern revolutions. What was then the nature of this change, during which the communist regime, until then thought to be omnipotent, its coercive power and control ubiquitous, was overthrown and

25 This term was used by Jan Patočka, See, e.g., J. Keane, *op. cit., supra* n.9 , p.97.

26 G. Stokes, *The Walls Came Tumbling Down*, Oxford, Oxford University Press, 1993, p.78ff.

27 *Ibid.*, p.102ff.

28 See, for instance, the brilliant eye-witness account of the 1989 revolutions by Timothy Garton Ash, T. Garton Ash, *We The People*, London, Granta Books, 1990.

no shopwindow was broken? Was there something unique and original from the viewpoint of modern history? Why is it that some Czechs, instead of talking about the revolution, prefered to talk about "the coup of nice people against nasty people"?

I suppose that the most surprising feature, apart from the fact that the enormous force of people demonstrated in squares and streets of Czech and Slovak cities, towns, and villages was not accompanied by any violent acts, was an absence of "the People". This may seem a rather paradoxical or even false image of what actually happened. What else than the Will of the People can make a revolution in modern social and political conditions? The slogan "People, your power has returned to you", taken from seventeenth-century Czech scholar Comenius and quoted by T.G. Masaryk in his inaugural address as first President of Czechoslovakia in 1918 and used in a pop-song from 1968, became one of the most popular phrases during the Velvet Revolution and was adapted by Václav Havel for his New Year's address after he had been elected the President of Czechoslovakia in late December 1989. It is also no surprise that a historian and journalist Timothy Garton Ash named his book about the revolutions of 1989 "We The People".[29] He himself, however, shows a high sensitivity for the specific character of those events, when drawing historical parallels with other modern revolutions.[30] Who was the People, then, which made the 1989 revolutions possible? Was it the ultimate operator of human history, as sometimes understood by modern political philosophy, or did we witness some change of the meaning of this concept, when looking at all these revolutionary changes in 1989?

To illustrate this problem, I think it is useful to recall what people, marching through the Leipzig streets in October 1989, were chanting. They were chanting "Wir sind das Volk (We are the People)" and at the same time "Wir sind ein Volk (We are one people)".[31] This duality reflects, in my view, the whole nature of the 1989 revolutions. Obviously, these revolutions were an open political protest against the totalitarian communist regime which denied people any access to and participation in political life. People demanded free elections, the division of political powers, and civil rights protections – the well known institutional framework of western liberal democracies. People called for a reconstruction of the western model of liberal democracy, which was

29 *Op. cit.*, *supra* n.28.
30 *Ibid.*, p.131ff.
31 G. Stokes, *supra* n.26, p.140.

hidden behind the "Iron Curtain" and which, unlike the people's democracies of soviet models, seemed to work. In that sense, people were, of course, the People which asked for the liberal democratic and constitutional regime and therefore for the sovereignty through free elections and representation.[32]

How should one understand, however, the slogan "We are one people"? Its German formulation may be understood in terms of call for one united nation. This demand already exceeds any institutional framework, but should not be conceived only in its national or nationalistic meaning. Similar references to "people", instead of "The People"could be heard, for instance, in Budapest or Prague. Unlike a sovereign subject of history called "the People", people originally formulated their goals in a more existential and moral language and accused the communist regime of constant lies and propaganda. People refused to live any longer like "laboratory rabbits" for the project of real socialism and communism.[33] In this sense, people demanded something more than simply political reform. They demanded to be freed from totalitarian politics, they were fed up with ideological lies and communist politics with its various "-isms".[34] They wanted to live a decent life as people in their singularity, uniqueness and autonomy.

Talking about the absence of the People, this concept is understood in the sense of a historical agent that is united with one social and political vision which is to be brought into reality. People in the former Soviet bloc countries did not have to use as much political imagination as the French or the American People during their revolutions two hundred years ago, because what they were asking for in terms of a political institutional framework, was a model existing in western liberal democracies. Moreover, the events of 1989 in Czechoslovakia (but also in other former Soviet bloc countries) had a significantly pluralistic nature and their primary effort was to dismantle communist totalitarian systems. The common ideological denominator of this revolution was purely negative - to get rid of communist ideological lies.[35] Slogans chanted during the general strike or written on banners lacked any unifying ideology, complex

32 For the concept of a political sovereign, see, for instance, H. Heller, *Die Souverenität*, Berlin, Gruyter,1927.
33 See, for example, T.Garton Ash, *op. cit., supra* n.28, p. 50, 71ff.
34 See, for example, J. Urban, *loc. cit., supra* n.13, pp. 124-126.
35 T.Garton Ash, *op. cit., supra* n.28, p. 136ff.

political programme or propaganda. The ruling plurality and differences among political vocabularies and rhetoric were a characteristic of the Velvet Revolution. On streets and squares there was not the People, rather there were different people with their demands and ideals, people who had been united only by the repugnance felt for the communist regime. The only thing connecting people in November 1989 was a total disgust with the regime which provided them with a minimum welfare and economic security, but robbed them of important civil rights and liberties. They demanded the reconstruction of political democratic institutions, the very existence of which is entrenched in the concept of the sovereign people, but at the same time were rather cautious about using the term "the People", which was so heavily exploited by communist ideology and propaganda and which legitimated so many political crimes commited by the communist regime. In communist systems, the Party elite always spoke in the name of the People, but in fact permanently humiliated people's dignity. A good illustration of this revolutionary hostility are the names of the revolutionary organizations themselves. Instead of the cliché of the People, they used "Forum" which invokes an open public space with free access.[36]

In January 1990, there were about two hundred political parties and movements in Czechoslovakia which also illustrates how fascinated people were by the possibility of social and political plurality and how important the process of differentiation was at that time. Besides losing the communist party, there was one dominating political organization in each republic of the Czechoslovak federation - the Civic Forum in the Czech Republic and the Public Against Violence in Slovakia.[37] Nevertheless, the original structure of the Civic Forum - a revolutionary organization articulating political demands against the communist power, also corresponded to the People's absence. Dissidents with critical communists, intellectuals with workers, students with artists, catholics with atheists, neoliberal economists with defenders of "socialism with a human face" - all these people worked together and cooperated in the Civic Forum. Its organization was heavily decentralized and in fact anyone, anywhere (at factories, schools, administration, or army) could decide to form a local

36 In Hungary - *The Democratic Forum*, in GDR - *The New Forum, in the Czech lands - The Civic Forum*, in Slovakia - *The Public Against Violence.*

37 See, for example, M. Bankowicz, "Czechoslovakia - from Masaryk to Havel", in S. Berglund and J.A. Dellenbrandt, *The New Democracies in Eastern Europe*, Aldershot, Edward Elgar, 1991, p. 157ff.

unit of the Civic Forum together with other critical individuals. In the first weeks of the Velvet Revolution, this informal structure was a main characteristic of both revolutionary organizations (The Civic Forum and the Public Against Violence), because one of its primary tasks was to bring together all who were critical of the communist regime and who wanted to support revolutionary changes. The Prague Coordination Centre of the Civic Forum became a centre just because of its strategic position and due to the natural authority of former dissidents, striking university students and resolute artists who called for the general strike and opened theatres for public discussions.[38]

The important and unique role of the Civic Forum was to dismantle structures and institutions of communist power. Later on, the revolutionary force of the Civic Forum was transferred into a process of natural structuring and differentiation of the society. The Civic Forum had to be torn apart and disappear, so that its inner plurality of vocabularies and political differentiation could be transferred into a new-born world of democratic politics. This process of differentiation and adoption of "normal" political programmes and ideologies began to grow with the approach of the first free parliamentary elections in June 1990. These elections had undoubtedly a very strong impact on the subsequent process of generating political ideologies, propaganda and sophisticated programmes and strategies. The structure of the Civic Forum came under growing tensions, which were intensified by the local elections in the autumn of 1990. A year later, the whole revolutionary organization split and disappeared from political life in post-communist Czechoslovakia. As Gale Stokes states:

> In the place of the antipolitical leaders have come dozens of professional politicians of all stripes, many considerably less attractive than the historians, philosophers, and musicians that the velvet revolutions brought forth. ...[39]

The social revolutionary movements of the Civic Forum in Czechoslovakia, New Forum in German Democratic Republic, and Solidarnosc in Poland played an enormous role in the struggle against the communist system, but their structure indicates that they also had one very important general characteristic - they were anti-bureaucratic movements

38 T.Garton Ash, *op. cit., supra* n.28, p. 89ff.
39 P.G.Lewis, *op. cit., supra* n.12, p. 261ff.

opposed to bureaucratized power structures. They represented a different form of participation in political life - different from the communist one party model, but different also from traditional liberal democratic systems with their bureaucratized political parties. I believe that this is a consequence of their main function during their dissident activities and also during the revolutionary processes - to show that there is an alternative to seemingly omnipotent communist systems and to liberate the public from political repression and discrimination. In Czechoslovakia, the Civic Forum developed very quickly during the revolution, from a dissident nucleus, from which it adopted a lot of its ideas, principles and strategies, into a mass social and political movement. It is no surprise then, that the first leaders of the Civic Forum were famous dissidents and intellectual opponents of the communist regime.

All communist regimes in the Soviet bloc were always scared of a possible revolt of intellectuals and considered this social group to be a dangerous threat to its very existence. People like Kolakowski, Michnik, Lukacs, Konrad, Patočka or Havel, who could hold very different views, but always were independent and critical about official ideologies, had an enormously important "subversive role" and enjoyed natural authority and prestige amongst the public for their ethical and intellectual views. In Czechoslovakia, these dissident intellectuals and their ethical and political views also had a great influence on the character of the revolution in its first period.

The Velvet Revolution, more than a grand historical movement with a clear and complex vision of what was to come next and what was to be constructed and cut off from the coming brand era, was a succesful attempt to dismantle the regime which deprived people systematically of fundamental civil freedoms - freedom of expression, political choice, or freedom of opinion. The regime forbade them to practise the most important freedom which constitutes the main political, or rather existential, condition of any liberal and decent society, namely, in George Orwell's words in 1984, the freedom to say that "two plus two equal four" from which all other freedoms can be derived and follow.[40] This existential aspect and ethos accompanied generally the negative political will of Czech and Slovak people from the very first moment of the revolution.

The most crucial revolutionary demand and the first political or ethical goal was simply a renewal of the possibility of "living in truth". T.G. Ash

40 G.Orwell, *Nineteen-Eighty Four*, London, Penguin, 1990.

calls 1989 "the year of the truth".[41] Living in truth, originally Franz Kafka's expression, the ethical meaning and civil pathos of which was witnessed by all Czechoslovak and other Soviet bloc countries' dissidents, does not obviously mean living in the only ultimate objective Truth. This living means "only" a possibility for individuals to lay down horizons and limits of their own lives by themselves, to become autonomous beings with individual interests and goals. Living in truth involves the possibility of living within the heterogeneous space of many little "truths", together with them and in their neighbourhood - something severely prohibited and punished in totalitarian or post-totalitarian societies. The Velvet Revolution had exactly this strong pre-political, pre-constitutional, existential aspect of a dissident call for individual autonomy of human being, the possibility of its authenticity and intimacy

In this context, the Velvet Revolution was Havel's existential revolution in spite of all possible criticism that it failed because of the failure to achieve a political state without bureaucratic, instrumental and purely technical structures. Living in truth, formulated in negative terms, means a possibility of escape from the evil which destroys the intimacy of the individual, which constantly measures his/her actions and thoughts, which constantly exposes him/her to the light and judgements of the outside political and ideological world. The Velvet Revolution was a rebellion against such evil. It was guided by the desire for the possibility of authentic being, without any walls, and for the possibility of intimacy, which used to be systematically repressed by the communist regime. It was the event during which "... (H)istory has outdone Shelley, for poets were the acknowledged legislators of this world ...".[42]

This existential dimension of the Velvet Revolution is something deeply rooted in the ethical dissident discourse and in its criticisms of the principle of socialist legality. It is nicely illustrated by Ash mentioning his conversation with a taxi-driver from East Berlin who asked him in November 1989: "How much is the ferry to England?" - a question that would, a couple of weeks before, have been absurd and pointless, had re-achieved its common meaning.[43] This possibility of authenticity is something pre-political and pre-constitutional, because it does not rely exclusively on the political private/public distinction. It precedes all

41 T. Garton Ash, *op. cit., supra* n.28, p.131.
42 *Ibid.*, p.136.
43 *Ibid.*, p.63.

politics. As a political demand, it evolved from the critique of that neutralizing quasi-private world of post-totalitarian consumerism, which was guaranteed by the communist system under the condition of non-interference into the sphere of politics. The intimacy and authenticity of a human being ignore rules and judgements of any public auditorium. The common liberal private/public distinction in its political, constitutional and legal sense naturally had to be reconstructed in post-revolutionary Czechoslovakia, but already with respect to this existential call, involving the important freedom FROM the political. Duality of dissident strategy against the communist system and its law - duality of ethical and legalistic arguments, found its reflection in the 1989 revolutionary changes and the dynamics of political, constitutional and legal transformation which followed.

The Rule of Law and Call for Justice and Natural Rights as Revolutionary and Legitimation Demands

It is interesting to investigate traces of the legalistic/ethical duality of the dissident struggle against the communist system after 1989 revolutionary changes. Political and academic debates after 1989 were very much absorbed by the problem of the legitimacy/illegitimacy of the new/old political regime and by the legitimation strategy in the new social and political condition. They were confronted with a classical problem of modern political and legal philosophy - the relation between legitimacy and legality. How could the past communist system be criticized and condemned in legal or legalistic terms? It had its own constitution, legislation, laws and judiciary. Was it a legal state (*Rechtsstaat*)? If yes, does it mean that any tyranny is legal? If it was not a legal state, why has the new liberal democratic regime adopted a substantial part of its laws? Why did it suffice to abolish some constitutional provisions, talking about the leading role of the Communist Party, and have for nearly three years, until the split of Czechoslovak federation in December 1992, a Constitution passed by the communist Parliament? Why was this situation common to many former Soviet bloc countries?

Ambiguity and complicated relations between legitimacy and legality significantly influenced public debates about law and politics in Czech society after 1989 and still, nowdays, there are disputes about the character of the former communist regime - if it was legal, legitimate or illegitimate. The problem of legality and legitimacy is even ironically mentioned in one play given in the National Theatre in Prague.[44] Prevailing arguments, admitting the formal legality of the communist regime and denying its legitimacy, have been recently challenged by a seemingly bizzare opinion that the regime was legitimate, but definitely not legal. This opinion is grounded in the belief that legitimacy is just a private image of one's own good, while legality must correspond to certain general principles which the communist regime lacked.[45]

The theoretical and practical importance of the relationship between legitimacy and legality grows enormously at the moment of sudden political change and the reconstruction of legal systems. It is even tempting to say that, precisely against the background of these revolutionary changes in Czechoslovakia and, I believe, in many other former Soviet bloc countries after 1989, a revision and possibly new formulation of the whole question of the legitimacy of law and political domination can be achieved. I suppose that the dissident distinction between legal aspects and ethical aspects of the principle of socialist legality can help us in this enterprise.

It was an easily recognizable fact that, in spite of incorporating some constitutional and legal documents of the former regime into the new political and legal conditions, there was a substantial difference between the principle of socialist legality and the rule of law or legal state (*Rechtsstaat*) in their classical liberal and democratic meaning. Taking into an account the arbitrariness of socialist legality and the dissident critique of communist laws, it is hardly surprising that the rule of law became one of the most important revolutionary demands. The revolutionary vocabulary, besides its other features, was accompanied by a legal positivistic vocabulary demanding the re-establishment of legality, due process of law and generally binding impartial procedures. Legal positivism and a formal legalist approach had a strong critical force because qualities of law such as the regularity, foreseeability, security, iterability, or integrity - usually mentioned by legal positivists in their functionalist understanding of

44 It is the play *Strange Birds* (*Podivní ptáci*) by the distinguished Czech playwright and film director Antonín Máša, This play is one of first critical reflections of Czech post-revolutionary situation. See A. Máša, *Podivní ptáci*, Prague, ND Press, 1996.

45 V. Bělohradský, in: *Lidové noviny*, 6/9/95, "Byl komunismus legalní nebo legitimní?" (Was Communism Legal or Legitimate?) and a critical response by J. Přibáň, in: *Lidove noviny*, 17/10/95, "Krize legitimity a mýtus legalismu" (Legitimation Crisis and the Myth of Legalism).

systems of positive law,[46] became important values defending individual autonomy and security. These qualities provide efficient tools for criticizing a political regime which promotes to the judiciary according to momentary political circumstances and which legislates, not by parliamentary rules, but by the secret rules of the Central Committee of the Party.

The famous slogan of legal positivists "Justice according to law!" can really have a strong critical and reconstructive meaning when confronting the communist power which uses "quasi-natural law" arguments and schemes. The arbitrariness, the repressive and discriminatory nature of this power was often ideologically explained by reference to the principle of the historical role and law of the working class, which was to abolish economic exploitation and introduce the ultimate historical and social justice. The communist system was also backed by the principle of the subjection of the judicial power to the "objective" interests of the socialist regime, as formulated by the Communist Party, or rather its Central Committee and repressive forces of secret police.[47] As Otto Ulč writes about the system of justice, one of the key concepts was "classness", according to Viktor Knapp, who was a key figure in the communist jurisprudence, "a brilliant discovery of legal science".[48] Ulč describes his own experience and doubts about the concepts of socialist legality and condemns its arbitrariness:

> Nothing was more harmful to the pursuit of justice than the insistence on the implementation of the omnipresent enigma termed as "classness". ... in Marxist terms the concept of "blind justice" and "equality for all" is an idealistic delusion. Even after the successful proletarian revolution, the laws and the courts remain the instrument of the new ruling class designed to liquidate the political, economic, and ideological remnants of capitalism. ... We felt, rather, that the whole class-concept "discovery" was irrational, ambiguous and arbitrary. No one has ever been able - or willing- to define a class enemy. ...[49]

46 See, for example, N. MacCormick, *Legal Reasoning and Legal Theory*, Oxford, Clarendon Press, 1978.

47 For further information see, J. Pelikan, *The Czechoslovak Political Trials, 1950-54*, Stanford, Stanford University Press, 1971.

48 V. Knapp, "Predmet a system ceskoslovenskeho socialistickeho prava obcanskeho" (The Object and System of the Czechslovak Socialist Civil Law), Prague, NCSAV, 1959, p. 29. O. Ulč, *The Judge in a Communist State: A View From Within*, Ohio 1972, p. 31.

49 O. Ulč, *op. cit.*, pp. 30-31.

In contrast to this arbitrariness of socialist legality, supported by propaganda of the substantive natural, or rather quasi-natural, law and rights of a particular social class, represented by the political body of the Communist Party and its Central Committee, the liberal concept of human rights, civil freedoms and the democratic rule of law represents a strong political demand which was to be achieved through revolutionary action and subsequent social, constitutional and legal reconstruction.

Before moving to a discussion of constitutional and legal reconstruction after 1989, it is important to mention a striking fact - the persistence of constitutional and legal documents adopted by the communist legislation. This persistence, I believe, was possible only due to the already discussed attempts of communists to legitimate their political dominion by laws and create a political impression of the rule of law and legality. They adopted many rules and provisions, which, if applied and adjudicated according to the principle of even-handed justice, would lead to decent social and political conditions. These provisions, however, were typical "dead letter law" and contrasted with what may be called "socialist living law" - law of arbitrariness, instability and repression.[50] They show a characteristic of legal language and legality that the same words can have different meanings in different contexts.

An important attempt and constitutional goal of reconstituting liberal society which would protect human rights and civil freedoms came very soon after November 1989 and one of its patterns was, the European Convention on Human Rights, which played an important role in the whole effort of formulating liberal political and constitutional conditions. It clearly shows that a legal or legalistic approach and positivistic definitions of human rights and civil freedoms have a big advantage in current legal conditions - international legal documents which define and specify rules of human rights and civil freedoms protection. Of course, it may be argued that this part of international law is only contingent and that its attempt to provide a framework of human rights protection is only another attempt to define some legal foundations which, nevertheless, remain artificial, temporary, historical and therefore arbitrary. I do not want to discuss the problem of international human rights documents and covenants as a new *ius gentium*, but it is a fact that these documents facilitated the task of

50 This concept builds on the socio-legal distinction between "living law" and "law in books". See, for instance, R. Cotterrell, *The Sociology of Law: An Introduction*, London, Butterworths, 1992.

legislating new constitutional provisions of human rights and civil freedoms in Czechoslovakia.

Dissident appeals to international covenants on human rights could thus finally be legally recognized and international legal documents have been incorporated to the Czechoslovak constitutional and legal system. Article 10 of the Czech Constitution, adopted on 16 December 1992 and entered into force on the first of January 1993 with the split of the Czechoslovak Federal Republic, formulates a principle according to which:

> International treaties concerning human rights and fundamental freedoms, which have been ratified and promulgated and by which the Czech Republic is bound, are directly applicable and take precedence over an act of Parliament ...[51]

This principle, interpreted from the viewpoint of legal enforceability, means that international documents on human rights have the binding force of constitutional laws and all legal documents must convene to their provisions and regulations.

International human rights and civil freedoms documents became an integral part of the Czech constitutional and legal system. Another part of the Czech constitutional system, the Charter of Fundamental Rights and Freedoms (adopted by the Czechoslovak Federal Assembly in January 1991 and after the split of the Czechoslovak federation incorporated into the Czech constitutional system), is in its structure and content significantly influenced by the European Convention on Human Rights and by the United Nations Universal Declaration of Human Rights. Besides traditional human and political rights, it also recognizes a relatively wide range of economic, social and cultural rights.[52]

Together with the incorporation of international treaties concerning human rights and fundamental freedoms into the constitutional system of the Czech Republic, there was an urgent need to formulate the principle of the people's political sovereignty in a new legitimate way and differently from the communist constitutional system. The Constitution of the Czech Republic mentions the principle of the sovereignty of the people in Article 2:

51 *The Constitution of the Czech Republic*, art. 10, Prague, 1993, translated by M. Gillis and V. Cepl.

52 *The Charter of the Fundamental Rights and Freedoms*, Prague, 1993, translated by M. Gillis and V. Cepl.

> The people are the source of all state authority; they exercise it through the organs of legislative, executive and judicial power(article 2, section 1) ... State authority serves all citizens, and may be exercised only in cases, within the limits and in the manner provided for by the law(article 2, section 3)...[53]

These provisions have to be read carefully and interpreted within the context of the preamble to the Czech Constitution, beginning with these words: "... We, the citizens of the Czech Republic in Bohemia, in Moravia and in Silesia ...".[54] Here, the legislative purpose was to identify the people with the citizens of the republic - citizens with different political opinions, social traditions, history and cultural background. In the Czech lands, the principle of national sovereignty was strictly rejected during political debates preceding the adoption of the Constitution in December 1992 and, instead of it, the language of the Constitution supported a notion of pluralistic civil society. This principle of civil pluralistic society was not unfortunately echoed in Slovakia in the early 90s, where national and nationalistic interests began to play a more important political role and the principle of Slovak nation as a political sovereign was adopted in the constitution of new independent Slovakia.[55] The principle of a civil pluralistic society, substituting ethnic and national standards of political sovereignty, appears to have had an important symbolic role during the post-communist transformation and the reconstruction of political pluralism of civil society represents one of crucial political issues in other post-communist countries, too.[56] It is somehow artificial and unrealistic to make such a strong distinction between the principle of civil and national political sovereignty because it is a plain fact of modern European history that nations are political entities.[57] Nevertheless, ethical and revolutionary demands for the civic virtues of pluralism and diversity have found their formal legal expression in different provisions of the Czech Constitution and support a larger socio-political and cultural or ideological transformation of the country.

53 *Supra* n.51.

54 *Ibid.*

55 The Slovak Constitution uses the principle of the political sovereignty of Slovak nation in its preamble.

56 See, for example, J. Kurczewski, *The Resurrection of Rights in Poland*, Oxford, Clarendon Press, 1993, p.451.

57 See, for instance, V. Havel, *Summer Meditations*, New York, Vintage Books, 1993, chapter 2.

Apart from these legalistic achievements of the legal and constitutional reconstruction after 1989, it is also possible to trace another, from positive lawyers' perspective, a much more subversive and suspicious strategy - the strategy of the implementation of natural rights and ethical discourse into the language of the Constitution and the Charter of Fundamental Rights and Freedoms. The Charter explicitly mentions the inviolability of the "natural rights of man" in its preamble, which has the function of providing guidelines for the interpretation of the individual provisions of the Charter.[58] Interpretative difficulties and the rage of legal positivists are also caused by the oath of a judge of the Constitutional Court, contained in the article no.85 of the Czech Constitution, according to which a judge promises, besides adherence to constitutional acts, independence and impartiality, to protect "the inviolability of natural human rights and of the rights of citizens".[59]

These references to natural rights discourse and principles are, to a great extent, determined by the complex situation of political, constitutional and social transformation of Czech society in the beginning of the 90s. It was as if the incorporation of international legal documents, together with the new constitutional legislation, was not sufficient for the protection of human rights and civil freedoms and for the legitimation of the new liberal political system; as if the laws, though not being taken completely sceptically, were just a part of the legitimate legal and political order and therefore it was necessary to look for a more general and universal legitimation and interpretive strategy. This "infection"[60] of the post-communist Czech constitutional system by natural rights vocabulary, I believe, has a lot to do with the dissident ethical position, standing behind the legal or "legalistic" critique of the communist regime in the late 70s and 80s. For legal positivists and many public lawyers, this infection represents a dangerous and unwanted element because it can shake the whole logical and semantic structure of individual provisions of the Constitution and the Charter of Fundamental Rights and Freedoms. It is a sort of dirt in the analytically clean language of the law.

Looking carefully at the whole process of political and legal transformation of Czech society after 1989, it is, however, possible to

58 *Supra* n.52.

59 *Supra* n.51.

60 For the term "infection" and its role in a legitimation of law strategy see J. Přibáň, "Beyond Procedural Legitimation: Legality and Its Infictions", in (1997) 24 *Journal of Law and Society*, pp. 345-346.

realize that this natural rights vocabulary is not so rare or bizzare and that it is impossible to blame legislators for a "slip of the tongue". Together with a necessary positivistic legal strategy of post-communist constitutional and legal reconstruction, it is possible to see the development of extra-legal arguments, based on natural rights and principles of universal humanity. Extra-legal, mainly political and ethical arguments may be found in decisions of the Czech Constitutional Court.[61] Many acts of legislators were primarily inspired and initiated by the call for historical, social and natural justice. One explanation of this whole tendency could be that every revolution and complex reconstruction is done in the name of justice and natural universal rights, the Velvet Revolution not being an exception. Former dissident demands for human rights and ethical criticisms of the principle of socialist legality are therefore echoed in the system of the reconstructed positive law.

Positive legal procedures and rules obviously constitute an important condition of modern political liberal domination. They can fight back against communist ideology and its dangerous language of the natural ultimate law of one social class. The double legitimation strategy, which was dicovered in the dissident discourse and which later appeared in the new constitutional and legal documents of the Czech Republic, nevertheless indicates that these rules and procedures can hardly be the only source of a legitimate liberal political and legal system. There remains a question, if legitimate law and political domination are not, to the same extent, conditioned by some extra-legal arguments and vocabularies. In other words, can the formal concept of legality and legal procedures generate all the conditions of legitimacy themselves, or is they also dependent on some external environment which is different from the system and rule of positive law?

The political, legal and social transformation of Czech society during the last eight years clearly demonstrated that there are legitimation limits to the system of positive law, and that the principle of legality, though being the necessary and effective filter of momentary political interests, cannot fulfil many post-revolutionary demands of citizens and their call for the principle of historical or natural justice. In Czechoslovakia between 1989 and 1992 and later in the Czech Republic, many hopes of civil and moral rehabilitation, restitution of property, or punishment of the political crimes died in the bush of legal rules and procedures.

61 See especially the judgement of the Court n.14/1994Sb.

Legislators, however, also failed in their attempts to incorporate demands for moral rehabilitations and justice into the text of legal documents. This failure is evident, for instance, in the Act on the The Lawlessnes of the Communist Regime,[62] or in the highly controversial Act of Lustrations.[63] Any law explicitly invoking the idea of justice paradoxically produces new conflicts, naturally cannot establish justice in its complexity, and even, as in the case of the Act of Lustrations, can cause new injustices, though they seem minor, when compared with injustices organized by the communist system. The Act on Lustrations was originally intended and proposed as an effective defense of the new administration institutions against former high communist officials, which would be an understandable and, I believe, justifiable act of the new democratic power, similar to the process of denazification in Germany after 1945. In its final adopted version, this Act however affected a large number of citizens and its application was so extended by legislators as to become just an instrument used in the political struggle causing, moreover, harm to many people who did not represent the communist regime, but only participated in its persistence.

This and other examples of the new post-revolutionary legislation clearly show the limits of any system of positive law in relation to the demand for justice. Even the legislation intended primarily to bring justice can do harm and produce injustices. Law simply cannot directly speak the language of justice. The duality of natural and positive law discourses, typical of dissident criticisms of the communist power and also of the post-revolutionary situation, cannot obviously lead to any kind of synthesis and a "new" harmony between positive law and natural rights. They can only create new paradoxes and conflicts in relation to which it is possible to re-think concepts of liberal legislation, civil society and the rule of law.

Conclusion

The political and legal transformation of Czech society after the 1989 Velvet Revolution involves several interesting developments which have a close relation to common legal philosophical and sociological topics. I have suggested that the post-1989 political and legal reconstruction in Czechoslovakia and later in the Czech Republic could be understood only

62 The Act n.198/1993Sb.

63 The Act n. 451/1991Sb., further discussed by Gillis, *infra* ch. 4.

if some typical features of anti-totalitarian dissident strategies were taken into an account. International legal documents protecting human rights and civil liberties provided great support for the dissident "legalistic" strategy, the primary purpose of which was to unveil the real character of the communist system, its principle of socialist legality and its illegitimacy. Nevertheless, the dissident legal discourse had larger ambitions and, besides emphasizing the fundamental necessity of the rule of law and due process of law, it sought to demonstrate the immoral nature of the regime, built on ideological lies arbitrarily used to legitimate political repression and violence. Legalistic dissident discourse turned out to be efficient because it proved the immorality of the regime of "lies". It is, nevertheless, important to remember that all those legalistic accusations of the communist system were grounded in the ethical vocabulary and calls for different political and social values. Legal struggles used to function as a part of a more general legitimation strategy. Ethical foundations of dissident activities, indicating the language of natural rights and universal humanity values, integrated legalistic demands into their own structures.

Analyzing the dynamics of the Velvet Revolution, it is no surprise that this legitimation/illegitimation strategy - one of the central issues of Charter 77 and other dissident movements - has also become one of dominant political and academic topics in Czech society after 1989. Was the former communist regime, in spite of all dissident efforts to show its systematic disregard of the principles of legality, ultimately legal because the new liberal democratic regime has adopted some of its laws? Legislators, concerned about this situation and its possible political or social implications, came up with a rather interesting solution - legislating explicitly the values of universal humanity and principles of natural rights and incorporating them into Czech constitutional documents together with international human rights and fundamental freedoms treaties. The main task of the reconstruction of the rule of law, legality and constitutional system of divided and limited political powers was supplemented by ethical or natural rights vocabularies, which represent such a hostile discursive territory for any legal positivist. On the other hand, post-revolutionary attempts to legislate directly some calls for historical or natural justice created a very problematic legal and social situation and failed in achieving their goals. It became clear that justice can never be fully legislated and that law must operate according to its own rules and principles and is impossible to be substituted by the principle of justice.

It is possible to trace both modern legitimation strategies - legal positivist legitimation by legality and naturalist legitimation by universal values and natural rights - in post-communist Czech society and it has also been pointed out that this duality has its roots in dissident activities in Czechoslovakia in the 70s. After the Velvet Revolution, one of the first political tasks was to introduce the rule of general legal rules and procedures which would replace the rule of political arbitrariness and instability. Qualities of law such as predictability, stability or foreseeability, usually described by analytical jurists as value-free standards of governing human conduct, had an exceptional value for anyone subjected in the past to the rule of socialist legality. At the same time, however, the revolutionary development and its inner dynamics soon raised a question, whether everything that new legislators legislate for or declare as law is automatically legitimate. This question became even more urgent after some legislative failures.

The question of legal legitimacy can hardly be resolved by a withdrawal from a legalistic strategy and invocation of a larger political procedures of democratic elections and representation of a legislative body. Legitimation or legitimacy by vote is, of course, fundamental for any liberal democratic society and therefore all revolutionary organizations in the former communist Eastern Europe countries demanded free elections as the very first and crucial revolutionary goal. Free elections represent the most typical and symbolic procedure of a democratic system of political representation.[64] Procedures for free elections were therefore a vital way of manifesting popular support for revolutionary changes and legitimate outcomes of the revolution and the whole process of political transformation. This legitimation by vote, in spite of its fundamental role, however, appears to be insufficient, especially when the problems concerning who is the People are taken into consideration.

The modern concept of the sovereign political People was severely damaged by a communist political propaganda or ideology of "the People's democracies" and I have tried to illustrate the hostility of Czechs, Slovaks and Germans to the introduction of the term in its to connote the sovereign. "Forum" appeared to be a more suitable word than "the People". This informal and pluralistic character of the Velvet Revolution is reflected in the Constitution and in its provisions about the sovereignty of the people which have only a procedural character through free democratic elections

64 See, for example, P.S. Wandycz, *The Price of Freedom*, London, Routledge, 1992, p.265ff.

and vote by referendum. There are basically two ways in which the people can be understood today in Central Europe. The first way is the pluralistic and informal way promoting the individual autonomy and respect for differences among individuals or collectivities of any social or ethnic origin. The second is much more dangerous because it identifies the people and its governance of the state with a particular nation. I believe that the whole ethos of the Velvet Revolution and also of all other 1989 revolutions clearly favoured and pointed to the first way, although later developments in some countries of the region indicated a preference for national or nationalist rhetoric in political life and the importance of the notion of a political sovereign nation.

I suppose, therefore, that legitimation or legitimacy, as witnessed against the background of the 1989 revolutionary changes in Czechoslovakia, can hardly be understood as belonging exclusively to the legalistic strategy, or to the strategy of democratic procedures which would determine the legitimate character of legislation. It is always supplemented and "infected" by ethical demands of justice, humanity and natural rights. They are ambiguous and therefore dangerous because easily misused by political demagogues and tyrants. Communist ideologies, or more recent nationalist ideologies are just some of many examples. They are, however, also inseparable from any legitimation strategy, be it dissident, revolutionary, or liberal. Legitimacy by vote or by law does not itself, for example, formulate and protect principles of minority rights or civil disobedience. They come to the legal system from the outside world of civil society and the law legislates them because it is forced to do so by civil and political pressures. Legitimation is therefore at the same time within and outside the limits of law and legislation, as demonstrated by the "legalistic" dissident strategy of the Velvet Revolution. It is always about law because every modern political power governs by law, but at the same time it is about law's ethical background and implications. This supplementary character and dangerous nature of ethical discourse strategies in modern law and politics is something that still makes the problem of legitimacy and legitimation one of the most challenging and intriguing questions of legal or political philosophy, social theory and everyday political and social life.

4 Lustration and Decommunisation

MARK GILLIS

Lustration Laws

A lustration law (alternatively referred to as a screening or a vetting law) has been a quite common feature in the post-communist legislative reforms of countries from the former Soviet bloc. Such a law requires that persons holding positions of importance or influence in the state administration submit to a background check into their personal records to ascertain any association with or assistance of the totalitarian regime's abuses. In the case that such compromising data is located, the law mandates either public disclosure or removal from office. The basic goal of lustration laws is to remove from state administration people whose personal histories renders them unreliable or suspect so that they cannot be trusted within a democratic state to state functions. There have been, of course, many variations on lustration law; some have had of quite broad application, others apply merely to certain professions (such as teaching or law). Nonetheless, this description captures the essence of the purpose behind such laws, discovery of compromising information, and the basic mechanism by which that purpose is achieved, disqualification from office or public disclosure of the information.

The Czechoslovak lustration statute can be taken as an example. It contains two long lists of positions or activities. The first list enumerates the current offices which persons are permitted to hold or perform only in the case that they can show they do not qualify under one of the categories in the second list. The second list lays down the offices or activities which, if held or engaged in during the communist regime, should disqualify the person from working for the state in the capacities cited in the first list. In short, there are present protected positions and previous suspect positions or activities. Examples of protected positions include all those filled by "election, nomination, or appointment" in "bodies of state administration", the army, security service, and police force, the staff working in the offices of the President, government, Parliament, and Supreme and Constitutional Courts, state radio and television. The suspect positions and activities include communist party offices from the rank of district secretary upwards, various offices related to the security police, activities in relation to purges after the communist takeover in 1948 and during the "normalisation" after 1968, and informing for the secret police. The last category became quite controversial because of the very large number of those who informed and the fact that the records of these activities were considered suspect. The law mandates that those who fall into the suspect positions or activities are *automatically* excluded, or removed, from the protected position, in most cases without any right of hearing or appeal.

The Hungarian lustration law and one of the Bulgarian lustration laws can be cited as further examples. The Hungarian law was similarly broad in scope as the Czechoslovak; however, rather than mandating disqualification or removal from the protected office, it gives the person the option either of resigning voluntarily or facing public disclosure of the incriminating information. The Bulgarian law affected only very limited protected positions, for example in teaching and banking.

Of all the significant issues facing the nations of East and Central Europe, it is curious that so much attention has been focused on the issue of lustration, an amount far in disproportion to its actual theoretical interest and significance for the countries concerned. Much of the commentary suggests that lustration is viewed as somewhat of a test case of whether countries with formerly repressive regimes can succeed in adopting western, liberal models. As the assessments of it seem to be almost uniformly negative, it is safe to assume that the commentators entertain serious doubts as to whether these countries are passing the test. However, such a conclusion would be quite off the mark, since what has been written so far gives a fairly distorted picture of the situation in that it merely applies labels to the process without presenting convincing reasons as to why the labels are appropriate. To illustrate this tendency, I will refer to the analysis in several pieces that seem to me to typify the prevalent negative view. In particular, I will refer to two articles by Prof. Herman Schwartz,[1] a

1 H. Schwarz., "Lustration in Eastern Europe" (1994) 1 *Parker School Journal of East European Law*, 141, and H. Schwarz., "The Lustration Decisions of the New Central European Constitutional Courts", in A. Rzepliński (ed), *Constitutionalism & Human Rights Vol. 2* (Papers of the International Conference: Constitutional Courts in Central and Eastern European Countries in the Period of Transformation, Warsaw, 9-11 September 1994) Warsaw, 1995.

report written by Morton H. Sklar and Krasimir Kanev,[2] and the book by Tina Rosenberg.[3]

It is difficult to know to what one should attribute this tendency. After all, everyone, even the sternest critics of lustration, acknowledge that decommunisation or purging of the governmental apparatus is a necessary process. For example, Prof. Schwartz quotes Wolfgang Nowak to the effect that '"[T]o move forward from the past . . . society must remove those people from office who harmed it"' and himself goes on to comment that "[t]he need to face the past cannot be ignored. One way or another, that need will manifest itself."[4] Nonetheless, they strongly criticise the form it has taken without consideration of why it has happened that way, and they offer an alternative approach to dealing with the situation without really demonstrating that their proposed rules would be either viable or sensible.[5] In the end, one is left in doubt as to whether they are not simply opposed to lustration in any form but are failing to acknowledge that view.

To correct what I perceive has so far been unbalance debate on this issue, I will offer some basic points that as yet have been little considered and which argue in favour of lustration in general. These points will dispute the general condemnation that lustration is nothing more than revenge, the former oppressed now turning the tables on their former oppressors, an unjustifiable violation of basic human rights. I will argue that, in view of the unique historical circumstances and the overriding value of ensuring the transition to a secure democratic society, such a measure was more than justifiable. While focusing most specifically on Czechoslovakia and the Czech Republic, I will examine the nature of the transition which post-totalitarian countries needed to undergo, the motives for adopting a lustration law, and the alleged necessity to link it to human

2 M. Sklar and K. Kanev, *Decommunisation: A New Threat to Scientific and Academic Freedom in Central and Eastern Europe* (Report issued by the Science and Human Rights Program of the American Association for the Advancement of Science, September, 1995).

3 T. Rosenberg, *The Haunted Land: Facing Europe's Ghosts after Communism*, New York, Vintage, 1995.

4 See H. Schwarz "Lustration in Eastern Europe" *loc.cit,* at p. 161; see also, M. Sklar & K. Kanev *op. cit* at p. vii. "The goal of removing from positions of influence those public employees of a repressive regime who secured or maintained their jobs at the expense of the human rights of others is a necessary and desirable one."

5 For example, Schwarz presents a set of model rules, Rosenberg concludes that lustration, as well as political trials, are not an appropriate way to deal with the past, and all of them (including Sklar & Kanev) insist on any lustration determinations being made in individualised hearings accompanied by due process protections.

rights abuses. Lastly, I will examine in more depth the Czechoslovak lustration law and the Constitutional Court decision concerning it.

The Nature of the Transition

To begin with, many commentators fail to give sufficient and sensitive consideration to the actual nature of the historical context in which the lustration issue is playing out, a transition during which the post-totalitarian nations confront some very serious and complicated problems. They tend to assume that the toppling of the communist leadership in 1989 marked the decisive end of the past regime deal, and they deal with the issues associated with lustration in the abstract as if the context of the transition were not a very significant influence. This blind spot may account for the tendency to attribute solely sinister motives to lustration, such as bloodlust or the desire for revenge. Because of this, when lustration supporters in the former communist states and critics in Western Europe and the U.S. discuss lustration, they have in mind quite different things. They tend to talk past each other; westerners only pay attention to that information responding to what they want to hear but not to the objections that their views miss the point.

The most evident and overarching problem is that the transition was and is so immense a phenomenon that it is impossible to fathom it all and manage it. It involves the overhaul of the political and legal systems, the economy, social relations, professional standards, the society's values, the police and army, and so on. With everything in flux, there is no firm ground underfoot. What in established western countries is taken for granted as the foundation of the society, is in these countries shifting sands. All changes had to be undertaken at the same time and carried out by persons who have little or no experience in democratic institutions or in making decisions. In addition, these massive changes needed to be carried through with precipitous speed and thoroughness. What might be called the revolutionary "window of opportunity" only stays open for a relatively short time, before two counter tendencies kick in: the desire to go back to doing things as people were used to doing them, and the need to return to a sort of normalcy. I believe this has much to do with the return of former communists to power in many countries.

The Hungarian Constitutional Court, in its judgment on the Hungarian lustration law, acknowledged that the particular characteristics of a period of transition held special significance for the assessment of laws enacted during that period. It declared that, by the time the Hungarian Parliament had adopted the law in 1994, "the change of system not only occurred but in many respects came to pass, without the personnel changes incorporated by the lustration acts or similar changes actually having occurred". The Court went on to state, "[t]he Act must therefore be examined in view of present-day, normal legal conditions characteristic of a constitutional state. Owing to the passage of time, the legal peculiarities of the transition period can today hardly be validated within the framework of obligations presumed by a constitutional state ...". The Constitutional Court also made it clear that the unique historical situation accorded the legislature a measure of constitutional manoeuvrability not necessarily identical with its obligations under the provisions of the Constitution under consideration.[6] This passage strongly suggests by implication that the special circumstances involved in a period of transition could have been invoked earlier to justify more flexibility in assessing whether a particular measure conformed to constitutional principles.

Nonetheless, the commentators either ignore or downplay the problem the transition poses for the creation of the rule of law. They are working on the assumption that, in spite of the trauma and upheaval involved in the transition and which post-totalitarian societies are even now, in some respects, undergoing, they can and should respect, in their entirety and in all cases, the complete and sophisticated rules societies of the West developed and refined over many years while they for the most part enjoyed social peace and democratic maturity. However, in the transformation from a totalitarian to a democratic, law-based state such a proposal is simply impracticable and amounts to denial of the need for a transition. Dr. Istvan Pogany made the point succinctly in a recent essay that "constitution making, the formal act of drafting or revising a constitution, does not lead automatically to constitutional transformation".[7] Unfortunately, neither does the change of those in leadership positions. The rule of law is not something that can be introduced by flipping a switch. To make an analogy, if the ground is rock hard, arid soil in the desert, you cannot simply plant a tropical tree there and expect it to grow. Or you could say if there is fertile soil, but it has been salted, the crops you plant will fail. If the new governing system, or rule of law, is viewed as that delicate tree and those who must implement it are the soil, then we would

6 Decision No. 511/b/1994/27 or Decision 60/1994 (XII.24) AB, Section III(3)(c) of the judgment; see also S. Zifcak, "Hungary's Remarkable, Radical, Constitutional Court", 3 *Journal of Constitutional Law in Eastern and Central Europe* 1 at 8-9, 21.

7 I. Pogany, "Constitution Making or Constitutional Transformation in Post-Communist Societies?", (1996) 44 *Political Studies*, 568.

say that the rule of law cannot be achieved if the soil is bone dry or salted. The soil must first be properly repaired.

The key problem in achieving the rule of law is not, as the commentators would have it, to simply start applying the sophisticated rules that have been worked out over time, but to ensure that there is a solid foundation for such application. Rule of law is not merely a set of rules; in addition, it involves a certain institutional culture, an overall approach to the functioning of legal and governmental institutions, or as Pogany has put it 'the character and habitual mode of operation of a society's political and legal institutions".[8] The rule of law as an institutional concept would make little sense, and the application of the sophisticated rules that characterise a rule of law systems would be practically meaningless, unless we can feel some assurance of a commitment to those principles on the part of the state actors themselves, those who apply these rules. Such rules are not self-applying, so that the application of beautiful rules by those not suited therefor (by nature, temperament, training, life experience, or what have you) would make of the law-based state a charade. This means that there must be a process of decommunisation, a way to ensure that state officials have a certain indicia of reliability and commitment to the new regime and level of qualification, before we can make the assumption that the sophisticated rules of a law-based state would be properly applied. Thus, the creation of the institutional foundations of the law-based state is logically prior to being certain that the principles will be of effect. The specific principle of the law-based state that arises most often in the context of lustration, and which will be dealt with here, is due process.

Where such an institutional culture does not already exist or has no background, it has to be introduced. Many years are required to foster and develop it; but the proper conditions must exist for it and it must be carried out before the revolutionary window of opportunity closes. This is where the transformation runs up against a seemingly unresolvable paradox: only those in government can institute such changes, but, apart from personnel

8 I. Pogany, *op. cit.*, p. 568. In addition to the problem of adapting institutional structures and personnel to the rule of law, there is the additional problem of adapting substantive rules and principles of these societies' legal orders to the rule of law (and visa versa). This also constitutes an immense and complex problem that goes beyond the scope of this article. See, V. Cepl and M. Gillis, "Making Amends after Communism", (1996) 7 *Journal of Democracy* No. 4; W. Laczkowski, "Constitutional Courts in a Period of State System Transformation", in *Constitutional Court in Poland in a Period of State System Transformation*, published by the Polish Trybunal Konstytucyjny (Constitutional Tribunal), Warsaw, 1993.

changes at the very top of the government after 1989, the people that make up the state apparatus, on the whole, stayed the same, and among them were many who were not competent or eager to institute such changes. To put it in a simple and straightforward way: the state is not capable of lifting itself by its own bootstraps. So in order for the state to emerge from this stalemate and bring about the transformation of its approach to government, it was necessary to intervene into the state apparatus and clean it out. The situation in these countries could prove intractable unless some extraordinary measure like lustration is employed. Keeping this in mind, it should be noted that the lustration law in Czechoslovakia, for example, was adopted by a democratically elected Parliament (which lustrated itself before adopting the law) and introduces a process in which no individualised determinations are to be made so that it does not require or allow the exercise of discretion by administrative or judicial bodies. That is, it introduced a legislative model of lustration, a fact whose significance will be further clarified below.

While it is universally acknowledged that some cleansing of the governmental apparatus is necessary, the means that have been employed to accomplish that end have been criticised. However, little thought has been given to the issue of why, if the method is so contrary to decency and basic principles, it is employed in nearly all cases (even in an a country like Germany, that already has a properly established rule of law system)[9] or to whether alternative means would be at all effective. In addition, the critics do not seem to take into consideration a host of problems that would certainly be encountered in trying to comply with the requirement that due process standards be applied.

For example, the insistence that any person subject to lustration must be given the due process rights of a full hearing, including the procedural protections of a trial and the opportunity for appeal to a court, in the course of which it must be proven that he did something wrong or caused harm in

9 It is of interest that the German Constitutional Court recently overturned the termination of some state employees under the lustration act there. The Court overturned the terminations for some of the reasons cited by lustration critics: the need for individual determinations, and the need for assessing whether the person in question has changed his or her attitude, so that they no longer constitute a risk to the transition. It must be noted, however, that the Court rejected the complaint by Heinrich Fink on the grounds that he held such an important position (which seems to agree with the Czech approach). In any case, the German decisions do not undermine the reasoning of this essay, as the former East Germany presented an exceptional situation: since it was incorporated into a country with a fully developed "western" legal system, the main problems of the transition that necessitated the resort to a solution like lustration did not actually exist in Germany.

the past or likely would in the future (always in relation to human rights, see below). Even if one concedes this to be the case (and I do not), time constraints and limited resources alone would have made it nearly impossible to meet this requirement. The state would have had to hold hearings concerning tens of thousands of persons, to marshal all the evidence to prove these cases, and to offer judicial review afterwards.[10] For the transformation to succeed, time was of the essence, and the process had to begin and proceed as quickly as possible. In a sense then, the process of transformation would be held in abeyance pending the resolution of these hearings (since the persons in question must certainly remain in their position pending the outcome of the case), which could take up to several years. The end result could very well have been that the transformation would in a genuine sense have arrived stillborn. If analysed with the principles of American constitutional law in mind, it can quite justifiably be argued that this situation presents a compelling government interest in comparison with which citizens interests in obtaining or retaining certain key positions, or in having mini-trials to resolve the issue, is minor indeed.

Even if the problem of time pressure did not exist, it is hardly likely that such hearings would prove what actually occurred during the communist era. It is true that concrete evidence may be lacking to prove specific, serious wrongful acts. In fact, as the Czechoslovak Constitutional Court pointed out in its lustration case, evidence on specific instances is lacking precisely because the agents of the totalitarian government disposed of or hid the records prior to handing over power.[11] As the state is meant to investigate and root out wrongdoing, if it is the state that commits wrongful acts, those who committed the wrongs are in a position to ensure that the facts did not see the light of day. Yet again, this circumstance does not correspond to the ground rules of a normally functioning democracy (where the rule of law can be taken for granted). Still some commentators mentioned here would draw the conclusion that such cases cannot be

10 See T. Rosenberg., *loc. cit*, n. 3 *supra*, at p. 404: "Communist repression should not be judged in a court of law (indeed, could not be, as the sheer number of cases would overwhelm even the most sophisticated judicial system)." While the comment goes to the propriety of prosecuting the leaders of the former regime for policies, it nonetheless amply points out the problem involved in judicial determination concerning activities engaged in by a substantial portion of a society's population.

11 "The possibility of separately proving collaboration by individual clandestine collaborators and the extent of their collaboration was in essence deliberately thwarted by the orders and procedures of the directors of State Security bodies, that is, by the intentional discarding of almost 90% of the files." Author's translation of CSFR Constitutional Court decision on the Lustration Law.

pursued. They would say that if the state cannot muster enough evidence then the case probably is not good, and in any event, we must place this burden on the state to keep it honest.

This conclusion is seriously misguided in that it is based on the assumption of a normally functioning democracy; it fails to take into account that the state was entirely dysfunctional. To draw the facile conclusion that nothing can be done, so that it is necessary just to forget about it, is terribly simplistic and foolish. Such cases need to be pursued because it is critical to the proper functioning of the democratic state, and resort is made to the best available evidence, such as records of participation in secret police activities. Rather than force this situation into a false comparison with criminal law principles, I see a rather closer resemblance to the tort principle of *res ipsa loquitur*. We know that a wrong occurred and that the persons in question were in control of the instrumentality which brought about the wrong when it occurred, but we do not have more specific evidence to prove the actual event. Nonetheless, the law in this field does not throw its hands up and declare that nothing can be done.

In addition, if it is attempted to prove by use of state bodies that a great many persons holding positions in government are unreliable, we are stuck back in the bootstrap paradox. For example, the position of a judge is lustratable, which to a certain degree expresses the belief that many in that position, as of 1989, may not be trustworthy to carry out their duties. Yet, it is insisted that the courts should be the ultimate decision making bodies as to individual cases of lustration. While independent courts may be the guarantee of individual rights, truly independent courts are not achieved alone by the mere introduction of guaranteed tenure and salary. It is also necessary that, through the process of training and selecting judges, only those who we have some reason to believe are fair, objective, and committed to the protection of individual rights are selected. But, it is well known that the communist system *did not* value or seek out these characteristics, rather the opposite. Following the revolution the judiciary became a closed system, keeping in for life those of questionable qualifications, virtue and reliability.[12] So unless and until there are some grounds for believing that, just following the changes, the courts would be truly independent and would be eager to uphold the newly introduced

12 See N. Kritz, "The Dilemmas of Transitional Justice" in *Transitional Justice Vol. I* at xxv-xxvi: "In order to enhance the power and independence of the judiciary as part of the democratization process in post-communist Poland, a law was enacted establishing the irremovability of judges. One consequence, subsequently recognized, was that many tainted communist judges thereby became entrenched in the new court system."

governing principles,[13] it would have been absurd to rely on them to administer lustration properly.

In regard to the question of the suitability of the judiciary to perform decommunisation, it is appropriate to quote Justice Boštjan Zupančič of the Slovenian Constitutional Court.

> Due to the lack of democratic tradition in Central and Eastern Europe the legal mentality (legal culture) itself has failed to transcend the pandectistic fetish. ... I believe, however, that there has been an evolution from the mere cognitive attitude of the hypertrophied legal formalism as the lawyer's normal defense, namely the clinging to the semantic form as the empty shell of former agreement --, to the cynical attitude characteristic of the members of the whole legal profession in certain Central and East European countries today. I think it is only natural that at some point extreme legal formalism should evolve into a "*selective* legal formalism". This is no longer simply a "professional" *cognitive* approach. Legal formalism is then no longer naively "prescriptive". It becomes an "instrumental" means of *semantic manipulation* to achieve preconceived political results having nothing to do either with the letter or with the spirit of the law. The *cynical* habit of using law as a smoke-screen for politically palatable decisions is the natural next step for the morally disoriented members of the legal profession.
>
> Formalism can cynically be used as a language game into which extraneous hidden political agendas can readily be translated. The end result of this is the schizophrenic discrepancy between what is being said and what is really meant. In other words, legal formalism then becomes the high art either of intelligent deception in one extreme or self-deception in the other (less intelligent) extreme. In most cases, however, the two cognitive extremes converge and overlap.[14]

13 See, for example, countless Constitutional Court cases on restitution where, even several years after the revolution, the ordinary courts have taken a uncompromisingly unfriendly approach to the rights and claims of those seeking back property. The need to introduce governing principles was a main theme of the Czech lustration case and one of the principle dilemmas. The case expressed the problem and the aspiration beautifully and inspirationally, and it is a pity that this aspect was largely overlooked. For example: "A democratic state has not only the right but also the duty to assert and protect the principles upon which it is founded". "A law-based state which, after the collapse of totalitarianism, is anchored to the democratic values enthroned after that change, cannot in the final analysis be understood as amorphous with regard to values."

14 B. Zupančič, *From Combat to Contract or: What Does the Constitution Constitute?* (unpublished manuscript).

So I must reiterate that an outside intrusion into the system was necessary. It was imperative to apply an approach that could roughly be called legislative, meaning that a defined category of persons are excluded from certain government posts merely for meeting the criteria for exclusion from that group. Critics insists that any valid approach should be more judicial in character; that is more concerned with the individual merits of the case, the justice of a particular persons actions and sanctions for them, that it should be tied to specific findings in the context of a hearing with procedural guarantees. This shows their view of lustration as some sort of punishment rather than a prophylactic measure. The concerns outlined above with regard to resources, evidence, and the doubtful reliability of decision-makers means that a judicial case-by-case approach would be futile in this context and a legislative approach must be applied instead. The legislative approach avoids all of those problems, admittedly at the cost of not providing individualised determinations.

The Purposes which Motivate Lustration

Much has been written about the purposes that a lustration statute should or may serve, and most conclude that they serve some forbidden or unjustifiable purpose rather than that which all recognise to be proper, safeguarding and assisting the transition.[15] I would first like to make a general comment about the discussion of motives or intent behind a statute and then to discuss some of the purposes that might actually have animated such statutes and whether or not they are proper.

As is well known, the issue of the purpose a statute is meant to serve is inherently problematic, and in constitutional law this murky issue is generally viewed as indeterminate, thus irrelevant. To begin with, we cannot ever know what really motivated representatives in casting their vote, and their public pronouncements about the law's purpose are viewed skeptically. In the usual situation, a statute can have several and even conflicting purposes, some noble and proper and others less so, and the statute ultimately adopted is generally a compromise between them. Further, even if all representatives had perfectly honourable intentions in voting for a statute, their motives can always be recast in a sinister light. For example, progressive taxation is not an effort to balance social

15 See T. Rosenberg, *loc. cit* p. 327: "The purges fulfilled their unstated primary goal, sifting out a sudden excess of public servants. They were not designed to help Germans deal with the past or build a democratic political culture."

inequalities but revenge on the rich, and criminal laws are not a means to protect public safety but a vicious attack on the poor. As there is no way to conclusively determine what actually motivated the representatives, it is necessary to analyse the actual provisions and to determine whether there is a legitimate purpose and then to decide whether the statute actually advances that purpose.

A common charge made against lustration statutes is that they are inspired by ignoble motives such as desire for partisan political gain and revenge and that such purposes are not justifiable ones for lustration. For example, I would suppose that some supporters of the lustration law were motivated either primarily or secondarily by the possible partisan political gain their party would receive by satisfying public clamor for a lustration law. However, I assume that politicians generally act with the thought in mind of satisfying, at least to some extent, their voters. Why would such an intent, in and of itself, be considered reprehensible? This charge is meant also to refer to an effort to discredit and weaken rival political parties. Schwarz charges that the Czechoslovak statute was "politically motivated" in that ODS supported it.[16] However, this assessment of the situation cannot be accepted. If one party's view of the public interest is that certain persons are not fit to be in public office, the fact that the allegedly unfit persons are in a rival political party does not automatically invalidate this view. In the ODS' view, Dienstbier's party represented a past and a political philosophy that had done great harm to the country, so it was perfectly legitimate for ODS to follow through on its views. In any case, the suggestion that Dienstbier's party was unjustly harmed by lustration is laughable; that party fell out of the political scene because it was ineffectual. In both the 1992 and 1996 parliamentary elections, it failed to reach the minimum 5 % vote threshold to enter Parliament. The fact that "[l]ustration fever died down almost immediately"[17] after the 1992 election would more properly be attributable to the fact that it was an issue already decided by Parliamentary vote and an election, so that interest in debating it waned. In addition, Schwarz neglects to mention that, following the 1992 election, Czechoslovakia went through its death throws, leading to the split of the country six months later. Understandably, all attention was focused on that matter.

16 See H. Schwarz, "Lustration in Eastern Europe", *loc. cit.* p. 152: "It was apparently no coincidence that those most affected by the law were former dissidents who ran in Foreign Minister Jiří Dienstbier's party."

17 Schwarz, *id.*

In addition, Prof. Schwartz makes the charge that "revenge seems to be a primary goal of much of the lustration legislation".[18] Although this is an entirely unsubstantiated assertion (and, as I have discussed above, it is one not capable of being substantiated), I will discuss it nonetheless. This claim could be taken to mean that those voting were motivated by a personal animus against their former oppressors. While at least some of the representatives undoubtedly felt personal animus against those targeted by the lustration law, I cannot believe that this was the prime motivation for most, otherwise they would have opted for much more severe measures (which was entirely possible).

There is still another sense in which "revenge" may have motivated the legislatures, that is, about the voters' desire to sanction the regime's agents. I would certainly agree that there is an element of this purpose in the statute, but with regard to this sense, I cannot agree with the critics that this would be an illegitimate purpose for the statute. If the legislature was attempting to give expression to the people's justifiable anger at the perpetrators of communist abuse and, at least in part, to vent and channel this anger rather than let it seethe and turn into a destructive rage, in my view such a purpose is entirely legitimate. Just as one of the accepted justifications for criminal punishment is to prevent people from taking private actions for revenge, this is also a sensible and understandable motive for lustration.

There are those who will nonetheless argue that it is better to forgive and forget. Fine counsel, but clear thinking will reveal that the normal run of humanity do not just forgive and forget; they desire some sanction. And can you blame them after the traumas they have suffered over two generations or more. While many of the compassionate people in the west who suffered along vicariously, as it were, may be willing to "let go of their anger", they should at the same time be understanding if those here who actually suffered cannot bring themselves to do so. It rankles enough that one time "committed" communists are in a position to reap benefits from the economic changes, but it would be considered too much to let them wield political power as well.

Much is made of the fact that many former dissidents are against lustration. But this in fact proves nothing in particular, for why should the views of a particular group of people be entitled to greater weight, to be a more decisive criteria. While charges are hurled from this corner that lustration is nothing but mere revenge, this is an accusation, not a real argument. One could just as easily hurl the accusation that those who

18 Schwarz, *ibid.*, p. 160.

oppose lustration are trying to shield wrongdoers from being affected by legitimate measures (possibly also because they themselves are implicated in the wrongdoing). In the Czech Republic, for example, many of the most committed dissidents were former communists who condemned the regime after 1968. But they also had been supporters of the regime before that time and understandably may feel some solidarity with people who are now suffering consequences for supporting the regime. Some may also have been implicated in the condemned conduct of secret police informing.

Now, I would agree with Schwartz that if the sole actual purpose of the statute were to accommodate people's desire for revenge, it would merit a very searching analysis and might not present sufficient justification for the statutes that were adopted. But this is clearly not the sole justification for the statute. I only wished to point out that retribution or revenge may have been one of the purposes of the statute, and if so that does not, of itself, make the statute suspect.

Lastly, the charge's that lustration is motivated by revenge has drawn much attention from the main point of lustration, to assist in effected the transition. Instead of making groundless and speculative charges, it would have been far more sensible to devote greater attention to the issue of whether, and to what extent, lustration actually can or has contributed to the transformation of society generally in terms of excluding unreliable persons from positions of influence. If those criticising the policy had demonstrated in any way that lustration had no practical effect in advancing the transformation, then their arguments advancing the revenge theory would have been more credible.

Linking Lustration to Human Rights Abuses

Another legitimate purpose for lustration, one acknowledged to be so by all is "to prevent the transition to a free, democratic society from being undermined".[19] I feel that this is the major purpose and justification for lustration, as I have discussed above. However, most critics believe that the transition could be safely protected with a statute that is far more narrowly tailored and restricts the people affected to only the very worst offenders. They propose limitations on the scope of lustration that would entirely

19 See T. Rosenberg, *loc. cit.* at 397: "A country emerging from dictatorship to democracy has . . . [an obligation] to its future: to ensure that dictatorship never returns. The nation must create a new, democratic political culture."

defeat this goal. They would hem it in by the proviso that "the focus of lustration should be on threats to fundamental human rights".[20] I simply cannot understand the basis for this formulation. Schwarz does not explain the reason, and he presents it as if it were a self-evident proposition. I suspect, once again, that he is confounding lustration with a criminal sanction, the imposition of which can only be justified if the person has committed a serious and identifiable wrong that is harmful to society, so that he wishes to limit its reach thereto (human rights violations can sensibly be categorised as a type of crime). Since a criminal sanction is so serious, Schwartz and others still insist that only a criminal type procedure is acceptable in these circumstances. But since the first part of the equation is false (lustration is not a criminal sanction), this is a misplaced effort and the need for the procedure also falls out. I do not wish to go over these arguments again as they have been sufficiently covered elsewhere.

It would be a serious error to focus on human rights abuses as the main danger to the transition. Once the transition to a democratically elected government is made, it seems to me that the danger is not that agents of the state will commit human rights violations. Those that would threaten the transition are, unfortunately, more clever than that. The perceived danger is that they will impede or fail to implement reforms, they will not foster an institutional culture that is characteristic of a law-based state, and they will implement certain reform measures in such a way as to undermine their purpose. The problem presented in relation to such people is well characterised by Neil Kritz:

> These, after all, are the same people who kept the engine of the repressive state operating; it is unlikely that many of them have undergone a sudden epiphany that has turned them into committed democrats. Even if they do not actively attempt to sabotage the changes undertaken by the new authorities, these people are set in the old ways and will serve as obstacles to the process of democratic reform.[21]

One example is with privatisation where there is the danger that people will manipulate the process of privatising large firms so that former

20 Schwarz; Other authors also link a successful transition to weeding out human rights abusers. See also A. Zidar, *Lustracija: izločitev nasprotnikov demokracije z javnih položajev*, Ljubljana, Nova revija, 1996 from the Afterword in English at 234: "[t]he need to prevent people who violated human rights in the past from continuing to occupy public functions . . . because they could threaten the transition from an unstable post-socialism to a stable democratic liberal arrangement."

21 N. Kritz, "The Dilemmas of Transitional Justice" in *Transitional Justice Vol. I* at xxiv.

managers succeed in maintaining control of them by grabbing ownership (where they used to control them through management). This problem seems to have been especially acute in the former Soviet Union. Nonetheless, Prof. Schwartz explicitly states that lustration should not include "those who [might] obstruct or undermine the move to a private market economy".[22] And why not, one might ask. Prof. Schwarz does not bother to make an argument for this position; he merely assumes that a goal such as the transformation of the economy is a luxury, not a necessity, so that it would not offer sufficient justification for a measure such as lustration. There are some, however, who believe that a genuine reform of the economic system is absolutely essential to the transformation of society.[23] Certainly, one cannot deny that economic power gives one political power. If the economic relations that existed under communism are not properly reformed, those that managed the economy under communism are in a position to grab much of it and wield undue and unearned economic and political power, thus thwarting the transformation in large part. It is, of course, much easier to make such a categorical statement as Schwarz does, if you come from a country where the basic foundations of a market economy and the right of ownership have never been threatened.

The case of Slovakia can serve as an example of a transformation that appears to be in danger of derailing, but where human rights abuse are not *yet* a problem. In that country, it seems in the last two years as if Mečiar is intent on having the decisive influence on every issue in the country, to which purpose he has tried to force out the President (either by legal or extra-legal methods), to intimidate the Constitutional Court, and to bring television and the press under his control.[24] He is working toward consolidating state power in his own hands, which goes against the model of diffuse power characteristic of a law-based state. All the while, few blatant or overt human rights violations are occurring, but the transformation is being threatened, so much so that the European Union and the U.S. have both felt the need to issue quite frank warnings about Slovakia's chances of entering NATO and the EU. This fact was made

22 H. Schwarz, Lustration in Eastern Europe, *loc. cit.* p. 163.

23 See generally, V. Cepl and M. Gillis, *loc. cit.*; Cepl The Road out of Serfdom, Vera Lux, Vol. XII, No. 1 (1992).

24 "The ruling coalition persists in its campaign to curb President Kováč's powers as the trend toward monocratic government in Slovakia continues." See, "Constitution Watch: Slovakia", (1995) 4 *East European Constitutional Review*, No. 3, at p. 29 (1995), quoted in Pogany, I., op. cit., at 581.

quite plain in July, 1997, when NATO did not invite Slovakia to join (did not, in fact, include it among the serious candidates), and the EU Commission recommended negotiation for admission with five Central European countries, including Estonia but not Slovakia.[25]

In this context, it would be good to remember the statement made by Schwartz that in Slovakia lustration was "not widely used".[26] Since the dissolution of Czechoslovakia, lustration has continued to be "not widely used" in Slovakia because, while it has not been repealed there, no ministry has been given the authority to issue lustration certificates, so that, in effect, it became a dead letter. This is significant because it is believed that many leading people in government would be subject to lustration and, in addition, the incriminating secret police files of some (including PM Mečiar) have conveniently disappeared.[27] I would not attempt to prove any correlation between the Slovak government's hostility to lustration and the problems with the transformation (such things are not amenable to proof, in any case), but I will state my view that lustration *might* have helped to prevent this situation. At least someone in Slovakia must agree or why else would the file pages containing Mečiar's information be missing. In addition, it shows that limiting the safeguarding of the transitions to preventing the danger of human rights abuses is a misplaced priority because the danger to democratic transformation lies not in overt human rights abuses, but in the subtle deception by those holdovers from the former regime who are not committed to fostering the democratic system.

In addition to having a tenuous relation to the transition, the trimming of a lustration statute to reach only those who would engage in human rights abuses would, in fact, be so unduly and unjustifiably restrictive as to positively ensure that lustration would not be the least bit efficacious in facilitating the transition. Schwartz' conception is as follows. The sole legitimate purpose is to prevent people from committing human rights abuses in the future. In addition, it would only be fair to apply it to persons if it can be proved, in a full-blown procedure requiring specific evidence, that they committed human rights abuses in the past. Moreover, the resources in terms of time, people, and money that this process would require would ensure that only a handful of such cases could be brought. The criminal law bug-bear is responsible for the insistence that you show

25 See *Mladá Fronta Dnes*, 16 July 1997, "Brusel se rozhodl jednat o přijetí šestice členů" ("Brussels Has Decided to Negotiate the Admission of Six Members").

26 Schwarz, Lustration in Eastern Europe, *loc. cit.* p. 151.

27 See Rosenberg, *loc. cit.*, pp.76-77: "While Mečiar was the Slovak Interior Minister, in possession of the files, someone tore six pages out of the StB register that contained his name."

specific human rights abuses, or in the case of informants, the provision of particular information that actually harmed someone and where the informant knew or had reason to know it would. Prof. Schwartz is imposing a criminal law model upon this issue, making sure that the large number of people who should be affected by lustration cannot possibly be reached.

Such a narrow approach in fact would have been harmful to the development of a rule of law state, not assist it, since very few who should have been would actually have been disqualified by it and many more would have been "cleared" or "exonerated" because of a lack of evidence. I believe the citizens would have been appalled by the spectacle of former agents of the old regime retaining positions now because of the state's inability to prove a case or because those agents are very clever at hiding the evidence or bribing people. The people's first experience with a democratic state would leave them with the impression that it is ineffectual and has tied its own hands instead of properly dealing with a situation that cries out for a solution. This will not raise respect for the rule of law.[28] At its early stages, in order for a law-based state to develop, a country needs breathing space, a certain protective cover, training wheels, if you will.

An issue related to the historical context and the need for decommunisation is the suggestion that, in applying lustration, the present leaders are acting like the communists. The fact that many former dissidents have objections to lustration is taken as conclusive proof that such is the case. The Sklar and Kanev pamphlet explicitly makes this argument where it states that lustration exhibits "many of the same totalitarian features embodied in the communist system that it seeks to replace".[29] Such charges grotesquely distort the situation and are the use of verbal hyperbole of the highest order to buttress a weak argument. They smack of the habit of applying a generally acknowledged term of grave condemnation (for example, "racist" or "totalitarian") to all situations, to the point where it becomes a mere label and loses any meaning at all, all the more so its power to command moral assent. As the word itself implies, it is not possible to be a little totalitarian. The new regimes can be

28 See Rosenberg *ibid.*, at 337: "The ban on *ex post facto* justice has begun to give rule of law a bad name in the East Bloc - to those who advocate punishment, it has become synonymous with letting communists off the hook. 'We expected justice, and we got rule of law' one former dissident commented."

29 Sklar & Kanev *op. cit.* at 3; see also, Rosenberg., *loc. cit.*, at p. 85: "Lustrace was perpetrating human rights violations, and the arguments used by some of its increasingly fierce supporters replicated the thinking of the old regime."

compared to the old totalitarian ones when they actually act like them. That would mean ensuring that all former communists were denied any work whatsoever in all significant fields, their property would be confiscated, thousands would be imprisoned, tortured, even executed, leaving all others in terror of suffering the same fate unless they kept quiet and went along with it. The relatives of such people would also suffer harsh sanctions, such as exclusion from educational opportunities, jobs, and political participation. All this and more that was done is too well known to require an extensive exposition and is stated succinctly and powerfully in the Czech Parliament statute on the Lawlessness of the Communist Regime.[30]

The criminal rampage which the communists wreaked upon these nations over the forty years of their reign was a hideously ugly situation which did inestimable harm to the societies, political and legal cultures, economies, not to mention the psychological scars it left on the people. Schwartz and others write as if all of these facts are irrelevant to an assessment of the situation, but they cannot be ignored. If lustration appears harsh and unnatural, it must be remembered that it is a reverberation of the damage caused by the communists and a necessary remedial measure for it. Taken in this light, lustration must be viewed as a mild and restrained response in an effort to return these nations to a normal and acceptable situation.[31] It makes sense to compare it to the situation where a seriously addicted person is given another type of drug in order to wean him off the first one, or the homeopathic method of medicine where a substance that is dangerous to a person is administered to them in small dosages so as to prevent the danger that the person would succumb to a larger exposure. Under normal circumstances, it would be unethical and illegal for a doctor to administer such substances to a patient. In context, however, it is both an effective and appropriate procedure.

30 See Act No. 198/1993 Sb., on the Lawlessness of the Communist Regime and Resistance to It, zákon č. 198/1993 Sb., o protiprávnosti komunistického režimu a odporu proti němu.

31 In this regard, it is instructive to quote the dissenting opinion of Justice Blackmun in the Bakke case, in response to the argument that affirmative action is a violation of equal protection, or equality before the law. "I suspect that it would be impossible to arrange an affirmative action program in a racially neutral way and have it successful. To ask that this be so is to demand the impossible. In order to get beyond racism, we must first take account of race. There is no other way. And in order to treat some persons equally, we must treat them differently. We cannot - we dare not - let the Equal Protection Clause perpetuate racial supremacy."

The Czechoslovak Lustration Law and Constitutional Court Decision on Lustration

I would like now briefly to review the decision by the Constitutional Court of the Czech and Slovak Federal Republic upholding the lustration law (with some exceptions) in light of what Prof. Schwartz wrote about them. Using colorful language that suggests more than is eventually delivered, Prof. Schwartz characterized the Czechoslovak law as the "most sweeping of all the lustration laws"[32] or the "most far-reaching measure"[33], which I take as criticism that the law reaches too far in an indiscriminate witch hunt. While it is true that the law applies broadly to affect many categories of persons and to exclude them from a wide range of positions, the law's broad scope indicates that the drafters actually took seriously the rational of system transformation and that the law is meant to serve the purpose, a genuine effort to protect the transformation by excluding from government those whom it is reasonable to believe are not trustworthy. If it had applied only to specific fields (such as one of the laws in Bulgaria which applied only to scientific and research institutes),[34] it would be open to criticism that it was motivated by the desire to punish a particular group of disfavored persons. The broad range of categories of previous activities and of present positions covered under the statute is complimented by the fact that the exclusion applies for the most part only to leading positions. For example, a person working in the university may not be the dean or vice-dean of a faculty, but this does not prevent him from teaching. This aspect also lends credence to the claim that the law is meant to assist the transition.[35]

The critics make what seem to be incompatible charges against the various types of lustration laws. Some laws, like the Czechoslovak, are criticised for being too "sweeping", and others, like the Bulgarian, for unfairly singling out people for harsh treatment. It seems to me that either one or the other of these solutions must be adopted. Either the law goes to

32 Schwarz, Constitutionalism, *loc. cit.* p. 142.

33 Schwarz, Lustration in Eastern Europe, *loc. cit.* p. 149.

34 See, Law for Temporary Introduction of Additional Requirements for Members of Scientific Organisations, the Bulgarian "Panev" Law, included in Sklar & Kanev, *op. cit.*, Appendix A.

35 See zákon č. 451/1991 Sb., kterým se stanoví některé další předpoklady pro výkon některých funkcí ve státních orgánech a organizacích České a Slovenské Federativní Republiky, České republiky a Slovenské republiky; see also English translation in Sklar & Kanev, *op. cit.*, Appendix C.

its logical boundaries, that is it affects everyone who might harm the transition (which is considered fair in the sense that it applies equally to everyone), or it affects only persons, only to those whom you can prove engaged in specific misconduct (which is considered fairer in the procedural but less fair in that only a few are singled out). To exclude either solutions is a disguised way of condemning the idea of lustration altogether and is reminiscent of argument used by opponents of the death penalty in America who lay down various criteria for acceptable imposition of the death penalty, one of which cannot be fulfilled without violating the other.[36]

In this context, it should be noted that the Constitutional Court actually widened the scope of the law by annulling Sections 2(3), 3(2) and 13(3), all of which provided for exceptions to the general exclusion because it violated the principle of fairness by not applying the same criteria to all similarly situated. Section 13(3) met one of Schwartz' general criticisms of lustration laws in that it made an exception for those who voluntarily repudiated their earlier behavior. It seems the Court was not against such an exception, but required it to be applied more generally, to all who had been rehabilitated, not just those rehabilitated under Sec. 2 of Act No. 119/1990 Sb. Apparently, the Court did not feel it possessed the power to extend the reach of Sec. 13(3) to cover these others, so it annulled that provision, perhaps expecting the Parliament might re-enact it in a more general form. However, no such amendment to the law was ever adopted.

From Schwartz' short commentary, it seems clear that, while perhaps he read the Czechoslovak lustration decision carefully, he did not read it sensitively; he only saw what he was looking for, all the while failing to pay much attention to the arguments the Court actually advanced in its reasoning. He wrote that "the key issues seemed to be grappled with - but not really".[37] Evidently his view as to what was "key" differed from that of the Court itself, but he never informs us what exactly these "key" issues are. Certainly the Court discussed many "key" issues that bear on the

36 For example, they argue that the death penalty should be imposed only in the case of the most heinous crimes, so that a wide-range of the defendant's particular life circumstances must be considered by the decision-maker as possible mitigating circumstances and other features. An additional criterion provides that it not be imposed arbitrarily and capriciously. Unfortunately, the application of the first criteria inevitably results in violation of the second: the extremely exacting procedures ensure that only a few of all those who committed horrible crimes will suffer this penalty and no definite or legitimate explanation for the actual selection can be found, because so much is left to discretion in individual cases.

37 Schwarz, Constitutionalism, *loc. cit* p. 142 (emphasis added).

justification for lustration, and a more detailed discussion of the case will bring that many of them are quite significant, if not persuasive.

The Court began with a quite extensive discussion of the facts. For example, it described at length the communist personnel policies which ensured that all persons in any position of influence were loyal to the regime and which provided justification in the Court's view for the system-wide approach to reforming the ranks of government employees. It underlined what the democràtic regime is up against in trying to reform the government. Next, it discussed the role that secret police repression played in the communist hold on power, the orders (issued while the revolution was in progress) for infiltration of the new regime by secret police agents, and the destruction of materials in the Ministry of Interior. It concluded that the ordered infiltration and destruction of materials "created a real and potentially very perilous source of destabilisation and danger, which could easily threaten the developing constitutional order". The Court also pointed out that the intentional destruction of files excluded any realistic "possibility of separately proving collaboration by individual clandestine collaborators". One cannot seriously dispute that these facts are crucial for determining whether it is necessary and justifiable to exclude from government those who worked with the secret police.

Schwartz also states that the "essence of the decision . . . is that collective liability is acceptable" and that there was "no discussion of *why* an approach that is usually condemned . . . is acceptable in this situation".[38] Statements like this convince me that he disregarded what the Court actually wrote because it did not conform to his conception of the problem. If the Court did not reason according to his liking (this is group liability, which is justified exceptionally only in the following cases, and the facts show that this is one of those cases), is no reason to mischaracterise the opinion by saying that no attempt was made to confront the issue. A careful reading of the case will show, however, that the Court did not duck this issue. It extensively discussed a democratic state's proper course of action when confronted with the situation described in the previous paragraph.

The Court enunciated some very broad principles about the duties of a democratic state when faced with the need to deal with a totalitarian legacy. It declared that a "democratic state has not only the right but also the duty to assert and protect the principles upon which it is founded" so that it cannot disregard the fact that personnel policy was made "in accordance with the now unacceptable criteria of a totalitarian system".

38 Schwarz, *ibid.*(emphasis added).

Further, "persons employed in state and public bodies" must possess "loyalty to the democratic principles upon which the state is built". It is clearly arguing that a democratic state has a *duty*, not a discretionary power, to ensure that those who carry out it actions conform to the principles of the state. It is possible that, in formulating such a view, the Court drew upon the jurisprudence of the German Constitutional Court referred to as militant democracy. As a consequence, it concluded that "it cannot deny the state's right . . . to lay down . . . conditions or prerequisites crucial for the performance of leadership or other decisive positions if . . . its own safety, the safety of its citizens and, most of all, further democratic developments are taken into consideration". In essence, it was referring to the necessity of protecting the foundations of the democratic state from being undermined. In this context the Court analogised to the many clauses in basic rights' provisions of constitutions or treaties that allow for exceptions which are "necessary in a democratic society . . . for the security of the state, for the protection of safety or of public order", and made reference to the laws in developed democratic states which allow for background checks on all applicants to government service, as well as the exclusion of those who fail some test of reliability. Whether or not Schwarz and others are persuaded by such considerations, they cannot assert that the Court made no arguments to justify the resort to an extraordinary measure such as lustration.

In over thirty pages of reasoning, the Court decided that lustration was permissible and did not violate anyone's rights, or "offend against either constitutional acts or international conventions". Prof. Schwartz made a contrary assertion to the effect that "[t]he Court did admit that this might produce 'formal violations' of people's rights, but it glossed over this."[39] The Court, however, said something quite different, so I have to believe that Prof. Schwartz was working with a less than perfect translation. What the Court actually wrote was that, "if compared with the preceding legal order, these conditions might appear to be, from a formal perspective, a restriction on civil rights".[40] The phrase "might appear to be" makes it perfectly clear that the Court was not admitting, nor did it believe, that the law violated anyone's rights. The actual significance of this quote is seen only when viewed in conjunction with other statements made by the Court. For example, it stated "[T]he adoption of the Charter of Fundamental

39 Schwarz, *ibid*.

40 Author's translation of the Czech original, which reads: "Ve srovnání s předchozím právním řádem se tyto podmínky mohou jevit z formálního hlediska jako omezení občanských práv."

Rights and Basic Freedoms . . . fundamentally changed the nature and the value system of our entire constitutional and legal order" and "a new foundation for the law-based state was established in this way". With these statements, the Court is drawing a distinction between the former legal order and the present one by referring to the difference between formal legality and material legality. It characterises the former as "the observance of any sort of values or any sort of rights . . . [as long as] they are adopted in the procedurally proper manner" and the latter as "respect for those norms that are compatible with the fundamental values of human society as they are expressed in the Charter of Fundamental Rights and Basic Freedoms". In effect the court is condemning and discarding the style of legal thinking by which the former regime could adopt and enforce laws that were in clear contradiction with the stated basic principles of the state and with basic rights enumerated in the Constitution and treaties. In the present legal order, it is not correct just to mechanically apply some legal provision taken out of context of the system as a whole and not assessed in relation to most crucial principles of the legal order. Another way to state this is that the whole legal order is infused with and must be adapted to the basic principles of the Charter. One of these is certainly "the duty to assert and protect the principles upon which it [a democratic state] is founded".

This last point is further illuminated by an additional quote:

> ... in the contemporary building of a law-based state, the point of departure for which is a sharp break with the values of the totalitarian regime, the state may not adopt a criteria of formal-legal and material-legal continuity which is based on a differing value system, not even under the circumstances that the formal normative continuity of the legal order makes it possible.

This statement seems to be in response to an argument that comes under the rubric of legal continuity and legal certainty and is commonly made by the proponents of the old order: there is continuity with the old law, so that until they are repealed, the rules that are formally adopted must be respected as understood then and that rights gained must also be respected, maintained and protected. If honoured in full, such a principle would be very effective in keeping the legal order from changing very much at all. The Court sees this argument for what it is and with the above-cited passage, it rejected it.

Prof. Schwartz' statements to the contrary notwithstanding, the Court also discussed the reliability of secret police files quite extensively, and it decided that some files served as a justifiable basis for lustration decisions but others did not. A great deal of evidence was taken concerning these files, and the Court concluded that the files kept on persons who fell under Sec. 2(1)(b) of the statute, the "clandestine collaborators" were quite reliable and could serve as the basis for a lustration decision. Substantiated testimony showed that the persons in this category had agreed to collaborate, so that they were aware of their status and voluntarily consented to it. In addition, it was a strict practice that people in this category were closely and regularly monitored to ensure that they were loyal and performing their tasks, so the claim that some agreed but never caused any harm is not believable. In contrast, the Court seriously doubted that the files on those under Sec. 2(1)(c) could reliably show either agreement to collaborate (or even actual knowledge that they were in contact with the secret police) or the provision of any information, damaging or otherwise. It only indicated that a secret police agent had made contact and was attempting to recruit the person. As a result of this finding, the Court annulled Sec. 2(1)(c).

Conclusion

I attended the Constitutional Court Conference in September 1994 when Prof. Schwartz presented his paper The Lustration Decisions. Another participant in the conference, Prof. Marek Zmigrodski of Poland, made comments on Prof. Schwartz' speech that merit repetition. He said that "Prof. Schwartz has entered dangerous ground" and that "scrutiny of Central and East European states, especially hermetically sealed ones is very challenging indeed." In reaction to Schwartz' analysis of the Bulgarian cases, he said "I am not Bulgarian, but I speak Bulgarian. I studied there and became well acquainted with the country, nonetheless, I am still not sure whether my studies of it are legitimate".[41] I could say the same about myself in relation to the Czech Republic. I am not Czech, but I have lived here for over five years, studied the language and legal system, and feel that I am well acquainted with the people and the country. Nonetheless, I still have doubts whether I am yet truly competent to assess the society and legal system and make definitive judgments concerning it. I certainly would not dare to make quick and facile ones.

A further problem I have with virtually all the critical commentary is that, by focusing on a very narrow issue, they miss a more crucial point. As

41 Author's notes from comments as simultaneously translated from Polish; see also A. Rzepliński (ed) Constitutionalism and Human Rights, *supra note 1*, note X, at p. 158.

I mentioned above in relation to purposes of lustration, it would have been far more sensible to devote greater attention to the issue of whether, and to what extent, lustration actually does contribute to the transformation of the society generally in terms of excluding unreliable persons from positions of influence. Considerations of the extent to which the means employed have proved effective shows much about the motivation and justification for lustration. Unfortunately, this avenue of inquiry was never taken.

Despite the fact that I have devoted my attention to the issue of lustration in this essay, I would suggest that it is now time to pass on to other important issues. Schwartz asserted that lustration has divided societies and exacerbated tensions,[42] but in my view, at least as far as the Czech Republic is concerned, he and others have greatly exaggerated and melodramatised the affair. In fact, there has been a general lack of interest in lustration for a long time (disinterest may be a better explanation for the drop in lustration fever than Schwarz' theory of a politically motivated scheme). From the beginning most people thought it was basically a correct approach to take. They objected more to the fact that the statute was not stronger and did not effect more governmental positions; they are convinced that too many people in government are those who were there before, and they are disgusted with such a situation. Otherwise, they have simply put it out of their minds and gone on with life. For better or worse, many post-communist nations have chosen to adopt a lustration law, and some are even now considering some form of it. It appears that a great many people simply do not accept the argument that lustration violates principles of a democratic, rule of law state, and they are convinced that it is an appropriate means to effect the transformation toward such a state. As there are countless other serious and pressing issues about the development of solid constitutionalism in the Czech Republic and other countries, such as, for example, the willingness of ordinary courts to be sensitive to new constitutional principles, I think it is time the critics devote their attention to some other issue and stop beating a dead horse.

42 H. Schwarz, "The Czech Constitutional Court Decision on the Illegitimacy of the Communist Regime", (1994) 1 *Parker School Journal of East European Law*, 398.

5 The Protection of Human Rights in the Czech Republic

VLADIMÍR SLÁDEČEK

Introduction

The protection of human rights is secured by a system of institutions in the Czech Republic, but it is not proposed to deal with every part of this system here. We shall not analyse the role of fundamental protective mechanisms relating to the police, prosecuting authorities, administrative agencies and ordinary courts (including judicial review of administrative action, the so-called administrative judiciary). The main emphasis is on the Constitutional Court's role in the protection of (fundamental) human rights and freedoms guaranteed by the Constitution of the Czech Republic and other constitutional laws, in particular the Charter of Fundamental Rights and Freedoms (hereinafter "the Charter").[1] Under the Constitution, the Constitutional Court is an independent part of the judicial branch, with the authority (separate from the ordinary courts) to defend fundamental rights and freedoms.[2] Considerable attention is also devoted to the institution of the ombudsman, a relatively new but important mechanism for the protection of human rights in the sphere of public administration, complementary to the Constitutional Court, the establishment of which has been recommended by the Council of Europe.[3]

1 This constitutional law was originally adopted by the previous state - the Czech and Slovak Federal Republic in 1991. It was in part inspired by the *International Covenant on Civil and Political Rights*, the *International Covenant on Economic, Social and Cultural Rights*, and the *European Convention on Human Rights and Fundamental Freedoms*. It consists of six chapters: 1. General Provisions, 2. Human Rights and Fundamental Freedoms, 3. Rights of National and Ethnic Minorities, 4. Economic, Social and Cultural Rights, 5. Right to Judicial and Other Legal Protection, 6. Joint Provisions.

2 See art. 4. It can be also illustrated by the wording of the vow of Judge of the Constitutional Court: "I promise, upon my honour and conscience, that I will safeguard the inviolability of the natural rights of Man and the rights of a citizen, abide by the constitutional laws and decide according to the best of my conviction, independently and impartially" (art. 82 para. 2).

3 See Recommendation No. R (85) 13 of the Committee of Ministers to Member States on the Institution of the Ombudsman.

This chapter is thus divided into three parts. The first outlines the history and development of the institutional protection of fundamental human rights and freedoms in the territory which now constitutes the Czech Republic. The second analyses the constitutional basis and legal regulation of the judges of the Constitutional Court as laid down by legislation.[4] It also deals with the Constitutional Court's practice, the results of its activities and some problems relating to the Court. The third part is devoted to unsuccessful attempts to establish an ombudsman-type institution in the Czech Republic. In particular reference is made to a proposal for a "Public Defender of Rights".

Historical Outline of the Development of Constitutional Judicial Review

The first institution which can be regarded as a judicial body to protect the fundamental rights of citizens was the Austro-Hungarian Imperial Court established in 1867. Yet dealing with complaints alleging infringements of rights seems to have constituted a very small part of its activities, since it was only a negligible part of its jurisdiction. A complaint was confined simply to the *political* rights guaranteed by the Constitution when the appropriate legal administrative procedure had been exhausted. The effect of the decisions taken in such cases, however, seems to have been, according to the legal literature of the time, very questionable. The Imperial Court had no power to quash administrative acts.

After the creation of the independent Czechoslovak Republic in 1918, the jurisdiction of the Imperial Court was transferred to a newly-established Supreme Administrative Court. Here again there were problems in practice. The Supreme Administrative Court had no power to examine the constitutionality of legislation, it was only entitled to scrutinise the legality of administrative acts. Furthermore, although the Constitution was later amended in 1920 to establish a Constitutional Court, this was designed to be a specialised judicial body exercising abstract control over the constitutionality of statutes. It did not have jurisdiction to entertain individual complaints concerning the constitutionality of administrative acts. Even within its restricted field of competence its performance was rather poor, which was partly due to its inactivity resulting from vacancies on the Court from 1931-1938. The events of the Second World War meant that the Constitutional Court in practical terms ceased to exist in 1941. It is

4 Act No.182/1993 Collection of Laws.

worth mentioning that after the forced split of the Czechoslovak Republic and the establishment of the Slovak State supported by the Nazis, legal provision was made for a "Constitutional Senate", a special body intended to defend constitutionality in the newly-founded State, but it was never established.

The liberation of the country in 1945 did not mean the reestablishment of the Constitutional Court, although it was formally still entrenched in the Constitution. Instead detailed discussions took place among legal experts about the creation of a newly-constructed constitutional court. One idea was to widen the jurisdiction of the court to individual complains of citizens against any official act that infringed constitutionally guaranteed rights, in those cases where the ordinary courts had no jurisdiction. However, the communist coup d'état in February 1948 interrupted all such discussions. The provisions of the Constitution adopted in May 1948 was deliberately influenced by the ideology of the new regime. A constitutional court protecting human rights was not wanted in the emerging and evolving totalitarian system. The official argument of the time was that such an organ "was more or less of a bureaucratic nature and in reality its position would be above the National Assembly". Only a very peculiar abstract control of constitutionality of legislation was allowed, whereby the Presidium of the National Assembly had the right to scrutinise the constitutionality of statues. Such a dubious power existed in a slightly modified form until 1992, but it was never exercised.

The events of the Prague spring in 1968 brought some fresh hope for the protection of human rights. A constitutional law, though adopted after the occupation of the country by the Soviet troops (and other "friendly" armies), nevertheless retained provisions for a constitutional court of the Czechoslovak Socialist Republic.[5] This law envisaged not only abstract constitutional control, but also certain safeguards for the protection of constitutionally guaranteed rights and freedoms for citizens in the form of a limited right of individual complaint.[6] Nonetheless, the so-called normalisation period began in 1970 and consequently the necessary implementing legislation never materialised. The Constitutional Court

5 Act No. 143/1968 Collection of Laws on the Czechoslovak Federation.

6 "The Constitutional Court shall decide on the protection of constitutionally guaranteed rights and freedoms, if they are infringed by the decision or other acts of a Federal organ, provided that the law does not grant other judicial protection" (art. 92). It should be noted, that existence of republican constitutional courts was envisaged.

existed only on paper written in the Constitution, a fact observed outside Czechoslovakia.[7]

The events of the "Velvet Revolution" towards the end of 1989 opened the way for the establishment of a regular constitutional judiciary. By the end of 1990, Václav Havel, the new President of the Republic, presented a Bill on the Constitutional Court of the Czech and Slovak Federal Republic. Contemporaneously, a similar proposal was submitted by a group of members of the federal parliament. The presidential proposals were the subject of negotiation in parliamentary committees and, after some amendment during its legislative progress, the law was approved by the Federal Assembly in February 1991.[8] An Implementing statute followed in November 1991, after an unsatisfactory delay due to the Government's failure to act, and was based on a bill submitted by a group of members of parliament.[9]

The Constitutional Court of the Czech and Slovak Federal Republic (hereinafter the "Federal Court") consisted of twelve judges appointed for seven years. They were appointed by the President of the Republic from candidates nominated by the Federal Assembly, the Czech National Council and the Slovak National Council, each of which put forward eight candidates. In addition to a president and two vice-presidents, it was envisaged that the Federal Court would operate both in plenary session and through four three-member panels.

The Federal Court's jurisdiction was defined very broadly. It was entitled to exercise abstract control over the constitutionality of federal statutes, legislation of the Republics and implementing regulations; to decide the jurisdictional disputes between federal state authorities, federal and republic authorities and between the Czech and Slovak authorities; and to interpret federal constitutional legislation. From our point of view, the most important aspect of its jurisdiction was its power to entertain complaints by an individual alleging that his fundamental rights and basic freedoms, as guaranteed by a constitutional law or by an international treaty on human rights ratified and promulgated by the CSFR, had been infringed as a result of a final decision in legal proceedings, to which he was a party, of a measure or of some other action by a public authority.[10]

7 H.F. Zamudio, "A Global survey of governmental institutions to protect civil and political rights" (1983) 13 *Denver Journal of International Law and Policy* 52.

8 Const. Act No. 91/1991 Collection of Laws.

9 Act No. 491/1991 Collection of Laws, on the organisation and proceedings before the Constitutional Court of the CSFR. A plenary session of the Court later adopted Organisational and Procedural Rules of the Constitutional Court of the CSFR.

10 Article 6, Constitutional Act No 91/1991 Collection of Laws.

After first receiving the approval of the Federal Assembly the judges of the Federal Court were appointed by the President of the Republic in January 1992. Ensuing political developments which ended in the break-up of the Federation[11] meant that the time in which the Federal Court had been active was quite short.[12]

By the end of 1992 implementing legislation had not been prepared to establish the new Czech Constitutional Court envisaged by the Czech Constitution and it was proposed that an interim judicial body should be set up. The Court for the Protection of Constitutionality of the Czech Republic was not established, because the necessary constitutional law was not approved by the Czech National Council.

Early in 1993 a special working group co-ordinated by the Ministry of Justice was put in charge of drafting a bill on the Constitutional Court. On June 16, 1993, the Act on the Constitutional Court[13] was approved by the Czech National Council and it came into force on July 1, 1993. The Court started to function from July 15, 1993, when twelve of the fifteen judges were appointed, the three remaining vacancies being filled later. The first decision concerning the constitutionality of the Act on Lawlessness of the Communist Regime[14] was adopted in December 21, 1993.[15]

The Constitutional Court of the Czech Republic

The constitutional basis of the Constitutional Court is to be found in articles 83-89 of the Constitution. These provide that the Constitutional Court is the judicial authority charged with upholding the Constitution. It consists of fifteen judges appointed by the President of the Republic with the consent of the Senate for a term of ten years. In fact the judges installed in 1993 were appointed with the consent of the Chamber of Deputies, because the first Senate was not elected until 1996.[16] A Judge must be over

11 See eg, A.K. Stanger, "Czechoslovakia's Dissolution as an Unintended Consequence of the Velvet Revolution" (1996) 5 *East European Constitutional Review*, 40.

12 The Federal Court functioned from Februrary 2, 1992 to December 31, 1992. It delivered eight judgments and eight resolutions of a "principal character".

13 Act no. 182/1993 Collection of Laws.

14 Act no. 198/1993 Collection of Laws.

15 Act 91/1991 Collection of Laws envisaged the existence of a constitutional judiciary in both Republics (art. 20). The Constitution of the Slovak Republic, approved on September 1, 1992, contained provisions on a constitutional court, which came into operation early in 1993.

16 See, D. Olson, "The Czech Senate: From Constitutional Inducement to Electoral Challenge", (1996) 5 *East European Constitutional Review*, 47.

forty years old, have a university-level legal education, practical experience in the legal profession for at least ten years and be of good character. A Judge of the Court takes up his post by swearing an oath before the President of the Republic. The Judge is bound only by constitutional laws, including the Act on the Constitutional Court, and by treaties on human rights and fundamental freedoms ratified and promulgated by the Czech Republic (hereinafter "international human rights treaties").

A Judge of the Constitutional Court (hereinafter "the Court") enjoys wide immunities similar to those of members of Parliament. He cannot be prosecuted without the Senate's consent and he may be detained only if he has been caught in the act of, or immediately after, committing a criminal offence. The appropriate authority must immediately notify the Chairman of the Senate of the detention. If, within 24 hours of the detention, the Chairman of the Senate does not give his consent for the detained judge to be committed to court, the authority concerned must release him. At its first subsequent meeting, the Senate shall make a final decision on the permissibility of prosecution. This mechanism has been criticised, in particular by judges of the Court. The requirement of the Senate's consent instead of that of the Court in plenary session is considered to be an improper interference with the independence of the Judges of the Court. The right to refuse to testify, even after having ceased to be a judge of the Court, about matters which he came to know in connection with the exercise of his function is in a way connected with these immunities.

The Constitutional Court, by virtue of the powers entrusted to it by the Constitution, occupies a special position among state organs and the Judges of the Court bear a special responsibility for safeguarding constitutionalism (and partly also legality), and for the protection of fundamental rights and freedoms guaranteed in particular by the Charter as well as by international human rights treaties. In particular instances laid down in the Constitution and listed below, the Judges also bear responsibility for ensuring the observance of principles of democratic government. The Court is composed as a democratically established collective body, where all Judges are equal when they decide a case. The Court is empowered to discharge both abstract and concrete control of the constitutionality.

The jurisdiction of the Court laid down in the Constitution is quite wide, even wider than the jurisdiction of the previous Federal Court.[17] The Court is entitled to decide on the following matters:

17 This is partly due to the fact that the Federal Court's jurisdiction was confined to "federal" issues. The Republics' constitutional courts were envisaged as exercising "the rest" of the constitutionality protective function.

(i) the annulment of enactments of the legislature or individual provisions thereof, if they are in contradiction with a constitutional law or with ratified and promulgated international treaty on human rights, by which the Czech Republic is bound (hereinafter "international treaty on human rights");[18]
(ii) the annulment of other forms of law, such as delegated legislation, or individual provisions of such laws, if they are inconsistent with a constitutional law or with a statue or international human rights treaty;
(iii) a constitutional complaint of an authority of a self-governing region against illegitimate interference by the central authorities of the State;
(iv) a constitutional complaint against a final decision or some other act of a public authority affecting constitutionally guaranteed fundamental rights and freedoms;
(v) a legal remedy against a decision concerning the validity of the election of a Deputy or Senator;
(vi) in cases of doubt, the loss of eligibility for the office or about the incompatibility of membership of the legislature with any other office;[19]
(vii) the Senate's indictment of the President of the Republic;[20]
(viii) the President of the Republic's proposal to annul a joint resolution of the Chamber of Deputies and Senate;[21]
(ix) the measures necessary to implement an international tribunal's ruling which is binding for the Czech Republic if it cannot be implemented otherwise;
(x) whether a decision on the dissolution of a political party, or any other decision concerning a political party's activities, is in conformity with constitutional or other legislation;

18 Such treaties are applicable as directly binding regulations, taking precedence over the laws (art. 10 of the Constitution).

19 According to art. 22 of the Constitution the office of Deputy or Senator is incompatible with the office of the President of the Republic, judicial and other offices prescribed by the law.

20 According to art. 65, para. 2 of the Constitution, the President of the Republic can only be prosecuted for high treason by the Constitutional Court on the basis of an action brought by the Senate. The penalty can be the loss of office and disqualification for the future.

21 According to art. 66 of the Constitution the resolution is adopted, if the President of the Republic cannot exercise the office for serious reasons.

(xi) disputes on the demarcation of competence of central government authorities and authorities of self-governing region, unless the law confers jurisdiction to resolve disputes on another body.[22]

More detailed regulation, for example who shall be entitled, and under what conditions, to institute proceedings before the Court, procedural rules, is left to implementing legislation. As already mentioned, the Act on the Constitutional Court[23] is the relevant implementing legislation. As for the organisation of the functions of the Court, apart from the special independent role of Judges discussed below, the President of the Republic appoints a chairperson and two vice-chairpersons of the Court. The full Court is composed of all the Judges and there are four panels each with three members.

We shall not go in any detail into the organisational and procedural aspects and the jurisdiction of each component element of the Court, nor shall we deal with special proceedings following from the jurisdiction conferred by the Constitution. Although some of these touch, at least indirectly, on human rights issues we shall focus only on individual complaints to the Court. Any natural or legal person is entitled to submit a constitutional complaint, alleging that his fundamental rights and basic freedoms have been infringed as a result of a final decision in proceedings to which he was a party or of a measure or of some other action by a public authority. A constitutional complaint must be submitted within sixty days. Where it is proposed that a statute or some other legal provision should be annulled in whole or in part, the complaint should be accompanied by a proposal to that effect. The state of affairs of which the petitioner complains must have been the result of the application of the law which is claimed to contravene a constitutional law, international human rights treaty or some other legal provision. This means that individual complainants can indirectly initiate abstract constitutional review. In practice they often do so, but not infrequently there is little relationship between the decision contested and the constitutionality of the legal provision challenged. Quite often the application to annul a law is rejected, but the complaint against the act or decision is upheld.

22 The Constitution envisages that in some specified instances, if prescribed by law, the Supreme Administrative Court shall have jurisdiction (art. 87 para. 2). Nevertheless, the Supreme Administrative Court has not been established so far (even appropriate legislation has not been submitted to the Parliament so far).

23 No. 182/1993 Collection of Laws.

The Judge-Rapporteur (hereinafter "Rapporteur") on the case shall reject the complaint without holding an oral hearing and without the parties being present (rejection *a limine*), on any one of six grounds:

(i) the complainant fails to cure defects in the complaint by the deadline designated therefor;

(ii) the complaint was submitted after the deadline set for its submission;

(iii) the complaint is manifestly unfounded;

(iv) the complaint was submitted by a person who is clearly not authorised to submit it;

(v) it is a complaint over which the Court has no jurisdiction;

(vi) the complaint is inadmissible. A constitutional complaint is inadmissible if the complainant has failed to exhaust all procedural remedies afforded by the law for the protection of his rights or where the case is *res iudicata*.

This part of the Constitutional Act was often a target for criticism. The problem does not lie in the fact that a number of complaints are rejected without any hearing of the merits on account of grave procedural defects. This also happens in other constitutional courts and a vast number of complaints deserve no better fate. What has been problematic is that the rejection of some complaints on the ground that they were manifestly unfounded has appeared to be partly based on the merits. Thus a substantive ruling is made solely by a Rapporteur.

During debates on the Bill on the Constitutional Court, it was objected that the Rapporeur's power would be too great, by virtue of the finality of the decision. However, neither a proposed amendment based on a previous regulation of the Federal Court giving a right to the senate to challenge the Rapporteur's decision, nor one giving a right to appeal against the Rapporteur's decision was approved. Certain Judges, including the Chairman of the Court, are aware of the imbalance of such decision-making and are of the opinion that the law should be changed and the power to reject complaints as unfounded, or that all remedies have not been exhausted should be entrusted to a panel of the Court. There is no possibility of monitoring the problematic cases of rejection at rapporteur level, since the Court only publishes information on them selectively. There was, however, a very well known case of a journalist who lodged two complaints relating to the right to information. The first complaint was denied, perhaps quite legitimately, on procedural grounds. The rejection of the second was hardly acceptable. A written refusal to make information available was considered to be an administrative act which should first have been contested in an administrative court. An amendment to the Act on the Constitutional Court was proposed to tackle the problem and was passed by Parliament. According to this amendment to the Act on the Constitutional Court, coming into force on May 10, 1998, the powers of the Rapporteur to reject the complaint were limited and the jurisdiction of the panels extended. Under this amendment it is within the jurisdiction of Panel to reject complaints on the grounds that they were manifestly unfounded.[24]

If the Rapporteur finds no grounds for rejecting the complaint, he shall prepare the matter for consideration on the merits by a Panel.[25] The Rapporteur is responsible, usually with the help of his Assistant(s),[26] for the necessary procedural and preparatory work such as gathering evidence. The Rapporteur also arranges for notice of the complaint to be delivered to other parties concerned with a deadline for the submission of their views.

An oral hearing before the Court is prescribed, but, subject to the parties' consent, may be dispensed with if it will not contribute further to the resolution of the case. This procedure is used quite often in cases where it is manifestly obvious from the evidence that the complaint will be rejected in its entirety. At the oral hearing, the Rapporteur begins by outlining the contents of the complaint and of the state of proceedings up to that time. The report may not contain an opinion on the final disposal of the case. Then the parties are given the opportunity to put their arguments. All evidence relevant to establishing the facts is admissible, including a dossier of the evidence taken outside the hearing. Admissible evidence includes witness testimony, expert opinions, and statements from public bodies.

Following the hearing the Rapporteur presents his final draft judgment, the Judges confer and vote. The Court decision on the merits of the case takes the form of a judgment *("nález")* and all other issues (including the initial rejection of the complaint by the Rapporteur) by a resolution *("usnesení")*. In its judgment on the complaint, the Court either upholds or rejects the complaint in its entirety or in part. Where the complaint is upheld the Court annuls the decision of the public authority.[27] If a

24 No. 77/1998 Collection of Laws.

25 Where the constitutional complaint is accompanied by a proposal for the annulment of a statute or other law, the Panel shall interrupt the proceedings and submit a proposal for consideration by the Plenum.

26 An assistant to a Judge is nominated by the Chairperson of the Court on the basis of proposal of that Judge and must be a citizen of the Czech Republic with completed university legal education and at least five years of legal practice.

27 The expression "Public Authority" comprises ordinary courts, including the Supreme Court. It is not always the case that the constitutional court may deal with decisions of

constitutionally guaranteed fundamental right or basic freedom has been infringed by an act of a public authority rather than a decision, the Court orders the authority to cease infringing and orders it, as far as possible, to restore the *status quo ante*. The judgment must specify the rights or freedoms infringed, the relevant constitutional or treaty provision and the act by a public body which resulted in the infringement. After the written judgment has been prepared, it is sent to the parties and every judgment adopted by the Court is published in the Collection of Judgments and Resolutions of the Court *("Sbírka nálezů a usnesení Ústavního soudu")*. Publication in parts, usually two per year, is unfortunately very irregular and is sometimes delayed.

In the years since it became active the Court has become a stable, functional and respected part of the constitutional system of the Czech Republic. In the course of that time, the number of petitions received and decisions passed by the Court has increased.[28] An analysis of the Court's activity in 1996 reveals a particularly rich and generally positive picture in the context of electoral issues. Much publicised was a complaint against a decision made by the Central Electoral Committee (CEC) during the election to the Chamber of Deputies. The CEC ruled that the Free Democrat-Liberal National Social Party (hereinafter "SD-LSNS") was a coalition for electoral purposes, thus making it more difficult for the Party to win seats in the Chamber.[29] The Court overruled the CEC's decision which had not been correctly decided. The CEC was prohibited from forming a view as to whether the SD-LSNS list of candidates represented a coalition list and was ordered to disregard its conclusion declaring the SD-LSNS a coalition.

the courts. On the other hand it has to be noted, however, that the Court does not scrutinise the contested decision completely, it is not a kind of (super) revision. The Court inspects just constitutionality of decision (including procedural aspects). Vast number of complainants seem not to be aware of this relevant fact.

28 For instance in 1995 the Court received altogether 1,248 petitions, from which 997 were constitutional complaints. 667 complaints were rejected *a limine*. 89 cases were decided by the judgment (21 of them were adopted in the Plenary Session). Data for 1996 are still incomplete, because the second instalment of the Collection of Judgements and Resolutions of the Court for this year has not been published at the time of writing. It is only known that the Court received 1,427 petitions and 644 were rejected *a limine*. Roughly 28 judgements were adopted in the Plenary Session.

29 According to the Act No. 247/1995 Collection of Laws on Parliamentary Elections, the electoral limit needed for being elected to the Parliament makes 5% in the case of an individual political party while in the case of a coalition it makes 7% from the total valid votes.

In contrast, there was in 1996 a questionable decision on the requirement for the parties to provide a deposit.[30] This was challenged by some deputies who sought to have the relevant statutory provision annulled as unconstitutional. The application was rejected by the Court, but far from unanimously. Not only were there four dissenting opinions, but the rapporteur was replaced because he advocated the annulment of the provision. In the end, the application was rejected by eight votes to seven which, according to some, including myself, did not accord with the voting requirements of the Act on Constitutional Court. The nine votes required for a majority decision on the annulment, or the refusal to annul, legislation was not attained.[31] Furthermore the reasoning in support of the judgment was not coherent.

The Court gave persuasive judgments in cases involving the non-registration of candidates in the Senate elections. Registration had been refused mostly for negligible formal defects and the Court upheld most of the complaints. For the most part it founded its judgments on Article 22 of the Charter which provides that legal regulations in the sphere of political rights and freedoms, and the interpretation and application of such regulations, should facilitate and protect free competition between political forces in a democratic society. The Act on Elections, including its restrictive provisions, should be interpreted to ensure the broadest possible participation by citizens in voting or standing in elections, provided of course that legal certainty is secured.

Two judgments relating to the right to a fair trial are indisputably important. The first case was based on a complainant's application to annul a statutory provision accompanying a constitutional complaint, and the second, arising from a concrete case was based on an initiative of a panel of the Court. The Court decided to annul two provisions of the Civil Procedure Act that infringed Article 38 paragraph 2 of the Charter. The Charter provides that everybody is entitled to have their case considered in public without unnecessary delay, in their presence, with an opportunity to comment on all the evidence. In a challenge to the election of a member of a local authority, the Civil Procedure Act did not allow the person whose

30 According to Act No. 247/1995 Collection of Law, a political party or coalition, in case that its candidates list is registered in respective electoral ward, is obliged to provide a financial deposit of 200,000 Czech crowns. That bail should be paid back to those parties/coalitions that reached the first scrutiny.

31 According to s. 13 of Act on Constitutional Court the Plenary Session adopts decision if a majority of Judges present are in favour of it. And if the matter concerns annulment of laws it is adopted if at least 9 Judges present are in favour of it.

election was under challenge to participate in the proceedings.[32] Furthermore, the need for a hearing could be dispensed with.[33] The Court held that not only did provisions of the Civil Procedure Act not comply with the Charter, but it breached both Article 14 of the International Covenant on Civil and Political Rights and Article 6 paragraph 1, of the European Convention on Human Rights and Fundamental Freedoms.[34]

To complete the picture of human rights protection, the Czech Republic is a party to the European Convention on Human Rights and Fundamental Freedoms. So an unsatisfied complainant may have resort to the Convention procedures.[35] Complaints have already been lodged with the Strasbourg organs, but none has yet been considered on its merits. Most have been rejected by the European Commission for Human Rights, some of them paradoxically because not all legal remedies, by which was meant complaints to the Constitutional Court, had been exhausted.

Ombudsman in the Czech Republic: lost hopes (for the time being?)

It is hardly worth speaking about an ombudsman system before 1989. In the former Czechoslovakia, it was always unlikely that an ombudsman-style institution would have been created before the collapse of the totalitarian regime. The state was not and could not be eager to establish an independent institution focused on protecting human rights, even in the sphere of public administration. It was unrealistic to expect that from a

32 S. 200l of the Civil Procedure Act concerns complaints against a decision on verification of the election of a person to a local representative board. Only the complainant could be a party to proceedings. A member of such a Board was completely excluded.

33 S. 250f of the Civil Procedure Act enabled the judge reviewing an administrative decisions to decide the case without a hearing in "simple cases...or if only legal issues are to be adjudicated upon".

34 Some of judgements (including two electoral cases) appear in English: (1997) 4 *East European Case Reporter of Constitutional Law*,1. From the rich literature in Czech see e.g., V. Mikule, "Lidská práva pět let po Listopadu", *Listy* 2/1995, 69 V. Mikule & V. Sládeček, "O závaznosti rozhodnutí Ústavního soudu", *Bulletin advokacie* 8/1995, 35; J Filip., "K otázce ústavnosti volebních kaucí" *Časopis pro právní vědu a praxi* 2/1996, 273; V. Kratochvíl, "Nad jedním rozhodnutím Ústavního soudu ČR" *Kriminalistika* 3/1996, 202; V. Sládeček, "K jednomu aspektu práva na spravedlivý proces: judikatura evropská a česká", *Právní rozhledy* 9/1996, 397; V. Adamus, "Odmítnutí návrhu podle zákona o Ústavním soudu", *Správní právo* 1/1997, 18, 39; V. Ševčík, "Ústavní soud ČR a soudy obecné - pokus o vymezení vzájemných vztahů", *Bulletin advokacie* 5/1997, 7-2.

35 The jurisdiction of the Czech Constitutional Court is wider than that of the organs of the Convention. Thus the complaints concerning social, economic and cultural rights have no chance of success in Strasbourg.

state which never established the Constitutional Court required by the Constitution. There was a "Socialist *Prokuratura*" having some of the formal features of the ombudsman when exercising, to some extent, similar functions.[36] Nevertheless, its main purpose lay in representing the state in criminal proceedings. A considerably smaller part of its activity was devoted to the protection of citizens by ensuring observance of law by administrative agencies. It must be stressed that any resemblance to an ombudsman was purely formal and unsurprisingly its impact was negligible. The ruling Communist Party's evident influence upon and interference with the Prokuratura's activity often hindered the taking of appropriate action.

Quite noticeable results, however, could be observed in the activities of the Prokuratura after the elimination of political influence from 1990 to 1993, when it ceased to exist. Unfortunately, the State Prosecution service that replaced it did not have jurisdiction to oversee public administration, given that no ombudsman-type alternative existed. Both unofficial and official attempts were made to establish an ombudsman in Czechoslovakia in the period between 1990 and 1992. A draft bill "On the Defender of Human Rights and Civil Freedoms of the Czech and Slovak Federative Republic", seems to be the most important product of the period, although it has never reached the legislature. Nevertheless, there was one genuine, if meagre, outcome of this period. In 1990, the law on the "General Inspector of Armed Forces" was passed.[37] The creation of this institution was to a certain extent influenced by the tradition of the Czechoslovak Republic before World War II and influenced by the German "Wehrbeauftragter" (Defence Commissioner).[38] The General Inspector resembles a kind of specialised ombudsman, though only as regards its more limited

36 See, e.g., G.B Smith, "Soviet Union", in G.E. Caiden (ed.), *International Handbook of the Ombudsman. Country Surveys*, London, 1983 pp.165ff.; L. Czubinski, "Inspection of Law Observance by the Prosecutor in the Polish People's Republic", in: J.C. Juergensmeyer, & A. Burzinsky (eds.), *Parliamentary and Extra-Administrative Forms of Protection of Citizen s Rights*, Colloquium Co-Sponsored by the College of Law of the University of Florida and the Institute of State and Law of the Polish Academy of Science, 1979 pp. 9- 23; C.T. Reid, , "The Ombudsman's Cousin: The Procuracy in Socialist States", [1986] *Public Law* 311; H. Bader & H. Brompton, "Remedies Against Administrative Abuse in Central Europe, the Soviet Union, and Communist East Europe (Ombudsmen and Others)" [1986] *Annals of the American Academy*; S. Frankowski, "The Procuracy and the Regular Courts as the Palladium of Individual Rights and Liberties - the Case of Poland", (1987) 61 *Tulane Law Review* 1307.

37 Act No. 540/1990 Collection of Laws.

38 See, e.g., E. Lohse, "West Germany Military Ombudsman," in D.C. Rowat, (ed.), *The Ombudsman*, London 1968, p. 119ff; P. Wolf, *Defence Commissioner*, Bonn 1992.

jurisdiction. The main task for the General Inspector lay in the supervision of the armed forces, on behalf of both the national and republican legislatures. However, although several votes were taken in the national legislature, no appointment was ever made. As a consequence of the split of Czechoslovakia at the end of 1992, the legislation ceased to be in force. A new draft bill on the institution, prepared by the Ministry of Defence, has not been introduced in the legislature and more recently the idea of such an specialised institution has been completely abandoned.

The debate on a general ombudsman continued in 1993 in the newly established Czech Republic and still goes on. Initially the cabinet and a majority of the members of the legislature seemed lukewarm, if not hostile, in their attitudes towards the issue. This was partly due to the fact that the significance and purpose of the institution was not entirely understood. Usually those opposing the institution observed that judicial protection sufficed. Additionally, the lack of support for the issue was and still is in part due to some undesirably partisan views that are expressed. These views are a reaction to the fact that some of the legislators who spoke in favour of the ombudsman belong to "left wing" parties.

President Václav Havel regularly expresses strong support for the institution. Furthermore, both scholars and members of organisations for the protection of human rights (such as the Czech Helsinki Committee) call for the establishment of the institution. In this respect, two international expert seminars dealing with the ombudsman, which took place in Prague in June 1993 and June 1994, seem to have been events of importance. During these seminars, draft bills on a general legislative ombudsman were presented. The first draft bill (1993) was prepared at the Law Faculty of Charles University.

The original draft was based on the legislation of, in particular, Denmark, Great Britain, the Netherlands, Poland, France, Portugal and Germany. Unfortunately, useful American model statutes were not available at that time, although the drafters were aware of their existence.[39] The envisaged ombudsman, generally speaking, a slight variation on the classical Scandinavian model. His expected focus was to be "only" on central public administrative agencies (subordinated regional entities

39 See, "A State Statute to Create the Office of Ombudsman", [1968] *Harvard Journal on Legislation*, 213; W. Gellhorn, "Annotated Model Ombudsman Statute", in V. Anderson (ed), *Ombudsman for American Government?*, The American Assembly 1968, pp. 159-173; American Bar Association, *Model Ombudsman Statute for State Government* 1974; B. Frank, "State Ombudsman Legislation in the United States", (1975) 29 *University of Miami Law Review*, 397.

included), albeit within all the existing spheres of government, with the exception of military affairs (this was connected with the existence of the above-mentioned special draft bill on an "Army Ombudsman").

Though not perfect, the Draft Bill served as a point of departure for some members of the legislature in the preparation of an official bill to be introduced in Parliament. The first important development was the so-called principles of legislation on *"A Public Protector of Rights"* introduced into Parliament in May 1995. Because of the new Rules of Procedure of Parliament - which came into force in August 31, 1995 - and in accordance with these rules, the principles were not dealt with by Parliament. A group of fifteen legislators submitted to Parliament a draft bill with the same title in the beginning of December 1995.

Although the Bill on the Public Protector of Rights was approved by Parliament in the first reading, the approach of general elections in June 1996, obstructive tactics by some of the parties prevented the Bill from undergoing the second and third readings required to become law. Nevertheless, the newly-elected Parliament introduced a new version of the Bill in September 1996. Once again the Bill was approved in its first reading and in its second reading in February 1997. Given the composition of Parliament and the prevailing opinion of deputies the proposed law was expected finally to be passed. The situation differed from that of two years before, since some of the coalition parties' deputies now favoured the institution. Nevertheless, in March 1997, a considerably modified law failed relatively narrowly to win approval in the third and final reading.[40]

40 These are the main features of the bill (which is a modification of original draft bill of 1993): The envisaged Public Protector of Rights/Ombudsman, is expected to focus his attention both to central and local administrative agencies. The Ombudsman is to be appointed by Parliament; his independence is, *inter alia*, guaranteed by the fact that reasons for which he can be removed from office are enumerated exhaustively. In principle, his connection with Parliament is ensured by the Petition Committee. The ombudsman has the right to submit reports to the Committee and to attend its meetings. He shall be enabled to speak at his own request.. A direct link to Parliament as a whole will be assured for the ombudsman, in particular, through annual reports, while individual Deputies and Senators may refer to him complaints which they have received. The Ombudsman is conceived as an officer acting on his own. He takes action not only on the basis of a citizen's complaint, but also on his own initiative It is not considered appropriate for the ombudsman to deal with complaints passed to him by state (governmental) authorities. The primary condition for initiating an investigation should be a citizen's application to the Ombudsman.. As is customary in other parts of the world, the Ombudsman is entitled not to pursue a submission under certain conditions. In his investigations the ombudsman has the necessary rights in respect of the parties (to ask questions, ask for materials etc.). Other governmental authorities are likewise obliged to co-operate when asked. If the ombudsman, during his investigations, finds a violation of

It can hardly be supposed that this Parliament will try again to work on such legislation. This is regrettable when we see that ombudsman institutions are being established (or at least legal provision is being made for them) in other former socialist states, such as Poland, Slovenia, Croatia, Lithuania, Russia, Hungary and Georgia. Nevertheless, the Constitutional Court can, to a certain extent, temporarily and partially, do the work of an ombudsman, though his main task and legal means are different.

a law or some kind of "maladministration" etc., he will propose measures to be taken for the purpose of setting things right. Where the relevant authority has not taken corrective action, the ombudsman notifies the superior authority, or even arranges for the case to be made public. Another option is to bring the case to the Petition Committee in Parliament. The Ombudsman is also entitled to initiate amendments to, and changes in, legislation. An important guarantee of the Ombudsman's independence is the reservation of a separate heading in the state budget.

PART II

SLOVAKIA

6 Does the Rule of Law (*Rechtsstaat*) Exist in Slovakia?

MIROSLAV KUSÝ

The Final Scene of the Division of Czechoslovakia

In 1992, when Czechoslovakia split, the prime ministers of both republics Mečiar and Klaus spoke with one voice. Nothing extraordinary is going on here, it is only an administrative affair. It will not affect the lives of citizens, everything will function as if there had been no split at all. It was a deliberate consoling lie and citizens were significantly affected from the very first day of 1993 when frontiers and custom offices became a reality - a reality the existence of which the Czech prime minister, Klaus, did not even "notice". Citizens started, step by step, to experience the effects of the split of Czechoslovakia in their everyday lives, especially Czechs living in Slovakia and Slovaks living in the Czech Republic. Especially those Czechs who used to perceive Slovakia as a part of their home and those Slovaks who were convinced that the whole of Czechoslovakia was their homeland.

Apart from these sentimental or psychological effects, the external consequences of the split have been and will be much more damaging. From the very beginning, political analysts said that, in spite of remaining in the same geographical position, the Czech Republic moved geopolitically towards the West and Slovakia towards the East. There is substantial evidence to support this opinion in the foreign relations established by the two republics after the split, the new quality of the historical relationships established in the newly defined geopolitical space and the new political relations of both republics with their neighbours and other countries.

The Czech movement towards the West and the Slovak movement to the East was obvious soon after the split. This was the responsibility of Mečiar's government and his political movement's parliamentary majority which, instead of mitigating and compensating for the negative geopolitical effects of the split, encouraged and opened the way to them.

In July 1997 at the NATO summit in Madrid, when the Czech Republic was named as one of three countries invited to negotiate entry into NATO, Slovakia was excluded. The division of Czechoslovakia was complete from an international perspective. This was not an unavoidable geopolitical necessity. If Slovakia, in this context, had a worse starting position than the Czech Republic, it definitely did not have a worse position in comparison to Hungary or Poland, the other two nominated for entry. Its historical ties with the East are not as strong as Poland's and the shaping its national culture by influences from the East is not different from the position in Hungary. Nevertheless, unlike Slovakia, the Poles and Hungarians succeeded and freed themselves from these relationships because they positively wanted to.

In Madrid, the Slovak Prime Minister behaved in the same easy-going and self-contained manner as when he divided Czechoslovakia: nothing special is going on, we lose nothing, we are not deprived of anything. Here was the same irresponsibility and the same lie. A lot was going on here and Slovakia was losing much more than many are ready to admit.

From a geopolitical point of view, Slovakia became an isolated island in a European sea. If the Madrid decision on NATO was a significant event in the process of integration into the European Union - and all experts and politicians believe that it was - then the catastrophe resulting from the negotiations with NATO will inevitably lead to the same catastrophe with the European Union. The European Commission Report, endorsed by the Council of Ministers, excluding Slovakia from the next candidates for the EU membership supports this view. It means that "Schengen-type" borders, which Slovakia now has only with Austria (representing only 127 kilometres, a small part of the Slovak border), will be created with Hungary, the Czech Republic and Poland. The only exception will be the 98 kilometre long eastern border with the Ukraine, which itself has a special treaty with NATO.

Schengen borders with Slovakia will have to be especially closely watched because Slovakia will be a strange element in the European body. It will be a 500 kilometres deep intrusion into Europe which will be attractive for and used by all those negative elements from the East which is exactly what led to the establishment of the Schengen-style borders.

The Slovak prime minister, Vladimir Mečiar, was then, in a certain sense, quite right when he suggested that "Europe needs us"- in the sense that Slovakia will be unnatural and unwanted within the compact body of the European Union. However, the fact that Slovakia was disqualified is evidence against Mečiar: European politicians prefer this cut into the European body to a threat of infection of European stability and democracy.

The political and economic consequences of this inevitable isolation from Europe will affect everyone living in Slovakia – governing coalition political parties and opposition parties, Slovaks and national minorities living in Slovakia. There is no need to put forward and fear catastrophic scenarios, but it is wise to be prepared, without any panic and media hysteria, even for the worst eventualities, for instance, for visa duty and custom regulations. Slovakia must certainly be prepared for the complicated conditions of its coexistence with the rest of Europe.

There is, however, one thing to be frightened of and against which we should warn -the threat of a radical turn by the Government coalition parties towards an autocratic political regime, to the flagrant violation of democratic game rules, the rule of law, to the obstruction of human and minority rights. Until Madrid, Mečiar's Government and his parliamentary majority had, at least formally, to reflect upon critical voices from abroad, upon reports and analyses addressed to Slovakia. After Madrid it became unnecessary because the Government and the parliamentary majority had, so to speak, their hands free for realisations of their own political goals.

These goals are clear: strengthening their positions, keeping the power for any price. The road to these goals leads via next parliamentary elections. The ruling coalition condemns a possibility which make up foundations of democratic game rules - possibility that it could lose the elections and would have to go into opposition. The coalition parties do not calculate with this possibility in their strategic plans and therefore are ready to play just one card, to keep the power by any means. All legislative efforts are subjected to this goal. All power actions target this goal. The coalition is ready to use even unconstitutional and illegal means, as is already witnessed in the referendum scandal, etc.

Madrid represented a hard blow to Slovak national confidence. As a "young nation and young state" we suffered, from the very beginning, from a need to manifest national strength. We were telling ourselves that we are equal among equals, especially equal with Hungarians and Czechs who represent immanent measures of our position in the world. In this respect, Slovak nation felt quite impressed and pleased with the propaganda of Mečiar's populist HZDS movement or with slogans of Slovak National Party: "Are not we as good as Hungarians? Look at our economic achievements, look at our historical treasures such as the altar in Bojnice, look at the Gabčikovo hydroelectric power plant, look at the stability of our currency, etc...". Although all expectations for Madrid were calculated as very low, HZDS supporters and nationalists did not want to believe that this can happen. "They cannot do it to us", they were persuading themselves, "Czechs yes, Hungarians yes, and Slovaks no?"

From this perspective, Madrid was a very cold shower for this false national self-confidence. Frustration together with attempts to find national enemies can be its only effect. The Government coalition will do all its best to present very emotionally political opposition as such an enemy of the nation. If it is necessary, they are ready to put it to national trial and outside the law. Let us recall the communist resolution of the question "Who is guilty?" - for our poverty, backward infrastructure, isolation from the outside world - in the 1950s. Let us not be consoled with that kind of optimism which tells that everything will turn all right. Psychologists have already a large collection of brilliant examples of what a frustrated nation may accept when it becomes convinced that it was innocent and betrayed by its enemies.

National minorities have, of course, to be mentioned here. They will also be frustrated by Madrid, although of a different kind when compared with Slovaks. The main question for Hungarians and Czechs living in Slovakia will be, now: "Why should we be affected by the result of Madrid together with Slovaks?". Their feelings of being unjustly separated from their own nations, which will enjoy the advantages of the integration to NATO and later the EU, will be radically enhanced.

If the government continues to rule in this current spirit of confrontation, it will lead to the increase of ethnic tensions and radicalisation on both sides. One can hardly expect that Hungarians in Slovakia will passively accept its worsening situation. The final scene of the split of Czechoslovakia, staged in Madrid, thus has a very bitter taste.

Opposition and Coalition

A current dividing line in Slovakia is not the political line between the right and left, liberals and conservatives, but primarily, after Vladimir Mečiar became prime minister, between the Government coalition and the Opposition. The political contest between them is not only a manifestation of their struggle for political power, but mainly of their struggle for the maintenance and development, or repression and abandonment of democratic principles of government. Slovak sociologist Vladimir Krivý has published empirical evidence and an analysis of this situation in the FOCUS project.[1] According to him, the dividing line between the coalition and opposition is a line drawn between supporters of an authoritarian and a democratic regime.

This struggle has gradually begun to dominate the whole of political life and thinking. It includes the Slovak-Slovak dispute about who are better and worse Slovaks and the Slovak-Hungarian confrontation. It is only some

1 V. Krivý, in an interview with *Domino Efekt,* May 9 1997.

of the leaders of the Democratic Left Party (post-communists) who still understand the current political development in Slovakia as a classical left-right political difference and thus leave room for manoeuvring between the two antagonistic political sides.

Even in 1997, events on the Slovak political scene were substantially determined by this dividing line and the solutions to every political problem became a matter of political prestige and confrontation. The coalition used all means at its disposal to achieve its interests. It used and abused institutional means at its disposal and gradually transformed political battle onto the level of an institutional crisis. Early in 1997 Krivý wrote that this "institutional crisis in Slovakia shifted from bad to worse in the last few months".[2] A lot of ordinary political problems have thus been changed into scandals, threatening the stability of the democratic regime and creating a negative image of Slovakia in the outside world. From the beginning of 1997, the National Council of Slovak Republic (the Slovak parliament) experienced some spectacular scandals, such as: the decision to deprive the MP, František Gaulieder, of his mandate and expel him from the National Council because of his resignation from membership of the HZDS parliamentary party; the appointment of a parliamentary candidate, although he was not legally entitled to be appointed; the Government's refusal to make nominations for the appointment of certain judges, in spite the fact that it is its constitutional duty. The Hungarian minority was cut to the quick when the Ministry of Education ordered the issue of school records in Slovak only. Since 1921 Hungarian pupils and students had been given their records in bilingual form. All these problematic decisions of the Government were accompanied by numerous protests, petitions and warnings from abroad - from the American Helsinki Committee in the case of MP Gaulieder, from the High Commissioner for Minorities, van der Stoel in the case of the language legislation, and the whole complex of the European Union institutions after the Government's boycott of the referendum.

The Slovak "Economic Miracle"

There is one sphere in which Mečiar's government has scored points and which was often used as a compensation for losses and faults in the sphere of political democracy: the national economy. It seems that this sphere is no

2 "Constitutional Watch" (1997) 6 East European Constitutional Review, No. 1, p.27.

longer a strong card for the Government. According to a leading expert in economic science and former deputy prime minister for economic affairs Brigita Schmognerova, also a deputy chair of the Democratic Left Party:

> ... the bubble of economic miracle in Slovakia is gone. The reason is not, as suggested by some politicians, our close ties with the Czech republic which has its own economic problems, but because we have analogous problems. In Slovakia, no fundamental structural changes have been made, no modernisation and innovation of industry. It cannot be resolved by short term administrative measures, such as implemented by the Government in the form of import deposits. Let us not be misled by the growth of GNP. We know very well how it was calculated in the communist regime. Under the cover is hiding anything but an effective growth.[3]

This conclusion completely corresponds to a general regularity discovered in the analytical report of Freedom House on the state of civil society, democracy and the free market in the countries of Central and Eastern Europe:

> Interrelations between democratic government and fundamental economic reform is so close that every country which consolidated its democratic political institutions, established a respect for human rights, promoted the press freedom and the rule of law and made up foundations for dynamic civil society, achieves an adequate progress also in economic liberalisation. These close interrelations between given political and economic factors is the most important finding of our report ....[4]

Brigita Schmognerova points to the current negative trends arising from the economic policy of the Slovak Government: the growth of unemployment to 13.5% in the first three months of 1997, the growth of state budget deficit from 8.3 million dollars in 1995 to 25.6 in 1997, a significant growth in the foreign trade deficit. In Slovakia, the deficit grew to 10.2% of GNP. In the Czech republic, its level of 8.4% is considered by the Czech Government as alarming. According to the author, all these "... figures clearly show that the Slovak economy, after a period of some

3 B. Schmognerova, "Zazrak sa nekona" ("No Miracle Is Happening"), *Plus 7 Dni*, June 9, 1997, p.14.

4 A. Karatnycky, "Introduction. Political and Economic Reform in East Central Europe and New Independent States: A Progress Report", p. 8 in: A. Karatnycky, A. Motyl and B. Shor (eds.), *Nations in Transit 1997. Civil Society, Democracy and Markets in East Central Europe and the Newly Independent States*, New Brunswick and London: Transaction Publishers, 1997.

success, turned in the middle of 1996 and ... last year figures begin to resemble the worst year after 1989, which was 1993 ...".[5]

This whole development has been accompanied by huge economic criminality, as we witness a penetration of state bodies by organised crime and the spheres of economy and politics becoming mutually linked together, when top political officials and leaders are involved in big business as owners or partners. This is "... even more dangerous because the Government is under the particular and real pressures of certain business and interest groups to such an extent that the Prime Minister has in fact become their hostage ...".[6]

Referendum

Both sides in current Slovak politics concentrated their efforts in a dispute about the referendum in May 1997. On 14 February, Parliament approved three referendum questions formulated by the Government Coalition, the first question concerning the integration to NATO and two other questions, at odds with the first, concerning the possibility of the deployment of nuclear weapons and military bases on Slovak territory. The Opposition suggested that the first question was irrelevant and the two other questions misleading. According to the Opposition, an orchestrated and expected negative answer to the first question was to justify the disqualification of Slovakia from the group of three other countries, the Czech republic, Hungary, Poland, which are going through the process of NATO integration.

The Opposition, without the post-communist Democratic Left Party, expressed its priorities in the successful petition for the direct popular election of the president. Within the limits of his power, the president put these two referendums into one and called for a referendum with all these four questions. During the referendum campaign, the Opposition took an initiative and recommended voters to answer "yes" to NATO integration and the direct election of the president, while it recommended a "no" to the two remaining questions. The campaign was ignored by Mečiar's HZDS movement while two other government parties campaigned for "no" to all four questions. Public polls suggested a majority support for "yes" which would have been perceived as an important opposition victory. At the last

5 B. Schmognerova, *supra* n.3.
6 *Ibid.*, p.15.

minute, the Government intervened unconstitutionally into the organisation of the referendum and ordered the Minister of Interior, who was technically responsible for the organisation, to withdraw the fourth question from the ballot. In the following legal and organisational chaos, only 10% of voters participated in the referendum and the Supreme Referendum Commission declared it void. The Opposition called for criminal proceedings against the Minister of the Interior and for his immediate resignation and, consequently, for the resignation of the Government, naturally without any success. The only member of the Government for whom the scandal had any consequences was the Minister for Foreign Affairs Pavol Hamzik, who immediately resigned.

The End of Democracy in Slovakia?

As a reaction to the referendum, some more radical journalists wrote that this was already a culmination of the coalition attacks against democracy and virtually the end of democracy in Slovakia. Luboš Palata, for instance, wrote in the Czech newspaper *Dnes* that "... by the boycott of the referendum, Slovakia crossed the border dividing democratic and undemocratic countries ... Slovakia crossed Rubicon during that weekend ... It is five past twelve ...".[7] In the Slovak weekly magazine, a similar commentary was written by Karol Wolf, who in an article entitled, "Mečiar has completely discredited himself and Slovakia" asserted that, after the referendum "Slovakia appeared on the list of European countries which are not to be considered democratic".[8]

Very emotional statements of this kind, shifting on a black and white scale, are too simplifying and misleading. This time, fortunately, leading opposition politicians and the Slovak President showed greater restraint and understood the whole affair in a more sophisticated way. In spite of very critical judgements, none of them spoke about the end of democracy in Slovakia.

In this context, it is worth taking into account statements of European Union representatives. The European Union expressed its concern about the events accompanying the referendum and asked the Slovak Government to respect the rule of law and principles fundamental for the stability of democratic society. "Concern" is certainly not a term signifying the end of democracy in Slovakia.

7 *Mlada Fronta Dnes*, May 27, 1997.
8 *Domino Efekt*, May 30, 1997.

According to Herbert Bösch, "... the referendum certainly did not increase trust of the European Union in the political stability in Slovakia ..." and "... these events damaged the reputation of Slovakia and its goal of being accepted as a EU member, soon. ... We want to enlarge the EU and accept countries with stable democratic regimes and, in this sense, the referendum is an important issue. The stability of democracy in Slovakia seems to be problematic, not its very existence".[9]

The EU commissioner Hans van den Broek said during his recent visit to Bratislava that "already a long time before the referendum, the EU has expressed its deep concern about the stability of political institutions in Slovakia". After the referendum, he said only that "... the rule of law and democracy do not seem to be deeply rooted enough in Slovakia".[10] There is no doubt that the way the Slovak Government spoiled the referendum was deeply undemocratic, like many other governmental steps before. It was a very destabilising step. "... We do not think that democracy is stable in a condition when a government can put in question respect for the rights and duties of such institutions as the President, Constitutional Court or Supreme Referendum Commission", said van den Broek.[11] This does not imply, however, that Slovakia is no longer democratic and has become a totalitarian, unfree country. Sociologist and political scientist, Soňa Szomolányi, expressed a similar opinion when asked about the state of democracy in Slovakia:

> ... I do not think it is already gone. ... We are still confronted with problems of the consolidation of democracy. It is wise to evade two extremes in judging the current tate - hysteria and ignorance of emergency signs ....[12]

Fortunately, the foundations of democracy are much broader and deeper and can hardly be destroyed by a spoiled referendum or other anti-democratic activities; the scale of possibilities of different levels of democracy in different countries is much richer than can be resolved by a simple dichotomy that democracy does or does not exist.

Anti-democratic activities destabilise and make democracy weaker, but if they do not break and destroy its systemic foundations, there is still the possibility of defence by working through democratic mechanisms. Even a

9 Cited by the daily news agency of Slovakia.

10 *Ibid.*

11 *Ibid.*

12 S. Szomolányi, "Zaklady demokracie na Slovensku este existuju" [There are still foundations of democracy in Slovakia], *Domino Efekt*, June 13, 1997.

developed democratic country is not immune to a government's attempts to avoid, misuse, or even badly damage democratic game rules. What is important is its readiness and capability to face these challenges.

The systemic foundations of democracy enable various types and levels of development of democratic regimes in different countries. Sweden and Turkey are democratic countries but nobody will, nevertheless, say that they are democracies of the same type and level of development. Political scientists Robert Dahl, David Beetham and others have precisely and virtually unanimously defined the main characteristics of democracy from which European institutions have derived their own criteria. Slovakia fitted within these criteria and was accepted as a member of the Council of Europe: all member states of the Council of Europe are democratic countries. Slovakia, moreover, fitted within ten countries with association agreements with the EU and within the NATO membership candidates. Here, the demands were even higher than in the Council of Europe and countries like Albania, Ukraine, or Moldova did not satisfy them.

The Level of Democracy in Slovakia

Doubts about Slovakia's NATO membership which culminated in the referendum crisis then mean only that Slovakia was disqualified from membership of the first, prestigious group of candidates. According to the American Secretary of State M. Allbright, these "... candidates must fulfil the highest possible standards before they are invited to join NATO ...".[13]

As for the European Union, membership is conditional on a country having established stable institutions promoting democracy, the rule of law, human rights and the protection of minorities. According to Commissioner van den Broek, this is exactly what has been jeopardised by the referendum scandal. The Union expects: "... clear signals from the Slovak Government about its intentions to support the rule of law and democratic process in this country, after which necessary practical steps will follow ...".[14]

Where does Slovakia belong, then? Freedom House classified Slovakia as a free democratic country. The problem is, however, that Slovakia ended up at the bottom of the list of ten countries candidates for membership of the EU. In 1996, only Romania was behind, and it was classified as a country with limited freedoms. After Romania took stabilising measures through elections and Slovak destabilising steps through the referendum

13 *Study on NATO Enlargement*, Brussels, NATO, 1995.
14 *Supra*, n. 9.

affair, it became clear that Romania was moving towards the free countries and Slovakia towards countries with limited freedoms. The latest records of Freedom House proved this expectation in the Nations in Transit 1997 report.[15] We can console ourselves only with the fact that Slovakia still does not belong to the third category of unfree and undemocratic countries.

In this report Freedom House divides the twenty five countries analysed into three groups, according to the development of political democracy and three groups according to the development of a market economy. The first group is represented by consolidated democracies and countries are listed as follows: 1. The Czech republic, 2. Hungary, 3. Poland, 4. Slovenia, 5. Estonia, 6. Lithuania, 7. Latvia. The same countries, but in different positions, make up the group of the most firmly established market economies. In 1996, Slovakia fell into the group of governments in transition, behind Russia and Moldova and ahead of Bulgaria, Romania, Ukraine, Macedonia, Croatia, Albania, Armenia, Kirgizia, Georgia, Kazakhstan, and Azerbaijan. The same countries were classified as having economies in transition. The third group - called consolidated autocracies and consolidated static economies - consists of Belarus, Tadzikistan, Uzbekistan, and Turkmenistan.[16]

Albright and van den Broek had in mind these facts, when they spoke about the high standards of membership of both organisations. According to Albright, the NATO enlargement must strengthen the Alliance and not make it weaker, and this is why NATO will accept only countries with a level of development of democracy comparable to the standards of current NATO members. Universal European citizenship, according to van den Broek, presupposes that "... countries that want to become EU members cannot only declare principles of democracy, but must apply them in everyday political life ...".[17]

Western politicians, experts and analysts do not consider Slovakia to be a free and democratic country, but a country with limited freedoms. Our primary task should be, therefore, to revitalise democratic institutions and the democratic way of political decision-making, a complex consolidation

15 See M. Skak, *Democratic Consolidation in East Central Europe*, Aarhus, 1996. Following comments on the research by Freedom House come from this book.

16 A. Karatnycky et al., *supra* n.4, p.14. According to the published major parameters of transition, all countries with association agreements with the EU except Slovakia are considered as free. Slovakia belongs to the category of countries with limited freedoms, together with Ukraine, Russia, Moldova, Macedonia, Croatia, Albania, Armenia, Georgia and Kyrgyzia.

17 *Supra*, n..9.

of our democracy and the stabilisation of institutions guaranteeing the rule of law.

What Has to be Done?

Extensive opposition activities during the referendum campaign for the direct election of the president of Slovakia were not only some oppositional caprice. They were about how to avoid the threat that the new president would not be elected and most of presidential powers would be transferred to the current prime minister. The Opposition "successfully" organised the petition calling for a referendum and the Government "successfully" damaged the referendum. Citizens boycotted the referendum without the fourth question concerning the direct election of the president. This result was interpreted by both sides as their own victory. After the case of referendum, the Opposition scored points in the political battlefield. It revealed how far the Government coalition was ready to go in "deforming the democracy and the rule of law".[18] Today, the Opposition is faced by the question of how to continue its politics. The calendar of 1998 was presidential elections in the spring, parliamentary elections in the autumn. Originally, the Opposition considered even a double possibility of "civil disobedience" and keeping their positions in legal and constitutional structures. It preferred the second alternative and, within its limits, "... to build the united democratic forces, mobilise citizens and prepare itself well for elections ...".[19]

This decision has a fundamental importance for the strategy of further steps of the Opposition. Concrete political actions are a crucial indicator. If the Opposition still supposes that Slovakia does not belong to the group of unfree countries, it means that it concentrates on the real chance of rectification by legal democratic means, by legal control of the Government and by a legal contest for the power. Today, the main task in Slovakia is not to let the Government cross the line beyond which the Opposition ends up in prisons and illegality. This would be a territory of unfree antidemocratic countries in which it is necessary to fight for the power by completely different means. The law on the direct election of the president would be a strong weapon in hands of the Opposition. The whole initiative was badly damaged by the Government's illegal act, but also by the Constitutional

18 O. Dostal, "Opozicna stredna cesta" [A middle road of the opposition], *SME*, 7.8.97, p.4.

19 Taken from the proclamation of the vice-chairperson of the Christian Democrats, J. Figel, for the daily newspaper *SME*, 10.6.1997, p.2.

Court decision in this case. The Court upheld the legitimacy of the four question referendum, but it also stated that its possible positive answer to the fourth question would involve only a binding recommendation to the parliament to adopt an adequate constitutional act on the direct election of the president. After this decision of the Constitutional Court, the situation changed qualitatively. In this context, it made no sense for the Opposition to struggle for a new referendum on this concrete question.

Slovak citizens have had bad experiences with referendums, anyway. In 1992, the referendum on the Czechoslovak federation was not organised at all, in spite of the fact that 2.5 million people signed a petition for it. In 1994, the Government's referendum on the so-called 'dirty money' was wrong from its very beginning and citizens ignored it. In 1997, the referendum inasmuch as it concerned NATO was in large part illogical and the Government destroyed it. It was a miracle that citizens were persuaded by the Opposition to sign the petition supporting the fourth question. Now, it seems impossible that after all these negative experiences a miracle could happen again.

The unsuccessful referendum should have led to a new strategy of the Opposition, to a new definition of its priorities before elections. The Opposition did not achieve this and the election of a new president remained in jeopardy.

> There is still a strange silence of the Opposition which makes impression that the Opposition has already resigned. The Opposition parties drafted a constitutional law on the direct election of the president, but now it seems that they only passively wait what is going to happen. This position can hardly lead to a solution of this problem ...[20]

The state of the Opposition in Slovakia, its fragmentary nature, its search for a political identity, is an expression of a more general critical situation which is discussed often as a "crisis of the Slovak political elite".

The Slovak Political Elite in Crisis

This discussion was opened by an article written by Peter Weiss, one of leaders of the Democratic Left Party, and having as its title the heading of this section. According to him, "... in its integrative ambitions, Slovakia was

20 *Ibid.*, comment by O. Dostal.

disadvantaged by the critical state of its political elite ...".[21] Not only the crisis of the current power elite, but of the political elite as a whole, both in the Government and also in the Opposition. In other words, it is a crisis of part of Slovak politics which is manifested in the behaviour of its actors.

The power elite is in a state of decline, in a state when it does not know how to carry on and shifts more and more towards solutions based simply on force. The elite of the opposition groups and coalitions is fragmented and as such political powerless. As a whole, it is still being born, searching for its integrated identity. When it finds that identity, it will become able to act. The extent and scale of its integrated identity will be a measure of its political capacity to act.

On the other hand, the crisis of the political elite does not mean a crisis in the whole Slovak society. Its political scene lives its own "wild" life which unpleasantly influences other parts of social life, but it does not take them over. There is a growing gap between politics and other parts of the life of Slovak society. Fortunately, people do not live by politics as much as politicians tend to think. Political life is perceived as a kind of theatre which is being played out somewhere else and mediated only by television or other media, as if it is not the citizens' business. This remoteness even blurs the fact that this political crisis damages Slovakia's, and therefore its citizens' own interests.

The crisis of the political elite is furthermore not a crisis of the whole cultural elite of Slovak society. The current power elite is not even part of the cultural elite. If Weiss says that, "... in this country, the concept of an elite should only be used with the adjective "political" in quotation marks ...",[22] he probably has in mind the power elite, which really does not belong to our current cultural elite. Weiss himself mentions examples of the vulgar and dirty language of the top state officials and representatives, their rude morals and immorality. This is, however, not true of the rest of the political elite, quite apart from the cultural elite in general. The cultural elite faces some problems caused by the power elite. The political crisis makes its life harder, but it does not signify its own existential crisis.

However, I can hardly agree with Peter Weiss's interpretation of the origin and formation of our new political elite before November 1989. He concedes that, "... unlike Poland and Hungary, where former communist state-parties started to reform themselves from inside and change while being still in power, ... in Czechoslovakia the ruling gerontocracy, which

21 P. Weiss, "Kriza politickej elity" [The crisis of the political elite], *Forum obcianskej spolocnosti* [Civil Society Forum], June 1997, n.2, p.20.
22 *Ibid.*

did not want even perestroika, had to be removed from power by crowds of dissatisfied people in streets ...".[23] It is true that, unlike in Poland and Hungary, the Czechoslovak Communist Party did not have a reform faction because reformers were completely excommunicated during the extensive party activities after 1968. Within the structures and nomenklatura of the Czechoslovak Communist Party and the Slovak Communist Party, after 1968 there remained only anti-reformers, whose programme was so called normalisation - a political counterpoint of perestroika - until the end of 1989.

How can Peter Weiss say at the same time that "... this regime was eroded mostly because of the middle rank nomenklatura members ..."?[24] Undoubtedly, a gerontocracy obstructed this nomenklatura because of the generation gap and its power was a source of dissatisfaction for younger nomenklatura generations, which could not get any higher in the power structures. However, it can hardly lead to the conclusion that this generation conflict involving the middle rank nomenklatura people and their 'neglected potential" generally involved any attempts at democratic reforms of the system. They, like the anti-reform nomenklatura officials, were interested only in transferring communist power into their own hands. Representatives of this group, later forming the Democratic Left Party, still, in November 1989, fought for communist power and represented the Party against the new democratic forces in the first public debates in the media in 1989 and 1990.[25]

Unlike in Slovakia, the communist parties in Hungary and Poland, according to Weiss, "... handed over their power during the round table negotiations and in democratic elections, which enabled them to keep a certain necessary minimum of personal continuity ...".[26] This power, however, was handed over to the anti-communist opposition, civic dissident activists, who in Poland, for instance, were represented by Solidarnosc or KOR. Personal continuity of communist power survived, at most, only until the first free elections.

There is then no significant difference in this respect between Slovaks and Poles or Hungarians. On the Czech political scene, the power was transferred in a similar way to the civic dissident movements, represented first by Charter 77. It involved anti-communists, non-communists, ex-

23 *Ibid.*, p. 21.

24 *Ibid.*

25 The Public Against Violence was a revolutionary organization which initiated and led all political talks during the Velvet Revolution.

26 *Loc. cit.*, *supra*, n. 21.

communists, but not "elements of the middle nomenklatura". In Slovakia, this type of dissent was missing as a social phenomenon, but there were so called "islands of positive deviation", still in existence in 1989, analysed and depicted by Soňa Szomolanyi, Vlado Krivý and Martin Bútora.[27] These islands were also born amongst anti-, non- and ex-communists and thus had nothing in common with the nomenklatura at that time.

The Slovak communist nomenklatura, including its middle ranking elements, was a reliable part of the communist regime in Slovakia and there was a huge "class struggle" gap between this group and dissidents. In some Party organisations present within the sphere of intellectual life, for instance in theatres, universities, the academy of sciences or the media, these "islands of positive deviation" started to appear towards the end of normalisation in the late 80s, but definitely not in the top positions occupied by "middle ranking representatives of the nomenklatura".

Peter Weiss recalls a well known fact that "... revolutions and coups open the way to politics for interesting persons, but also for many fraudsters of all kinds ...".[28] The Czechoslovak Velvet Revolution was certainly no exception. It promoted many mediocre opportunists of the sort who always try to adapt immediately to the conditions of a new regime. In the light of this fact, together with the landslide victory of the Civic Forum and Public Against Violence in the first free elections in 1990, Peter Weiss unjustifiably concludes that these elections:

> ...unexpectedly opened a large political space...for people, literally speaking, of chance who were brought to politics by a revolutionary wave. And this is why the main voice of the Civic Forum and Public Against Violence was not the voice of Charter 77 members or Prague Spring representatives, but of people,...who used politics for their own personal interest....[29]

This interpretation presents both the Civic Forum and Public Against Violence as organisations ruled by fraudsters and reduces the Velvet Revolution to primarily an event for gold-diggers. Weiss is here surprisingly close to nationalists and populists from the Government coalition, such as Slobodnik or Bolidsova. To present excesses as the rule and as characteristic means that the author ignores the fact that, from

27 See M. Bútora, V. Krivý and S. Szomolanyi. Pozitivna deviacia: "Kariera pojmu a epidemiologia javu v Ceskoslovensku na sklonku 80. rokov" ["Positive Deviation: The concept's career and phenomenon's epidemiology in Czechoslovakia at the end of 80s"] September 1989 (manuscript).

28 *Loc. cit.*, *supra*, n. 21.

29 *Ibid.*, p. 21.

November 1989 until the first free elections in June 1990, the foundations for democratic changes in our society were laid, which were later, after elections, the subject of legislation and constitutionally protected.

In Czechoslovakia in general and in Slovakia in particular, there was no room for the Polish or Hungarian way of yielding to a faction of communist reformers, simply because there was none. These factions in Poland and Hungary later formed "strong transformed political parties of a social democratic orientation", as mentioned by Weiss. In Slovakia, non-communist social democracy was too weak and social democracy within the Democratic Left Party was being born slowly and in a complicated way. This explains why the Left has not got a position in Slovakia as it has in Poland or Hungary, that it did not win elections and will not win in the near future.

This, nevertheless, does not mean that "...consensual politics were rejected before and after the 1990 elections...",[30] as suggested by Weiss. Such politics simply has different political partners from those in Poland and Hungary. This politics culminated in the Revolution of 1989, which, just because of that politics, was called "Velvet" or even "Tender". In Slovakia, it was even more tender than in the Czech lands. For instance, the Lustration law was never applied in Slovakia. Even after the 1990 elections and before the "hot" elections in 1992, political life was dominated by a consensual democracy. The end of consensus came with independent Slovakia. It did not, however, affect people with a communist past, but leaders of the Velvet Revolution themselves. Communists have, therefore, no reason to cry.

30 *Ibid.*, p. 22.

7 The National Elite and the Democratic Deficit in Slovakia

SOŇA SZOMOLÁNYI

Introductory Notes

As recently as 1994, Slovak accession into both the EU and NATO seemed quite likely to occur in conjunction with its most advanced Central European neighbours: Poland, Hungary, and the Czech Republic. Today, in all probability, Slovakia will be left out. Not only has Slovakia failed to join the first group of Central European countries to be invited to the first wave of negotiations on NATO expansion, but the country is no longer even mentioned as a likely candidate for the second wave. Similarly, the European Union appears increasingly decided against inviting Slovakia to the forthcoming membership talks.

International and domestic commentators alike attribute this remarkably rapid fall from Western grace to an increasingly apparent "democratic deficit". They refer specifically to the current government's disregard for the rule of law, its sub-standard human and minority rights guarantees, and its weakened democratic institutions. They also point to the relatively better, if still far from perfect, performance of Slovakia's neighbours: the Czech Republic, Hungary, and Poland. Increasingly, commentators have come to view Slovakia as the deviant country in Central Europe. Since then, several additional deviations from emerging Central European standards have occurred that render analysts more likely to group Slovakia among its neighbours to the east than with Poland, the Czech Republic, or Hungary.

A debate is raging over whether critiques of Slovak democratic practices, or lack thereof, are based on objective evidence or merely reflect the bias of a politically-motivated opposition and, possibly, of a conspiratorial international elite. Elite conduct of the debate deeply influences public perceptions of reality. The government portrays these problems as mere "growing pains" typical of any "young state". The opposition squarely blames the government and holds it responsible for practices which, in their estimation, cannot be reconciled with democratic norms. Hence this paper attempts to identify the role of the character and configuration of the national elites in the turbulent regime change in Slovakia.

National Elite Fails the Slovak People

A number of states from the former soviet bloc have applied for membership of the European Union. The European Commission has expressed the view that a number of applicants have still to make progress in their practice of democracy, but only Slovakia has been identified as failing to meet the necessary political conditions.

It is therefore reasonable to ask, who is responsible for Slovakia's "democratic deficit" - the national elite or the Slovak population?[1] Put another way, is it the political elites or the voters who eventually decide how the country will be governed? While the political culture of elites and general population are two sides of the same coin, the final composition of the ruling coalition is not determined by election results alone. Subjective decisions, accidents, and contingent moments also play a role. The final composition of the ruling coalition as well as specific power relations is shaped by the degree of consensual unanimity among the elite.

The political and economic elites that have power to make strategic decisions thus bear responsibility for the direction of the Slovak Republic. Individual or factional responsibility directly corresponds to their share of executive and legislative powers. In Slovakia, power is highly concentrated in the hands of the politicians of the ruling coalition. They have reduced Slovak politics to a "zero-sum game", excluding their parliamentary opponents from a wide range of important policy decisions and directions. Opposition leaders cannot be entirely exempted from responsibility, however. They have failed to demonstrate to the outside world that there is an alternative to the politics of the current regime. They have also failed to dispel the foreign stereotype that reduces all events in Slovakia to "the phenomenon of Mečiar".

Slovakia differs from its Central European neighbours in the absence of consensus over its foreign policy of the country and this includes division amongst opposition leaders. Slovak leadership also lacks diplomatic skills and retains a parochial view of the world and politics. Again, this includes a

1 I use the concept of elites in the sense of the following definition. "We define elites as persons who are able, by virtue of their strategic positions in powerful organisations, to affect national political outcomes regularly and substantially. Elites are the principal decision-makers in the largest or otherwise most pivotally situated organisations in a society. The national political outcomes they affect are the basic stability or instability of political regimes, the more specific democratic or authoritarian forms regimes take, as well as regimes' main policies": Field, J. Higley, M.G. Burton, "A New Elite Framework for Political Sociology" (1990) XXVIII *Revue Européenne des Sciences Sociales* p. 152.

number of opposition leaders. The effect has been to damage their image abroad as an effective and influential political force.

An empirical analysis of popular beliefs and attitudes indicates that at the attitudinal level of the general population Slovakia's capacity for EU integration is no worse than that of Poland or Hungary. The current ruling elite, however, fails to mobilise Slovakia's human capital for the country's interests. They appear to fear that standard democratic rules would endanger their power. It thus seems apparent that they give priority to their particular group and individual interests, while ignoring the broader interest of most Slovak citizens.

Civic political culture has never taken deep roots in Slovakia. But once again, this is not distinctly different from Slovakia's neighbours such as Poland or Hungary. The prevalence of populist beliefs and attitudes in those countries is about the same. Slovakia, however, deviates from its neighbours in another important respect: the extent to which extreme elements of society have been mobilised and pushed into the centre of the political system. A number of Slovak political parties, such as the far-right SNS (Slovak National Party) and the leftist ZRS (Association of Workers of Slovakia) would have been marginalised in Poland or Hungary. Yet, in Slovakia both are coalition members and their activity as the representatives of the state administration has strongly damaged the perception of Slovakia abroad. As a rule, they have operated with the silent consent of the major coalition party HZDS (Movement for a Democratic Slovakia).

To summarise, while Slovak society has contributed to the unique path of regime formation in Slovakia, empirical analysis demonstrates that popular patterns of political beliefs and behaviour are not significantly different from the populations of Slovakia's Central European neighbours. An explanation for Slovakia's democratic deficit must therefore be found in the configuration and attitudes of the national elite.

Prehistory of the Current Elite Configuration

At this point an empirical generalisation should be emphasised - where the issue of nationhood is not considered by a relevant segment of population to be satisfactorily resolved, it is likely to become a mobilising issue in the political struggle. In such countries political elites are predominantly occupied with the issue of nationhood and do ignore civil rights.[2]

2 U. Altermatt, *Das Fanal von Sarajevo. Ethonationalismus in Europa*, Zürich, Verlag Neue Zürcher Zeitung, 1996, p. 62.

In contrast, where nation-formation and state building are accomplished, the conditions for the development of a civic political culture are much more favourable. This was the case of the Czech lands, an exception, with its most developed civil society, among the East Central European countries before World War II. The historical fact is that the Slovak national issue was first of all a divisive issue among the Slovak political activists themselves. For Slovak elites the debate on nationhood has been a fundamental divide since the first Czechoslovak Republic (1918-1938), beginning with debates between two *Slovak* elite groupings, the "autonomists" on the one hand and "Czechoslovaks" on the other. Under the early First Republic, Slovak autonomists were politically represented by Andrej Hlinka and the People's Party. They fought against Czech-centrism and Prague's drive to create a "Czechoslovak" nation. Czechoslovaks, *many of whom were Slovak*, argued against Slovak autonomy on political and cultural grounds. They emphasised the kinship and unity of Czech and Slovak cultures as a means of unifying the Slavic peoples in the face of the threat of the irredentism of Hungarian and later Germanic claims. Czechoslovaks feared that greater Slovak autonomy would also mean greater Hungarian and Germanic autonomy and the eventual dissolution of the state.[3]

There was also a significant paternalistic cultural component to the Czechoslovak argument. Czechoslovaks associated coexistence with the Czechs with more rapid "progress" that would make up for centuries of neglect under Hungarian rule. Advocates of Slovak autonomy emphasised the need for cultural isolation of the Catholic, traditional, and anti-liberal Slovak culture from the "western-liberal, anti-religious" oriented Czechs.[4]

Following World War II, autonomist strains in the Slovak Communist Party were harshly repressed under Klement Gottwald in the early-mid 1950s, but they re-emerged in the form of a Slovak demand for federalisation (rather than democratisation) at the time of the Prague Spring. The legal issue of statehood and autonomy as a variant of its resolution again became the most crucial issue following the Velvet Revolution, particularly after Czechoslovak Federal Minister of Finance, Václav Klaus introduced an inflexible program of radical shock therapy

3 It is only slightly ironic that today's national-populists play on a similar fear.

4 For a good, even-handed review of these issues, see C.S. Leff, *National Conflict in Czechoslovakia*, Princeton, Princeton University Press, 1988, pp. 133-140; For a largely "autonomist's" view, see S. J. Kirschbaum, *A History of Slovakia: the Struggle for Survival*, MacMillan, London, 1995, pp. 169-179.

that generated national-populist complaints about "alien" solutions to Slovakia's problems once again being imposed from without.

A final, but closely related point, is that the configuration of elite concerns in Slovakia was significantly different from those of their Czech counterparts. The divergence dates back to the First Republic (1918-1938) and even before that, but emerges in the current generation of leadership in their reaction to the 1968 Prague Spring movement. Czech Prague Spring reformers sought primarily to gain greater political and economic liberties within a socialist or western-style social democratic framework. The goals of Slovak reformers were not as clear-cut. Given the rapid development of the Slovak economy under policies of equalisation, the need for economic revitalisation was not as pressing. Slovak communist reformers saw themselves first and foremost as "patriots". Their primary aim was "national self-assertion" rather than economic reform and democratisation.[5] While some Slovaks shared the aims of Czech reformers, a significant portion of Slovak Prague Spring participants fell into the hard liner (limited or anti-reform) camp on economic issues. One apparent fear of Slovaks was that "Czech-led" economic reforms would restore priority to Czech industry in planning and investment and thus set back nascent Slovak industrialisation. On economic issues, therefore, many Slovak reformers were decidedly in favour of the status quo.[6]

This cleared the way for a unique Slovak drive to establish autonomy within a federative Czech and Slovak republic. Czech reformers challenged the monopoly of the Communist Party on political life. They sought democratic reforms first above all else, trusting that additional reforms would come soon thereafter. Slovak reformers, by contrast, rejected the formula of "democracy first" and focused their challenge more on the location of party power and the demand for "symmetry" in representation in

5 J. Krejčí and P. Machonin, Czechoslovakia, 1918-92, Basingstoke, MacMillan, 1996, pp. 30, 45-46; M. Kusý, "Slovak Phenomenon", *Slovenská otázka, v 20.storočí*, Kaligram, Bratislava, 1997, 460-461; S. Abraham, "Early Elections in Slovakia: A State of Deadlock," [1995] *Government and Opposition*, 86; S. Abraham, "The Break-up of Czechoslovakia: A Threat to Democratization in Slovakia" in S. Szomolányi and G. Meseznikov (eds.), *Slovak Path of Transition – to Democracy?*, Bratislava, Slovak Political Science Association and Interlingua, 1994, pp. 13-40.

6 On the eve of his replacement by Dubček, Communist Party General Secretary Antonín Novotny even felt compelled to reassure Slovaks that "the overall economic development of the Republic must not overshadow the important task of the precedence of the development of Slovakia which does not yet equal the level of the Czech lands". Author's Interview with Miroslav Kusý, Department of Politics, Comenius University, Bratislava, Slovakia, December 18, 1996.; *New York Times*, Jan. 2, 1968, as cited in Leff, *op. cit.*, *supra*, n. 4, pp. 120-1.

Czechoslovak governing bodies.[7]

By its very demands, the Slovak reform movement was less threatening to the communist regime. Given the example of the Soviet Union, there was certainly nothing contradictory between federal forms of government and Leninist principles.[8] Unlike in the early 1950s, hard line Soviet and Czechoslovak communists were willing to accept that one could be both a good communist and a Slovak nationalist simultaneously - particularly if granting Slovaks some concessions would undermine their support of the fundamental challenges to one-party rule made by their Czech brethren. As one analyst has noted, their "need to consolidate Slovak commitment in crisis was paramount".[9] With Soviet approval, hard-liners thus granted Slovaks their demand for a federation. They had Dubček sign the Agreement on Federation in Bratislava in October 1968. On paper, at least, the agreement went far towards granting many of the Slovak reformers' demands.

When Dubček was finally ousted as First Secretary of the Communist Party in April 1969,[10] hard-liners replaced him with Gustav Husak, whose Slovak credentials had been well established by a lengthy prison sentence in the 1950s for "nationalist deviation". During Prague Spring, Husak had been a leading Slovak advocate of federalisation and was counted amongst the ranks of Prague Spring reformers. After the invasion, Husak's regime limited the extent and harshness of the post-invasion purge in Slovakia. Many Slovaks who had participated in the reform movement were allowed back into party ranks provided they signed a document approving the Warsaw Pact's "international assistance". Moreover, the apparent gains for

7 While Slovak insistence on federalisation was consistent in principle with Czech demands for democratisation, the establishment of an equal Slovak voice in governing on the principle of "one nation one vote" would mean that the numerically inferior Slovaks would be over-represented at the federal level. Many Czechs thus felt Slovak demands were undemocratic. The final compromise was a bicameral legislature in which representatives to the one house were apportioned equally between the Czech Lands and Slovakia with the other house proportionally representative. Real decision-making power remained in the hands of the KSC which continued to be organised along asymmetric lines. The majority principle also dominated the ministries, again a locus a real power in Communist systems and one where Slovaks remained in the minority. Leff, *op. cit.*, pp. 120, 127, 244-246.

8 Leff, *op.cit*, p. 124.

9 *Ibid.*

10 For a good although Czecho-centric account of politics during Prague Spring and its aftermath, H. Renner, *A History of Czechoslovakia since 1945*, London, Routledge, 1989, pp. 49-89.

the Slovak nation made signing such a humiliating document all the more easy: Slovaks benefited from the Husak regime's decision to pursue and even intensify policies of "equalisation", in effect continuing the redistribution of dwindling Czech prosperity to Slovakia.[11]

While the KSČ Party bodies and ministries continued to be governed on the principles of democratic centralism and national asymmetry, Husak pursued an aggressive Slovak affirmative action program at top Party levels. Henceforth, Slovaks would hold between 30 and 40 percent of all cabinet posts.[12] Czech '68 reformers, by contrast, were thoroughly purged - forced into exile, or allowed only to work as menial labourers. Moreover, while many could have and did sign documents "approving" of the Soviet invasion, they would for the most part, not be readmitted into political life or even the ranks of the Communist Party.

Thus, the line marking naked, opportunistic collaboration with a patently disliked regime was clearly drawn in the Czech lands. In Slovakia, it was blurred. It was therefore more easily crossed. This was by no means insignificant. Dissidents in Slovakia thereafter never had the clear, unchallenged moral authority of Czech dissidents. Indeed, Husak and other Slovak communists rationalised collaboration with the Soviet invaders as an "act of patriotism" that served the interests of the Slovak nation.[13] Husak took this tack in his persecution of Czech Prague Spring reformers, many of whom were charged with not being sufficiently attentive to Slovak concerns or including Slovaks in reform planning.[14]

Slovak anti-regime activism was muted after 1970. Concessions on federalism; greater top-level representation; moderated purges; and a continuation of the upward mobility and improved standards of living that

11 Krejči and Machonin, *op. cit, n.5,* p. 196.

12 According to C. S. Leff, the enhanced presence of Slovaks at top levels of leadership may have had something to do with the moderated purge in Slovakia. The new cadres may have been able to protect proteges from persecution. In sum, only 17 percent of cadres lost their positions compared to 42 percent in the Czech lands. Punitive measures likewise were often less harsh in Slovakia. Slovaks compromised by Prague Spring activities were generally only demoted. Czechs, by contrast, generally lost their jobs and were forced into menial positions or exile. Leff speculates that the fact that Slovak reformers could keep their jobs later contributed to the muted dissident movement in Slovakia. Slovaks retained a stake in the system. By contrast, Czech's had little left to lose. For anecdotal evidence of this, see testimony of Czech dissident, Jan Urban, Reformist cadres in both regions however were subjected to similar interrogations, surveillance and the lose of higher education abilities for their children. C.S.Leff, *op. cit.* n. 4, pp. 252-253, 261.

13 Krejčí and Machonin, *op. cit., supra,* n. 5, p. 193.

14 Leff, *op.cit*, pp. 243-244.

accompanied ongoing policies of equalisation, combined to produce a greater tolerance of the status quo in Slovakia and greater respect for a nomenklatura background after November 1989. In marked contrast to the Czech lands, most dissident activity in Slovakia centred around freedom of religious expression rather than a fight for civic and political rights. Of only seven Slovak trials involving secular dissidence during normalisation, only two involved ethnic Slovaks.[15]

This "Slovak phenomenon" reached far into Slovakia's intellectual elite where even "dissident" writers and artists could find accommodation with the post-68 regime if they focused their attentions on achieving national expression and goals rather than democracy. Some Slovak's even apparently joined the Communist Party in the 1970s, in an explicit effort to, "keep the spirit of reform alive".[16] Moreover, as young Slovak intellectuals grew into political life in the 1970s, they too, found conditions more accommodating than in the Czech lands, where intellectual life continued to be shaped by the exile or repression of leading thinkers.[17] By and large, the democratic agenda pursued by Prague Spring reformers and revitalised by the Charter 77 affirmation of the principles of Helsinki, had a smaller impact on political and intellectual life in Slovakia than it did in the Czech Lands.[18]

In sum, Slovakia's contemporary ruling elite were socialised as willing participants in the communist system, not dissenters. While this is also true of a majority of contemporary Czech ruling elite, Slovakia's communist era produced only a weak, and largely marginalised, civic dissident movement that, by 1989, lacked the ability to provide the strong national leadership of its Czech counterparts. Civic-dissident leadership in Public Against Violence, the Slovak counterpart to Civic Forum was limited to Miroslav Kusý, Milan Šimecka and a handful of others. Not only did these individuals have no desire to retain political office, but they found they needed to cooperate closely with moderate, reformist elements of the former communist Slovak nomenklatura to run the country.

There was also a significant paternalistic cultural component to the Czechoslovak argument. Czechoslovaks associated coexistence with the

15 As of the mid-1980s.

16 Krejčí and Machonin, *op. cit.*, p. 193.

17 P. Petro, "Slovak Literature: Loyal, Dissident and Emigre", in H. G. Skilling, (ed), *Czechoslovakia: 1918-88*; Basingstoke, MacMillan, 1991; M. Kusý, "Slovensky fenomenon" (1985) 15:5 *Listy*, 29.

18 H. G. Skilling, Charter 77 and Human Rights in Czechoslovakia, London, Allen & Unwin, 1981, as cited in Leff, *op. cit.*, p. 264.

Czechs with more rapid "progress" that would make up for centuries of neglect under Hungarian rule. Advocates of Slovak autonomy emphasised the need for cultural isolation of the Catholic, traditional, and anti-liberal Slovak culture from the "Western-liberal, anti-religious" oriented Czechs.[19]

Regional Comparison

Traditionalism, paternalism, and the lack of an elite of a civic-dissident-movement character enabled, but did not determine, Slovakia's contemporary elite configuration. While Slovakia possesses strong elements of traditionalism and paternalism, the same can be said about its neighbours. The Czechs are less traditionalist and paternalist, yet the difference is of degree rather than kind, and there are still some significant elements of paternalism and traditionalism in Czech society. The same can be said of Poland or Hungary.[20] And while civic political culture has never taken deep roots in Slovakia, this is again not distinctly different from Slovakia's neighbours. The prevalence of populist beliefs and attitudes in those countries is about the same.[21]

Two Austrian authors have presented evidence that there are not substantial differences between Central European countries as regards the attitudes of the general population. An exception is the Czech Republic. This is supported by the following data: In Slovakia 20% of respondents, in Hungary 22%, and in Poland 23%, preferred a single party system over one with competing parties. In the Czech Republic 6% expressed this preference. Another question was intended to identify the degree of the authoritarian attitudes: "Dictatorship may be better under certain circumstances." The number of those who agree with this statement was highest in Poland 17%, with equal support of 11% in both the Czech and Slovak Republics, and was lowest in Hungary where 8% expressed

19 For a good, even-handed review of these issues, see Leff, *op. cit.*, pp. 133-140; For a largely "autonomist's" view, see Stanislav J. Kirschbaum, A History of Slovakia: the Struggle for Survival, London: MacMillan, 1995, pp. 169-179.

20 For example, an empirical analysis of popular beliefs and attitudes indicates that Slovakia's capacity for EU integration is no worse than that of Poland or Hungary. See *Central and Eastern Europe on the Way into the European Union*.

21 S. Miháliková, Správa o medzinárodnom sociologickom výskume "Socio-politické, ekonomické a axiologické orientácie a premeny stredoeurópskych spoločností (porovnanie českej, slovenskej a rumunskej spoločnosti" co-ordinator Z.Strmiska, C.N.R.S. Paris.,1995-1997.

agreement.[22]

The Origin of the Disunited National Elite

A comparison of Slovakia with its Central European neighbours indicates that the country possesses the least robust accumulation of favourable conditions for democratic consolidation. Slovakia has a higher degree of ethnic heterogeneity and perhaps most importantly an absence of a sustained, historical experience of statehood. At the same time, the number of tasks that Slovakia has had to complete simultaneously is higher than in the Czech republic, Poland, or Hungary. The additional task of state-building, in particular, has complicated the change of regime. Perhaps most importantly, the circumstances and events under which the State was established had a significant formative effect on the values and configuration of Slovakia's national elite.[23]

The origin of the current disunity among Slovakia's elite is thus to be found in the problem of statehood and, to a lesser extent, ethnic diversity. Historically, this problem is not exceptional. The Czech lands, Poland, and Hungary experienced problems of state-building as early as the nineteenth century. In the Czech lands, for instance, civil society began to emerge simultaneously with the process of national emancipation in the second half of the nineteenth century. This paved the way for a smoother transition to statehood following the First World War. By contrast, the Slovak process of democratisation and state building have overlapped and been compressed into a relatively short time frame.

The road to statehood in Slovakia was compressed into several years. In 1991, Mečiar began to form a splinter political movement within VPN around old Slovak resentments against "Prago-centrism" or the rule of Slovakia from Prague. It was not ethnic differences, but resentments and fears generated by Mečiar himself as a weapon in the power struggle and the absence of developed civil society that made possible the success of populist nationalist politicians in Slovakia.

The radical economic reforms of Czech Finance Minister Václav Klaus

22 F. Plasser. and P. Uram, "Measuring Political Culture in East Central Europe" in Fritz Plasser and Andreas Pribersky *Political Culture in East Central Europe*, Avebury, Aldershot, 1996, p. 22.

23 As elite theorists assert, "nation-state formation has so frequently left a legacy of elite disunity and resulting regime instability as to constitute the modal pattern of politics in the modern world" Field et al., *loc. cit. supra* n. 2, p. 159.

and moral leadership of President Václav Havel came under particular attack from the disloyal opposition camp led by Mečiar. Klaus's reforms were labelled, "a Czech invention, created in the Czech environment for Czech conditions, and most importantly, inappropriate for Slovakia".[24] Havel was reviled for, among other things, taking a moral stand against the export of weaponry (as much as 65% of industrial defence production was in Slovakia).[25] Following and then surpassing the lead given by former religious dissident and Christian Democratic Movement leader, Jan Čarnogurský, Mečiar implied that, given local control over the organs of government, the transition would be smoother in Slovakia.

Anti-communism, which played an important role in placing the former communist nomenklatura in the Czech Lands on the defensive, had a less important role in Slovakia.[26] Mečiar took a public stand against the lustration (meaning, literally "purification") of Slovak officials with communist-era secret service ties and was supported in that stand by most Slovak elites. This weak anti-Communist stand allowed the industrial nomenklatura to begin to lobby aggressively for an active sectoral industrial policy and insider preference in privatisation.

At first, the civic wing of VPN, which after the split transformed into the Civic Democratic Union was almost entirely isolated on the political scene. Indeed, in the 1992 general election, VPN did not even poll the necessary votes to clear the 5% threshold. Yet the bitter fight over issues surrounding secession from the Czech Republic and Prime Minister Mečiar's intolerant and somewhat undemocratic leadership style created a new civic opposition, even as some former leaders of VPN disappeared from the scene.

An independent Slovak republic was established on January 1, 1993 due to a pact of the winners of the 1992 elections.[27] The decision was made without a referendum and against the will of the majority of the Czech and

24 Ivan Mikloš, "Economic Transition and the Emergence of Clientalist Structures in Slovakia," in Szomolányi and Gould, (eds), *Slovakia*, p. 60.

25 Zora Kominkova and Brigita Schmognerova, "Introduction," in Kominkova and Schmognerova, (eds), *Conversion of the Military Production*, p. 1.

26 Hilary Appel, "Politico-Ideological Determinants of Liberal Economic Reform: The Case of Privatization", *Paper presented to the Annual Conference of the North Eastern Political Science Association*, November 15, 1997.

27 This was not modern Slovakia's first experience of statehood. In March 1939, a Slovak state was established when Hitler threatened to divide the country and annex its parts to neighbouring states unless it acted quickly to create an allied, quasi-independent state.

Slovak citizens.[28] The "founders" of the Slovak Republic, however, never elaborated a concept for building the new state. The concept of an "ethnic Slovak nation-state", however, was strongly present in their policy. The preamble of the Slovak Constitution, for example, begins with a phrase: "We, the Slovak nation." Only later are ethnic minorities mentioned as "other citizens are" but not as a part of the "Slovak nation". This implies the exclusion of national minorities from participating in state-formation and had a profoundly alienating effect on Slovakia's ethnic Hungarian minority[29]

Formally, the principle of inclusive citizenship exists, but the founders of the new Slovak State have applied a principle of exclusion. This is not the formal, transparent exclusion that has afflicted ethnic Russians in the Baltic's. Rather, in their rhetoric, ruling elites informally frequently divide citizens into the categories of "good Slovaks" and ethnic Slovaks who were against the division of the former Czechoslovakia and independent statehood of the Slovak Republic. They also exclude ethnic Hungarians. The leaders of the ruling coalition derive at least some of their legitimacy from their status as "founders" of the independent Slovak State. On this ground, they claim the right to prevent all that were against the separation of the Czech and Slovak Republics from participating in building the new Slovak State. They often tell both opposition leaders and representatives of the cultural elite: "You were against it - you have no right to talk."[30]

Inter-elite antagonism has been further exacerbated since Mečiar was restored to power by the general election of fall 1994. Mečiar's party, Movement for a Democratic Slovakia, and its two coalition partners, have cobbled together a ramshackle social alliance founded on the financial support of the old industrial nomenklatura and voting strength of the rural, elderly and less educated. Educated, urban voters as well as new entrepreneurs in the finance and service sectors have tended to reject Mečiar's populism as has Slovakia's ethnic Hungarian minority. But there

28 For polling data, see Z. Bútorová, "Public Opinion", in: Bútora M.and Hunčík, P. (eds), *Global Report on Slovakia. Comprehensive Analyses from 1995 and Trends from 1996*, Bratislava, Sándor Márai Foundation, 1997, pp.265 - 286.

29 M. Kusý,.: "The State of Human and Minority Rights in Slovakia", in Szomolányi and Gould (eds), *Slovakia*, 1997, pp. 169-186.

30 HZDS continues to repeating this old refrain, asserting that the opposition parties, especially the Christian Democrats (KDH) and the Democratic Party (DS), as well as Hungarian minority parties, do not have the right to "tell people that they will build this state if they have declared openly that they disagreed with the establishment of the Slovak Republic." *CTK News*, December 3, 1997.

has been no clear focus for these interests and their votes have been spread out across a wide range of programmatic and association-based parties.

Elite Consensus and Differentiation

New elite theory makes predictions about regime types that are likely to endure or emerge on the basis of two variables, elite consensus and elite differentiation.[31] The higher the elite consensus and the greater the elite differentiation, the more likely a state will be able to maintain a stable democracy. Slovakia's elite procedural consensus, established during the Velvet Revolution, had already begun to weaken by the first dismissal of Prime Minister Vladimir Mečiar in March 1991, It has weakened even further since Slovak independence on January 1, 1993. Slovak elites, however, remain highly differentiated - increasing the chances that pacts and balances of power can be achieved that will maintain democratic practice in the face of fundamentally competing world views.

New elite theory contends that there are two components to elite consensus, elite unity and elite access to decision making. One of the most important ramifications of the issue of Slovak statehood has been the divisive effect it has had on Slovak elites since at least the First Republic. This is exacerbated by the uniquely Slovak world vision of many of Mečiar's national-populist supporters, a vision that simultaneously generates, reflects and reinforces the belief systems of Slovakia's less educated, rural and traditional cultural elements and is sharply opposed by the Opposition's more civic-democratic world view.

Opposition elites would assert that the issue at the core of Slovakia's inter-elite conflict is the current ruling coalition's fundamentally undemocratic approach to the conduct of democracy. The Ruling elites, the Opposition argues, fail to understand or respect democratic rules and norms. Instead, they conceive of politics as warfare in which the ruling coalition alters the rules of the democratic game in their favour. They play a winner-take-all strategy in which they subordinate the standard rules and

31 Under the new elite theory I refer to the new elite framework as it has been developed by Burton, Higley, Field, and Pakulski. M.G. Burton and J. Higley, "Elite Settlements" (1987) 52 *American Sociological Review*, 95-307; J. Higley and M.G. Burton, "The Elite Variable In Democratic Transitions and Breakdowns" (1989) 54 *American Sociological Review* 17; Field, J. Higley, M.G. Burton, "A New Elite Framework for Political Sociology" (1990) XXVIII *Revue Européenne des Sciences Sociales* 152; J. Higley and J. Pakulski, "Elite Transformation in Central and Eastern Europe", (1995) 30 *Australian Journal of Political Science* 415.

norms of democratic competition to retaining political power.[32]

Opposition perceptions are fiercely opposed by the unique world view of the ruling coalition elite. Their world view retains a strong, but by no means dominant, measure of popular assent.[33] The least cynical and most credulous among the ruling coalition elites picture themselves as the founders and the protectors of an independent democratic Slovak state. They argue that most of the current opposition elites were against independence and thus have no right to specify what is right for Slovakia, even if those opposition elites do so through the democratic process. Worse, they suspect opposition Slovak and ethnic Hungarian elites of being either naive or actively complicit in a conspiracy to grant Slovakia's ethnic Hungarian minority collective rights, in preparation for the eventual annexation of Southern Slovakia into the Hungarian Republic. They are loath to forget that Hungary did just that after Munich in 1938. Nor do they fail to stress more than "one thousand years of suffering" under Hungarian rule. They also warn that ethnic Slovaks have fared poorly in post-war Hungary and claim that as many as 25,000 ethnic Slovaks have been actively assimilated into the ethnic Hungarian population since the 1960s. Finally, they believe that a wide range of international interests is conspiring against Slovakia. They fear that many neighbours, such as the Hungarians, and possibly even the Czechs and Austrians, seem intent on compromising the territorial integrity of Slovakia. They argue that other interests, including international Jewish and financial conspiracies, are also complicit in the plot and, in addition, are intent on punishing Slovakia for its refusal to allow foreign capital into the privatisation process.[34]

However misguided, many ruling coalition elites thus see themselves as national patriots who possess the vision to see the "real" threats to Slovak sovereignty. These sentiments, however, overlap and intermingle with a wide range of actors with more opportunistic motives. Of particular importance is Slovakia's new industrial class which includes a number of

32 For more, see S.Szomolányi, "Identifying Slovakia's Emerging Regime", and G.Meseznikov, "Slovakia' Political Party System".

33 According to an October 1997 opinion poll, 55% blamed the governing coalition's unwillingness to observe democratic rules of the game for the EU's negative evaluation of Slovakia. 48% think that Slovakia has not met the EU's political criteria. By contrast, only 30% blamed the President and the Opposition for Slovakia's failure to integrate: IVO poll, Bratislava, October 1997.

34 The best indicator of the ruling coalition's world view remains the HZDS party daily newspaper, Slovenska Republica. Within that, the most strident views are consistently put forward by HZDS commentator and parliamentarian Roman Hoffbauer.

"privatisation groups" - loosely organised networks of Slovak entrepreneurs and the ex-communist nomenklatura with political connections and/or positions who have done extraordinarily well in the privatisation process. By linking themselves to Mečiar's ruling coalition they have gained insider access to power and wealth distributed through the privatisation process. An industrial elite lobbying the Government scuttled mass privatisation in 1995 and provided industrialists with significant influence in subsequent privatisation decisions.[35] Slovak industrialists now justly fear that opposition groups want to re-nationalise some key properties in preparation for distributing it to other actors.

Despite the opportunism of some industrialists and the clear willingness of the ruling coalition elites to deliberately construct threats, as a means of mobilising frustrated and frightened voters, some exceptional ruling coalition elites might indeed be entirely honest when they claim they believe in democratic rule. But given their perception of the dire threats surrounding them, they also believe that some compromise, or at least convenient redefinition of democratic principle, is entirely justified to retain their political and material position and counter threats to Slovak sovereignty. Industrialists and other opportunist elites, meanwhile, have gone along out of self-interest.

The ruling elite's highly xenophobic world view and their willingness to compromise the democratic rules of the game, vastly constrains their ability to make domestic alliances. As a result, extreme elements of Slovak society have been mobilised and pushed into the centre of political system. Since 1994, Mečiar's HZDS has had to rule in co-operation with parties that have nothing in common but a common populist approach, shared values and considerable opportunism. Hence the country is currently ruled by a combination of HZDS with *both* the nationalist-right SNS and the far-left ZRS. In a country with a stronger elite consensus, this combination would appear absurd. Moreover, HZDS's extremist coalition partners would have been marginalised. In Slovakia, however, they take advantage of HZDS' inability to create a centrist coalition. Indeed, they are almost Mečiar's only feasible coalition partners.[36]

35 Miklos, "Emergence of Clientalist Structures", in Szomolányi and Gould, (eds), *Slovakia*, 1997.

36 S.Szomolanyi, "Does Slovakia Deviate from the Central European Transition Path" in S.Szomolanyi and G. Meseznikov (eds.), *Slovakia: Parliamentary Elections, 1994*, Bratislava, Slovak Political Science Association, 1995. ZDS pragmatists and SDL "soft-liners" have maintained a flirtatious relationship over the years. Many speculate that a future coalition could be formed from a reformed SDL, shorn of its hard line opponents to cooperation with Mečiar, and a faction of HZDS that excludes its more extremist

Unequal Access to Decision Making

Slovakia's lack of elite consensus in fundamental political values and outlook has endangered Slovak democracy. Given the ruling coalition's conspiratorial and fearful world view, many industrial and coalition elites continue to feel that draconian measures remain necessary to fulfil their objectives. Behind such rationale, the administration of Prime Minister Vladimir Mečiar and his ruling Movement for a Democratic Slovakia (HZDS) have systematically sought to limit the access of opposition elites to decision making power. Indeed, they have taken a degree of control of Slovak political decision making procedures that is inconsistent with parliamentary practice in Western democracies. This was best illustrated in a night session of the Slovak Parliament of November 3-4, 1994.

The night session violated standard western rules and norms as well as established democratic practice in Slovakia. In a single sitting of Parliament, Mečiar's parliamentary majority denied its minority opposition meaningful participation in institutions vital to democracy. Specifically, the ruling coalition excluded opposition members from meaningful participation in bodies monitoring and supervising important state functions, including: the Supreme Control Office, Special Control Body (OKO), the General Prosecutor's Office, and the National Property Fund (NPF).[37] Opposition exclusion from OKO was particularly critical as that body monitors the security service. Mečiar's ruling coalition also selected top executives for Slovak Radio and the Board of TV and Radio Broadcasting from its ranks-effectively turning the public mass media into a partisan political servant.

The exclusion of the opposition extended to parliamentary bodies. The ruling coalition reduced the representation of opposition MP's on important parliamentary committees to levels far below their representation in Parliament. Nor did the ruling coalition allow opposition parties to choose specific MPs for those committee positions allotted to them. As of November 1997, the ruling coalition agreed to increase opposition representation on these committees and bodies. The EU co-chair of the

national-populist elements. See, Vladimir Jancura, "The Courting of Pragmatists", *Pravda*, September 23, 1997, p. 4. While such an alliance would be more centrist than the current coalition government, this alliance might still leave HZDS officials with a fundamentally undemocratic world view in charge and thus would not go as far as the elite pact advocated that we advocate below in building Slovak democracy.

37 Despite its majority, the ruling coalition did not actually form a cabinet until a month later. Until then, the Cabinet was actually in the minority opposition.

Joint EU-Slovakia Parliamentary Committee praised these moves, but added that they had not gone far enough to allay EU concerns.[38] Perhaps most importantly, by denying opposition elites regular access to decision-making procedures, these exclusions undermined consensual unity of Slovak elites and have made it more likely that Slovak political competition will be seen by elites as a zero-sum game. This has done enormous damage to Slovakia's democratic prospects.

Since late 1994, however, a number of additional steps have further weakened democratic institutions in Slovakia. HZDS has built a party-state apparatus that makes political orientation, or, rumour has it, a well placed bribe, prerequisite to favourable government treatment. This includes decisions as diverse as central state budget allocations to a village or a municipality, the award of government purchasing contracts or a favourable privatisation ruling by the Fund for National Property.[39]

More recently, in apparent violation of a constitutional provision, the ruling coalition expelled Member of Parliament Frantisek Gaulieder from Parliament after he resigned from HZDS. It has since refused to heed the Slovak Constitutional Court and European Parliament recommendations that he be reinstated. Finally, in May 1997, the Government unilaterally cancelled a referendum despite a Constitutional Court ruling that the decision on whether to hold the referendum rested with an independent referendum commission and not with the Government.[40]

An additional challenge to opposition elite access to decision making has been HZDS steps to monopolise channels for societal interest group representation. Darina Malova calls this mode of interest group representation "party-state corporatism". It typically consists of an effort by the dominant ruling party or parties to either establish party-affiliated or party-controlled interest group monopolies in a certain field, take control ("colonise") of existing societal interest groups, or establish and support parallel interest groups that compete with independent societal interest groups in their particular field. Malova demonstrates how this form of

38 Of vital concern to the EU is Slovak language legislation. For more, see Kusý, "The State of Human and Minority Rights,"*loc. cit.*, *supra*, n 29, p. 176.; M.E.S.A 10, Slovak Monthly Report, (November 1997): p. 1.

39 For more on state-party-society clientalism, see Mikloš, "Emergence of Clientalist Structures", and Krivý, "Slovakia's Regions and the Struggle for Power", in Szomolányi and Gould, (eds), *Slovakia*, 1997.

40 For more on these events, see Szomoláyi, "Identifying Slovakia's Emerging Regime" pp. 9-34. For a developed discussion of constitutionalism in Slovakia, see, Katarina Zavacka, "The Development of Constitutionalism in Slovakia", in Szomolanyi and Gould (eds.), *Slovakia*, pp. 157-168.

societal interest group representation has become a standard control mechanism of the current coalition over the past two years. Party-state corporatism is actually a more sophisticated way of establishing the hegemony of the ruling party under the conditions of formal democracy.[41]

Again, new elite theory would point out that the result of HZDS actions to deny equal access to decision-making for all elites is the likelihood that politics in Slovakia will come to be perceived as a winner-take-all form of political warfare. The fundamental challenge to the democratic rules of the game has led Western diplomats to voice repeatedly their displeasure and issue numerous informal complaints and formal diplomatic demarcates to the Slovak government. The Slovak government's apparently inadequate response to Western complaints and concerns, moreover, have led the governing bodies of the European Union and NATO to exclude Slovakia from the first wave of accession talks to both institutions.[42] The failure has had little impact on ruling coalition policies. Opposition Slovak elites speculate that these actions prove that the ruling coalition would rather subvert the 1998 election than risk losing it in a free and fair vote.

Elite Differentiation

While Slovak elites are polarised into divided elite camps, they are also highly differentiated as is characteristic of an industrialised society.[43] This is perhaps best demonstrated by the political groupings that have formed since 1989. In general terms the Slovak political party system may be characterised by "fragmented polarisation". In addition, to the seemingly untenable red-brown alliance combining extreme right (SNS) and extreme left (ZRS) into a single coalition with HZDS, the opposition Slovak Democratic Coalition similarly contains strange bedfellows - ranging from the conservative Christian Democratic Movement (KDH), the Democratic Party (DS) and the Democratic Union (DU) on the right, to the Social Democratic Party of Slovakia (SDSS) and Greens (SZS) on the left. Unallied to the Slovak Democratic Coalition, but still in the opposition, is Slovakia's successor party to the Communists, the Party of the Democratic

41 Darina Malova, "The Development of Interest Group Representation in Slovakia after 1989: From 'Transmission Belts' to 'Party-State Corporatism'?" in Szomolanyi and Gould, (eds)., *Slovakia*, pp. 93-113.

42 Duleba, "Democratic Consolidation".

43 Higley & Pakulski, "Elite Transformation", *loc. cit.*, *supra*, n.31, p. 417.

Left (SDL). The SDL has successfully shed its communist past and now functions well as a mainstream European social democratic party. Finally, the left-right spectrum is repeated across Slovakia's spectrum of smaller, loosely aligned Hungarian parties.[44]

The wide differentiation of Slovak parties demonstrates that the polarisation of its elites is not socio-economically based. Left and right are incorporated into all three of Slovakia's coalition groupings - Mečiar's ruling coalition, the Slovak Democratic Coalition, and the smaller ethnic Hungarian coalition. Perhaps as importantly, a major potential coalition partner for both SDC and the Mečiar's HZDS could be the Party of the Democratic Left. Indeed, it is hard to use class terms to explain how a communist-turned-social democratic movement could become a central coalition broker after the next election.

In short, Slovakia's political elite have not polarised over traditional "programmatic" issues that can be ranged on a typical left-right spectrum.[45] Rather, polarisation reflects each side's base in the wider continuum along axes of ethnicity, tradition and modernity, rural and urban behavioural tendencies, and past and present positions on issues of Slovak independence and identity. The implication is that there is little programmatically to bind the ruling or opposition elite poles. These political poles are entirely creations of identity and perception and a common fear of what would happen if power shifted, or does not shift, to the other pole.

Conclusion

New elite theory predicts that elite unity and differentiation are strong indicators of regime type and regime endurance. Applying this theory to Slovakia reveals a country at a crossroads. Abrupt socialist-era modernisation of the Soviet type has produced an industrialised country that

44 Meseznikov, "Slovakia's Political Party System".

45 *Ibid.* This not unique to Slovakia. As one analyst states, "Left, right, center: all these notions have a strange, and elusive meanings under postcommunism. Using interpretive Western paradigms would simply create false analogies and would explain little if anything." The author stresses that populism in particular cannot fit into a left-right spectrum. Hence post-communist conditions require new conceptual framework, one that can accommodate the "new version of radicalism in East Europe [that] combines themes of the left and right in a baroque, often unpredictable alchemy". See Vladimir Tismaneanu, "The Leninist Debris, or Waiting for Perón", (1996) 10 East European Politics and Societies, p. 504.

retains a strong remnant of traditionalism based on the elderly, the less educated and the countryside. These groups are mobilised and represented by a group of elites that are unlikely to embrace western conceptions of modernity in the near future. Instead, traditionalist elites have fuelled an ongoing debate over Slovakia's sovereign status and Slovak national identity and used populist mobilisation strategies that build on and reinforce the pre-modern elements of Slovakia's political culture. The result is a bitter elite divide along lines of traditionalism/modernity and national/ethnic identity.

In addition to this, Prime Minister Vladimir Mečiar has cemented his political position by using privatisation and state governance of the economy to reward political allies and cronies and punish enemies. In their effort to retain power in this conflict-ridden atmosphere, we have seen that Mečiar's current ruling coalition, with the support of industrialists, has exhausted democratic and even resorted to undemocratic means to reduce the opposition's access to formal and informal decision making channels. Some analysts even speculate that Mečiar and his allies might prefer to subvert the 1998 election rather than lose it in a free and fair contest.

Weak elite unity, however, is complemented by a rich differentiation of elites in Slovakia. While elites are grouped into the opposing poles described above, within each pole they maintain a diverse left-right spectrums of political parties. This hold true for all three major groupings comprising, respectively, the ruling coalition, the mainstream democratic opposition, and minority Hungarian parties. Such diversity holds promise that elite polarisation will not necessarily lead to an authoritarian solution in which one elite group would prefer to rule or be ruled by force rather than submit to a government of its opponents. Rather, a number of loose crosscutting elite configurations are possible that might prevent Slovakia's disunited elites from developing two monolithic and divided elite coalitions with irreconcilable interests and views of how Slovakia should be run.

One possible solution is for Slovak opposition parties to attempt to reach an historic agreement in which the opposition elites agree to recognise privatisation decisions by the current government in exchange for willingness of the new entrepreneurs to submit to democratic rules and norms and competitive market behaviour. [46]

46 The issue of the pact between the opposition political elites and the new industrial elite is developed in two papers that I have published jointly with John Gould: J. Gould, and S. Szomolányi, "Bridging the Chasm in Slovakia", (1997) 4:6 *Transitions*, 4:6, pp. 70-76 S.

The choice to accommodate the immediate interests of Slovakia's new entrepreneurs will be painful and difficult. Many of Slovakia's elites have gained their current status and wealth through inegalitarian and marginally legal or patently illegal procedures. But the growing polarisation of Slovak elites threatens the very existence of democracy in Slovakia. As it stands, the free and fair practice of democratic procedures could threaten too many ruling coalition elite interests. To secure victory and democracy, opposition elites need to act now to begin to create and capture the middle ground - a space where democracy is reconciled with the wealth and power of its new industrial elite. It would be the first significant step toward the gradual transformation of the un-unified elites to a consensually united national elite in Slovakia that would create a crucial favourable condition for the stability of a democratic regime in the country.

Szomolányi. and J. Gould, "Elity Víťaz neberie všetko", *Domino Forum*, (November 7-14, 1997), pp. 7-9.

PART III

HUNGARY

8 (Re)Building the Rule of Law in Hungary: Jewish and Gypsy Perspectives[1]

ISTVAN POGANY

Introduction

Those who belong to the predominant national groups in post-Communist societies (or their intellectual standard-bearers), frequently portray the collapse of Communist rule as an historic event of unique importance. Quite suddenly, stifling authoritarianism and an externally imposed ideology gave way to national self-determination. However, these momentous events, along with other land-marks of the twentieth century, have not been experienced in quite the same way by every national or ethnic group. In East Central and Eastern Europe,[2] perspectives on political

1 I should like to express my appreciation to the Airey Neave Research Trust who granted me a Research Fellowship in 1996. The bulk of the research for this chapter was carried out during the course of my Fellowship. I should also like to thank the British Academy for awarding me a generous grant which enabled me to undertake visits to Romania, Hungary and Slovakia during the course of 1996. In Hungary, I received a wealth of insights and materials regarding the Gypsy, or Roma, community from Dr. Péter Szuhay, a Curator of the Ethnographic Museum in Budapest and from Ms Angéla Kóczé of the European Roma Rights Center. All translations from Hungarian, unless indicated to the contrary, are mine.

2 Throughout the post-war decades, the entire region of Europe that lay within the Soviet sphere of influence was known as "Eastern Europe", irrespective of geographical considerations. The term "East Central Europe" was subsequently introduced to denote those former Communist states (most frequently Poland, Hungary and the former Czechoslovakia) whose history, culture, economic performance and political orientation appeared to render them closer, in certain crucial respects, to "Western" standards than the countries of "Eastern Europe", as properly understood. Personally, I remain resistant to the idea that the term "East Central Europe" has outlived its usefulness and that it ought to be discarded in favour of a new "Central European" zone in which some of the post-Communist states are linked together with, say, Germany and Austria. Terms such as "Central" or "East Central Europe" do not denote geographical distinctions as much as differences of history, economics, law and political culture. From a sociological perspective, the differences between even the most "Western" of the former "Eastern"

change frequently have an ethnic or "national" dimension.[3] For Hungarians in southern Slovakia or in the Transylvanian region of Romania, the onset or collapse of Communist rule may have been less (or no more) important than dismemberment from Hungary as a result of territorial adjustments following the two World Wars.[4] For many, if not all, amongst the Volksdeutsche communities (i.e. persons of German "nationality") uprooted from the Czech lands, Poland, Romania, the former Yugoslavia and Hungary in the immediate aftermath of World War II, the prospect of Communist rule would have been far less terrible than the fact of their expulsion from the countries of their birth and the simultaneous confiscation of their real and moveable property.[5] It scarcely needs stating that for Jews and Gypsies in East Central and Eastern Europe, neither the post-war process of sovietisation nor the eventual overthrow of Communist rule are necessarily the most decisive events to have borne down on them in the twentieth century.[6] An appreciation of the plurality and instinctiveness

states and "Western Europe" are likely to remain real and important for some time to come.

3 In an East European context, "nationality" is *not* coterminous with citizenship. The former connotes membership of a particular national group, such as Polish, Czech, Ukrainian etc. By contrast, "ethnicity" is identified with membership of an ethnic group that lacks national self-expression. The Gypsies, or Roma, are the preeminent example of such a community. Confusingly, the category of "national group" in Eastern Europe and in the post-Soviet states, in contrast to certain East Central European countries such as Hungary, frequently encompasses Jews who are seen as a national group in their own right rather than simply as a religious minority. This view is generally considered offensive by Jews who see it as evidence of an inability to treat them as an ordinary and integral part of societies in which they have lived for centuries.

4 In the peace settlement following World War I, Hungary was forced to cede one third of her former territory to the neighbouring states of Romania, Czechoslovakia, and the Kingdom of the Serbs, Croats and Slovenes. As a result of these territorial changes, 1,066,685 Hungarian speakers found themselves citizens of Czechoslovakia, 1,661,805 became Romanians and 452,265 were transformed into Yugoslavs (i.e. subjects of the Kingdom of the Serbs, Croats and Slovenes). See, generally, J. Rothschild, *East Central Europe Between the Two World Wars*, Seattle, University of Washington Press, rev. ed., 1977, at 154-56. Some of these territories were recovered by Hungary during, and immediately prior to, World War II as a result of Hungary's ill-fated alliance with the Axis Powers. However, after the conclusion of the War, Hungary was obliged to surrender these gains.

5 See, generally, on the expulsion of the German minorities from East Central Europe after World War II, J. Schechtman, *Postwar Population Transfers in Europe 1945-1955*, Philadelphia, University of Pennsylvania Press, 1962, esp. Chapters 3,5,9,11. For a somewhat emotive account of these events see A.-M. de Zayas, *The German Expellees: Victims in War and Peace*, Basingstoke, Macmillan, 1993.

6 Even if, as in the case of Hungarian or Slovak (but *not* Czech or Yugoslav) Gypsies, it could be argued plausibly that the collapse of Communist rule *has* been the most decisive

of individual and group experiences in countries such as Hungary, that have undergone complex, far-reaching and multiple socio-political changes during the course of this century, is essential for an understanding of the variety of contemporary responses to the enterprise of (re)building the rule of law.

The use of the term "(re)building", in preference to "building" or "constituting", is deliberate. Elements of the rule of law - as of the separation of powers - were already present in Hungary in the final decades of the nineteenth century and throughout much of the first half of this century.[7] Needless to say, notions of the rule of law do not have a determinate content. As understood by Dicey, the rule of law entailed, "the absolute supremacy or predominance of regular law as opposed to the influence of arbitrary power, and excludes the existence of arbitrariness, of prerogative or even of wide discretionary authority on the part of the government".[8] According to this conception, the rule of law requires, in addition, "equality before the law, or the equal subjection of all classes to the ordinary law of the land ...".[9] For the German jurist Franz Neumann, the rule of law signifies:[10]

> ... law that is not only reliably enforced but also general in application, applied uniformly to all cases within its terms. It is, therefore, predictable and

event experienced by these communities in the present century, the reasons for this may be very different to those that apply to the majority i.e. Magyar or Slovak populations. Thus, for Gypsies in Hungary and Slovakia, the collapse of Communist rule brought *increasing* social, economic and political marginalisation. On the problems experienced by the Gypsy community in present-day Slovakia see e.g. *Time of the Skinheads: Denial and Exclusion of Roma in Slovakia*, Report of the European Roma Rights Center, Budapest, January 1997). For details of the problems currently experienced by Hungary's Gypsy population see *infra*.

7 For a general survey of Hungarian politics and society during the latter half of the nineteenth century and the first four decades of the twentieth century see e.g. C. Macartney, *Hungary, A Short History*, Edinburgh, Edinburgh University Press, 1962, Chapters 8,9.

8 See A. Dicey, *The Law of the Constitution*,ed. E.C.S. Wade, London, Macmillan,10th ed., 1959 at 202.

9 *Ibid.*, at 202-03. More controversially, Dicey argued that the rule of law requires, in addition, that the "ordinary law courts" administer the law of the land. However, this final stipulation has been widely seen as a parochial misjudgement of the efficacy of Continental legal systems in which there is a separate tier of administrative courts. For an overview of notions of the rule of law, taking account of Continental as well as British definitions, see R. Cotterrell, "The Rule of Law in Transition: Revisiting Franz Neumann's Sociology of Legality", (1996) 5 *Social and Legal Studies*, 451, esp. at 452-455.

10 Cotterrell, *supra* n.9, at 452.

> calculable in its general consequences, permitting a sphere of freedom to the citizen. The Rule of Law is thus the enemy of particularistic regulation and administrative discretion.

Judged against these criteria, Hungary's pre-Communist legal order undoubtedly possessed elements of the rule of law. By and large, "the absolute supremacy or predominance of regular law" was a feature of Hungary's pre-Communist legal system, while law was reliably enforced, general in application and "applied uniformly to all cases within its terms". The law was therefore "predictable and calculable in its general consequences". In addition, "equality before the law, or the equal subjection of all classes to the ordinary law of the land" was at least formally recognised in Hungary during much (though not all) of the first half of this century and, increasingly, during the latter decades of the nineteenth century. For example, the preamble of Act XLIV of 1868, on the Equal Rights of the Nationalities, asserted that, "every citizen of the mother-land enjoys equal rights, whatever national group he belongs to".[11] Article 2 of Act XLIII of 1895, on the Free Exercise of Religion, affirmed that, "[t]he capacity to exercise civil and political rights is entirely independent of [membership of a] religious denomination".[12]

Various aspects of the separation of powers were also realised in pre-Communist, particularly pre-war Hungary. These included a bicameral legislature[13] in which censure of the government was commonplace (if generally ineffectual),[14] as well as courts of law benefiting from a tradition of independence and buttressed by a culture of legalism.[15]

11 See [1836-1868] *Magyar Törvénytár*, at 490.

12 See [1895] *Magyar Törvénytár*, at 306.

13 After World War II, the bicameral legislature was replaced by a unicameral "National Assembly", which was first convened on 29 November, 1945.

14 A vigorous parliamentary system did not necessarily connote a vigorous democratic system as well. Far-reaching restrictions on the franchise, in both the latter half of the nineteenth century and throughout much of the inter-war period, as well as the habitual manipulation of elections, were characteristic of Hungarian politics. For example, during the closing decades of the nineteenth century the ruling party retained control of Hungary through the redistribution of constituencies and through the exertion of direct pressure in districts where national minorities were numerically predominant. Macartney observes that, "[b]y these means the party regularly secured comfortable parliamentary majorities, but its rule was simply that of a clique ..." Macartney, *supra* n.7, at 179.

15 Significantly, the independence of the courts, in civil or criminal law matters, did not extend to the more politically sensitive domain of public law. A leading Hungarian scholar has observed that, before the establishment of a Constitutional Court in 1990, "the very idea of judicial review ... [was] ... previously unknown in the Hungarian constitutional tradition". P. Paczolay, "The New Hungarian Constitutional State:

However, these elements, though important in themselves, were never sufficient to constitute more than a shadow of a fully fledged Rechtsstaat. Strikingly, the reach of constitutionalism never extended far beyond Hungary's upper and middle classes. For the desperately poor farm labourers and "dwarf holders" in this predominantly agrarian society,[16] notions of liberal democracy or of the rule of law would have been not only incomprehensible as political concepts but absurdly irrelevant in terms of their daily lives. For them, law was often brutal and vengeful; it was exemplified by the csendörök, or gendarmes, who maintained law and order in the countryside, if necessary by thrashing peasants or agricultural labourers.[17] As a recent political memoir reminds us:[18]

> Hungary was never a state governed by the rule of law, a country in which rights were guaranteed to everyone. Only sporadically could one find certain bastions of the rule of law (for example, parliament, universities, the courts).

It is also important to bear in mind that in pre-Communist Hungary, particularly during the inter-war period and during the early years of the war,[19] the rule of law was understood in largely formalistic terms. The doctrine was equated, to a significant extent, with the certainty and predictability of legal norms, with the absence (in theory, if not always in practice) of arbitrary government and with the supremacy of the law. In effect, the horizontal dimension of the rule of law, which had been recognised progressively in the latter half of the nineteenth century, was abandoned. Thus, Hungary's adherence to the rule of law did not preclude the enactment of legislation curtailing the civil and political rights of

Challenges and Perspectives", in A. Howard (ed), *Constitution Making in Eastern Europe*, Washington, D.C., The Woodrow Wilson Center Press, 1993, 21, at 43-44.

16 The term "dwarf holders" refers to those peasants in Hungary, and in the neighbouring states, who did not own sufficient land to support themselves and their families, even at the barest subsistence level. See, generally, P. Gunst, "Agrarian Systems of Central and Eastern Europe", in D. Chirot (Ed.), *The Origins of Backwardness in Eastern Europe*, Berkely and Los Angeles, University of California Press, 1989, 53, at 80.

17 An elderly peasant in the town of Vaja, in north eastern Hungary, was asked recently how those who did not own land of their own had survived in pre-war Hungary. His reply is illuminating: "They stole from the big estate. I did it, too. If you got away with it, fine. If not, the gendarmes gave you a beating." E. Kalman Naves, *Journey to Vaja*, Montreal and Kingston, McGill-Queen's University Press, 1996, 42.

18 Z.Benkö, *Történelmi Keresztutak* ["Historical Crossroads"], Miskolc, Felsömagyarország Kiadó, 1996, 25.

19 In the latter stages of the war notions of the rule of law became largely redundant, particularly after the German-backed coup, in October 1944, which brought Ferenc Szálasi and his Arrow Cross movement to power.

particular segments of the Hungarian population defined by reference to race or religion in stark contradiction to the principle of "equality before the law, or the equal subjection of all classes to the ordinary law of the land". In introducing the Second Jewish Law in the Hungarian Chamber of Deputies on 24 February 1939, Deputy János Makkai remarked, "[w]e are obliged to solve this problem [the Jewish question] with parliamentary means which are the result of our present constitutional system ...".[20] Without a trace of irony, he added that "a measure of such great importance has not been realised anywhere in Europe by parliamentary means".[21] The rule of law was not a panacea for dictatorial, let alone oppressive, government in pre-Communist Hungary; it merely determined the means by which oppression was effected.

Jews and Gypsies in Hungary, 1918-1945

There have been numerous studies of the fate of East Central and Eastern European Jewry in the twentieth century,[22] while an increasing body of literature has focused on the plight of the region's Gypsy, or Roma, communities.[23] However, very few texts have set out to compare and contrast the experiences of these two peoples.[24] Yet, there is as much that unites these superficially dissimilar minorities as distinguishes them. Neither Jews nor Gypsies share a common ancestry with the majority

20 372nd sitting (24 February 1939), in *Az 1935 évi Aprilis hó 27-ére hirdetett Országgyülés Képviselöházának Naplója*, Vol. 22, 2.

21 *Ibid.*

22 On the fate of Hungary's Jews in World War II see, in particular, R. Braham, *The Politics of Genocide*, Vols I-II, New York, Columbia University Press 1981. For a general history of the Hungarian Jewish community see L. Gonda, *A Zsidóság Magyarországon 1526-1945* ["The Jews in Hungary, 1526-1945"], Budapest, Századvég Kiadó,1992.

23 See e.g. D. Crowe, *A History of the Gypsies of Eastern Europe and Russia*, New York, St. Martin's Griffin, 1996. Amongst a growing Hungarian-language literature see, in particular, L. Karsai, *A cigánykérdés Magyarországon 1919-1945* ["The Gypsy Question in Hungary, 1919-1945"], Budapest, Cserépfalvi Könyvkiadó, 1992; B. Mezey (ed), *A magyarországi cigánykérdés dokumentumokban 1422-1985* ["The Hungarian Gypsy Question in Documents 1422-1985"], Budapest, Kossuth Könyvkiadó, 1986.

24 For a brief but illuminating comparison see M. Brearley, *The Roma/Gypsies of Europe: a persecuted people,* London, Institute for Jewish Policy Research, 1996, esp. at 9-11. See, also, a brilliant essay by the Hungarian philosopher Ferenc Fehér: F. Fehér, "A Megvetéstöl a Gyülöletig: A Végig nem vitt "Végsö Megoldás"" ["From Contempt to Hatred: the Incomplete "Final Solution""], in A. Heller, *Az Idegen* [The Stranger], New York, Budapest, Jerusalem, Múlt és Jövö, 1997, 102.

population of any European state, unlike the numerous "national" minorities of East Central and Eastern Europe. Both Jews and Gypsies are presumed to have entered Europe at some point or points in time, investing them with an "alien" quality in the eyes of their "hosts". In the case of Jews, this sense of difference has often been rooted in, or at least accentuated by, the factor of religion.[25] In the case of Gypsies as well as of some Jewish communities (e.g. the Hassidim) the sense of difference has often been compounded by externalities such as dress or physical appearance.[26] In the absence of substantial immigrant populations of the type now found in many West European countries, Gypsies stand out as an exotic, "Asiatic" presence in East Central and Eastern Europe. Perhaps Jews and Gypsies have also suffered, in equal measure, from being reduced to racial stereotypes by the societies in which they settled. If Jews have been portrayed as materialistic, clannish and cerebral, Gypsies have been habitually labelled as dishonest, unreliable and indolent. Even the attribution of inconsistent stereotypical features to one or other minority has in no way diminished popular acceptance of their essential truthfulness.[27] Objectively, Jews and Gypsies shared a common, or at least similar, fate during the Second World War as both minorities were targeted for oppression and, finally, extermination by the Nazis and, to a greater or

25 Hannah Arendt has argued that Christian anti-Jewish sentiment does not represent the driving force of modern antisemitism. See H. Arendt, *The Origins of Totalitarianism,* London, André Deutsch, 1986), xi. However, this hypothesis may be less, or only partially, applicable to antisemitism in East Central and Eastern Europe. Even at the height of the War, when the fate of Jews in countries occupied by Nazi Germany had already been sealed and after Hungary had adopted a series of increasingly draconian anti-Jewish laws. Bishop László Ravasz of the Reformed (i.e. Calvinist) Church delivered a sermon on Good Friday 1942 in which he repeated and elaborated the ancient "blood libel" against the Jews: "His blood is upon us! It is doubly upon that race which raged there [at the crucifiction] ... This is what you did, this is where your road leads, such is the stigmatized people". Quoted in J. Pelle, *Az utolsó vérvádak* ["The Last Blood Libels"], Budapest,1996, at 60. One should bear in mind that Bishop Ravasz was not considered an extremist and was in no sense pro-Nazi in his views. Sentiments similar to those expressed by Bishop Ravasz have not been confined in this century to East Central and Eastern Europe. It was only in 1965 that the Second Vatican Council issued a Declaration, *Nostra Aetate*, which firmly stated that, "the Jews should not be presented as rejected or accursed by God". An earlier draft of the Declaration had gone further in proposing that Christians should never present the Jewish people as "guilty of deicide". However, this - evidently controversial - passage was deleted. B. Wasserstein, *Vanishing Diaspora*, London, Penguin Books, 1997, at 144-45.

26 On Hassidism see e.g. C. Roth, *A History of the Jews,* New York, Schocken Books, rev. ed. 1970, at 313-15.

27 For example, Jews have often been portrayed as ruthlessly militaristic (in Israel) and as lacking in physical courage (in the *diaspora*).

lesser extent, by their European allies. Subjectively, Jews and Gypsies have been widely perceived, particularly in East Central and Eastern Europe, as intrinsically different from other national or ethnic groups, as fundamentally unassimilable.

Of course, there is also much that distinguishes Jews and Gypsies in East Central and Eastern Europe, whether in terms of overall numbers, average incomes, educational qualifications, participation in the political, cultural or intellectual life of their countries, as well as in terms of their geographical distribution. In Hungary, as in the surrounding states, a significant proportion of the Gypsy, or Roma, communities continue to live in rural areas. By contrast, in the aftermath of the Shoah, which virtually wiped out Hungary's provincial Jewish population, the country's remaining Jews, numbering up to 100,000, have become almost completely urbanised; they are concentrated overwhelmingly in the capital, Budapest.

Yet, despite such differences, it is the similarities which are striking. Whether at the level of popular consciousness or in the writings of many of the region's most prominent intellectuals, Jews and Gypsies are united by the degree to which they, and they alone, have been identified as "rootless" and "alien".

In focusing on the period 1918 to 1945, for the purposes of this Chapter, there is an element of artificiality.[28] In certain respects, the period was exceptional insofar as it marked a departure from the liberal(ish) norms which had been progressively introduced in Hungary during the preceding half century and which, from 1990 onwards, have been reintroduced and extended. However, for Hungary's Jews, the period 1918-1945 remains crucial; the political and social consciousness of this community was shaped, to a significant degree, by its experiences during these years. For Gypsies, at least in Hungary, the critical period was both considerably shorter and much longer. As explained below, intensive, ideologically-driven persecution of the Gypsy community in Hungary endured from October 1944 until the end of the war. However, Gypsy consciousness has also been shaped by a centuries long experience of discrimination, marginalisation and oppression.

From Red and White Terror to Normalcy, 1919-1932: Hungary's Jews

In contrast to Hungary's Gypsies, who comprised one of the country's poorest and most underprivileged social strata at the close of the nineteenth

28 The material included in this chapter forms part of a larger study to be published as: *Jews and Gypsies in Hungary, 1848 to the Present.*

century, Jews were prominent in the commercial, professional and intellectual life of the country.[29] In large measure, the capitalist development of Hungary was due to the enterprise of Jewish industrialists and financiers. By 1900, and after a century of sustained immigration, Hungary's Jewish community comprised 830,000 persons, or 4.9% of the total population.[30] However, this figure had fallen to 473,310 by June 1920.[31]

For the great majority of Hungary's Jews, even more than for the non-Jewish population, the years immediately following the First World War represented a period of crisis, intermittent fear and uncertainty. Hungary emerged from the War a defeated power while its future borders remained undecided until as late as June 1920, when a peace treaty was finally concluded with the victorious Allies. Dismay at the territorial claims of her neighbours, at their apparent endorsement by the Allied Powers and at the impotence of the government of the liberal Count Mihály Károlyi, helped to create the conditions in which a Communist-led government, under Béla Kun, came to power in March 1919.[32]

The new government took office committed to the preservation of Hungary's ancient borders (for which there was overwhelming popular support), while at the same time determined to transform Hungary's archaic society along revolutionary lines. The lack of a genuine mandate for the Kun government's domestic reforms did not restrict either the scope or the suddenness of the changes introduced by the new regime, including the declaration, on 25 June, of the Dictatorship of the Proletariat.[33]

Titles and ranks were abolished, church and state separated, education secularised, out-of-wedlock children legitimated, and divorce facilitated. Revolutionary tribunals were authorized to administer politicized justice. Housing, transportation, banking, medicine and culture (including private art possessions) were socialized. Industrial and commercial establishments

29 By 1910, 12.5% of self-employed "industrialists", 54% of self-employed traders and 85% of self-employed persons in banking and finance were Jews. Macartney, *supra* n.7, at 191. As Macartney points out, the term "industrialist" was used indiscriminately, taking no account of the size of a particular enterprise. Thus, the scale of Jewish ownership of Hungarian industry was actually larger than these statistics suggest.

30 *Ibid.*, at 190.

31 Following the peace treaty concluded by Hungary, in June 1920, she was left with only "one-third of her historic territory, two-fifths of her prewar population, and two-thirds of her Magyar people". Rothschild, *supra* n. 4, at 155.

32 *Ibid.*, at 139-45.

33 *Ibid.*, at 147.

with more than twenty employees, and land not personally cultivated by the owner, were taken over by the state. Labor was proclaimed compulsory ...

In the face of Allied pressure and growing domestic problems, the new regime was incapable of recovering "Hungarian" territory that had already been occupied by Czech, Romanian and Yugoslav forces, in advance of a final peace settlement. At the same time, the government's uncompromising and frequently incompetent internal policies gradually alienated almost every sector of the population.[34] Kun abandoned office on 1 August, fleeing for Austria on the same day. His "Soviet" government collapsed around him. The Dictatorship of the Proletariat gave way to a vicious counterrevolutionary terror spearheaded by reactionary elements of the Hungarian gentry.

These events were to prove of decisive importance for future relations between Jews and gentiles in Hungary. Jews, who represented about 4.9% of the population in 1900 (830,000 persons) were particularly prominent in the 1919 Soviet formed by Béla Kun; out of a total of 45 commissars, 32 were known to be of Jewish extraction.[35] The identification of Hungary's Jews with the revolutionary excesses of the Kun administration proved enduring; in the popular imagination - as well as amongst a significant proportion of the Hungarian intelligentsia - Communists (and, paradoxically, capitalists) came to be equated with Jews. A book first published in Hungary in 1923, in the aftermath of the Soviet, served as both a vehicle for, and as an illustration of, this thinking. After listing 590 persons known to have been executed by the "Soviet" and the circumstances of their deaths, the author, Dr. Albert Váry, lists the individual members of the ousted revolutionary regime, including details of their religious origins or affiliations.[36] Even where a member of the Soviet had previously converted to Calvinism or Catholicism, or had abandoned the practise of religion entirely, the book is punctilious in exposing their Jewish origins. The sub-text of Dr. Váry's book is all too clear.

The over-representation of Jews in the Hungarian Soviet did not prevent Jews from also being over-represented amongst the regime's victims. Up to 11.9% of those executed and 18.4% of those imprisoned during the short-

34 See, generally, A. Janos, *The Politics of Backwardness in Hungary, 1824-1945*, Princeton, New Jersey, Princeton University Press, 1982, at 197-200.

35 On the reasons for the prominence of Jews amongst Hungary's radical political movements in the early years of the twentieth century see *ibid*, at 176-82.

36 The book was recently reissued in Hungary as: A. Váry, *A Vörös Uralom Aldozatai Magyarországon* ["The Victims of the Red Dominion in Hungary"], Budapest, Hogyf Editio, 3rd ed., 1993.

lived Soviet were Jewish.[37] Less surprisingly, perhaps, Jews also figured disproportionately amongst the victims of the "white terror" unleashed after the collapse of the Soviet in August, 1919.[38]

Executed mainly by déclassé elements of the lumpen gentry, who enjoyed the personal protection of Admiral Horthy ... the white terror killed five to six thousand victims, many of whom were Jewish. Countless were the beatings, tortures, rapes, castrations, and incarcerations, and many outstanding elements of Hungary's intelligentsia were driven into exile.

The acute need for economic recovery, in the wake of a war that had been as disastrous in economic as in territorial terms, led to the curbing of anti-Semitic excesses by 1922, largely at the instigation of Hungary's then Prime Minister, Count Bethlen.[39] However, if Jews were no longer the target of systematic terror by Magyar "patriots" enjoying the tacit support of the authorities, they remained at least partially alienated from the Hungarian state. As a deliberate policy, the "pragmatic" Bethlen administration ensured that Jews were no longer recruited into the civil service, into local government, or into the judiciary. The representation of Jews in the governing party or in the government was minimal.[40] As Andrew Janos has observed, these exclusionary policies had a significant impact on the national consciousness of Hungary's Jews:

> Gone were the days when the Jewish bourgeoisie conspicuously identified itself with grandiose national designs, whether they entailed independence from Austria, Magyar imperialism on the Balkans, or the cultural assimilation of recalcitrant ethnic minorities. The governments could still count on the economic support, but not on the political backing of the Jewish citizenry.[41]

The national consciousness of Hungary's gentile population, or at least of that substantial segment which occupied the Conservative end of the political spectrum, was expressed in the work of the acclaimed historian, Gyula Szekfü. In his most successful book - Három Nemzedék, or "Three Generations", first published in 1920, Szekfü condemned the Jews' influence on the political and intellectual life of Hungary. Szekfü, a

37 Janos, *supra* n.34, at 182, n.105. Dr. Váry's book, which methodically lists the religion of the Soviet's leading figures, rarely mentions the religious affiliation of the regime's victims.

38 Rothschild, *supra* n.4, at 153.

39 Janos, *supra* n.34, at 224.

40 *Ibid*, at 227.

41 *Ibid*.

complex and intellectually gifted figure who subsequently opposed both Fascism and Nazism, nevertheless had no compunction in writing:[42]

> ... as journalism has become entirely capitalistic and Jewified, a Christian Hungarian can only get a word in edgeways if he also serves the extremes and, competing with the Jewish newspapers, pursues and hunts for Hungarian, for public dissension ...

As one of Hungary's most respected contemporary historians has pointed out, in 1920 Szekfü was far from an originator but merely the "articulator of the anti-Semitism of the Christian middle classes".[43] His book became the "bible" of the counterrevolutionary era.[44]

From Red and White Terror to Normalcy, 1919-1932: Hungary's Gypsies

An elaborate survey of Hungary's Gypsy community was conducted in 1893, on the initiative of Hungary's Ministry for Commercial Affairs.[45] However, a detailed discussion of the condition of Hungary's Gypsies between 1919 and 1932, or indeed during the entire inter-war period, is impossible because of the lack of comparable information.

According to the 1893 survey, there were 274,940 Gypsies living in Hungary at the time of whom only 3.3% remained "nomadic"; the vast majority lived in settled communities.[46] Significantly, only 5.7% of the surveyed Gypsies could read or write, although nearly 60% declared that they had a trade from which they earned a regular income.

However, in the inter-war period, technological innovations, changes in the rural economy and in consumer preferences meant that many of the traditional Gypsy occupations were no longer viable. Gypsies who had formerly worked as blacksmiths, nail-makers, coppersmiths, wooden spoon makers, wooden trough carvers or as broom makers could no longer earn sufficient for their needs from these occupations.[47] Living on the periphery

42 G. Szekfü, *Három Nemzedék és ami utána következik* ["Three Generations and what Follows Afterwards"], Budapest, AKV-Maecenas, 3rd ed., 1934, reissued in 1989 with an introduction by Ferenc Glatz, at 337.

43 Ferenc Glatz, *ibid.*, at XXXII.

44 P. Gunst, *A magyar történetírás története* ["A History of Hungarian Historical Writing"], Debrecen, Csokonai Kiadó, 1995, 176.

45 See *A Magyarországban 1893. január 31-én végrehajtott Czigányösszeirás Eredményei* ["The Results of the Gypsy Census Effected in Hungary on 31 January 1893"], Budapest, Az Országos Magyar Kir. Statisztikai Hivatal, 1895.

46 The results of the 1893 census are discussed in D. Crowe, *supra* n.23, at 84-85.

47 Karsai, *supra* n. 23, at 26.

of villages in hovels that were frequently constructed of wattle or even of plain mud, without running water or electricity, most Gypsies were compelled to seek work as miners, labourers, brick-makers, saw-mill workers etc.[48] During the inter-war period, the standard of living of Hungary's Gypsies actually declined in relation to that of the ordinary population.[49]

While the economic plight of Hungary's Gypsies was acute, the community was at least spared unwelcome political attention. In contrast to Hungary's Jews, who were vilified alike for undermining Hungarian culture and mores (one of the arguments advanced by Gyula Szekfü in Három Nemzedék) and for their alleged support of international Communism, the Gypsies were virtually ignored by conservative, Fascist and even leftist politicians. As László Karsai has commented:[50]

> The Gypsy question was almost wholly absent from political arguments in inter-war Hungary. Quite simply, the conservatives didn't deal with them [the Gypsies], nor the extreme right "protectors of the race", nor those on the left.

Similarly, Karsai notes that, apart from brief news items about petty crimes, "the era's right-wing and extreme right [news] organs did not even mention the Gypsies for months, even years".[51]

The Road to Genocide, 1932-1945: Hungary's Jews

For Hungary's Jews, the resignation of the Prime Minister, Count Bethlen, in August 1931, marked a watershed. As premier, Bethlen had been committed to a programme of economic modernisation and of orderly political development following the successive ravages wrought by the First World War, the short-lived Hungarian Soviet and by the counterrevolutionary white terror. Bethlen was by no means a liberal or even a democrat in the Western sense. On his appointment as Prime Minister, Bethlen informed the National Assembly that: "democracy cannot represent rule by the masses, the blind rule of the raw masses ... Real democracy ensures the leadership of the intelligent classes".[52] Nevertheless,

48 *Ibid.*, at 27-29.
49 *Ibid.*, at 26.
50 *Ibid.*, at 35.
51 *Ibid.*, at 35.
52 175th sitting (19 April 1921), in *Az 1920 évi február hó 16-ára hirdetett Nemzetggyülés Naplója*, Vol. 9, 186.

Bethlen stood for rationalism and pragmatism in an age that came increasingly under the sway of extremist ideologies of both the Right and the Left.[53] Bethlen, who resigned from office as the effects of the Great Depression rocked Hungary's fragile economy and threatened its precarious political stability, was eventually replaced by Gyula Gömbös.

Gömbös, a former career army officer who had been closely aligned with Admiral Horthy and other Conservative elements in opposing the Hungarian Soviet, had become leader of the powerful radical Right movement in Hungary. Gömbös espoused an essentially populist and arch-nationalist ideology, hostile alike to Hungary's traditional ruling classes and to the country's Jews.[54] Although formal anti-Jewish measures were not introduced during his premiership (indeed, following his appointment as Prime Minister, Gömbös even described assimilated Jews as his "brethren" and "spoke effusively about the Jewish military heroes of World War I"),[55] nevertheless the tone of Hungarian politics underwent a significant and seemingly irreversible change. In 1938, the first of a succession of anti-Jewish laws and decrees were passed which gradually excluded Jews from the professional, business, cultural and intellectual life of the country and divested them of their property, all of which served merely as a prelude to the attempted physical annihilation of Hungary's Jews following the German occupation of Hungary in March, 1944.[56] As Randolph Braham records in his monumental study, The Politics of Genocide:[57]

> ... Hungarian Jewry ... became easy prey for the SS and their Hungarian accomplices ... The Final Solution program-the isolation, expropriation, ghettoization, concentration, and deportation of the Jews-was carried out at lightning speed. In late Spring 1944, close to 440,000 Jews from all over Hungary, excepting Budapest, were deported to Auschwitz within less than two months.

53 See, generally, on Bethlen's policies, Rothschild, *supra* n.4, at 158-71.

54 Janos, *supra* n.34, at 256-58.

55 *Ibid.*, at 260.

56 See, generally, on Hungary's anti-Jewish laws and on the subsequent fate of Hungarian Jewry, Braham, *supra*, n. 22; I. Pogany, *Righting Wrongs in Eastern Europe,* Manchester, Manchester University Press, 1997, esp. Chapters 2,5. It is worth recalling that the huge and administratively taxing business of identifying, assembling and deporting Hungary's Jews was, of necessity, entrusted by the Reich to Hungarian civil servants, gendarmes and other personnel. Eichmann, who had been sent to direct the operation, had no more than 150 to 200 German operatives under his command. See e.g. Pelle, *supra* n. 25, at 61.

57 Braham, *supra* n.22, at xxvii.

Adding spiritual insult to temporal injury, Hungary's leading ecclesiastics, both Catholic and Protestant, warmly supported the anti-Jewish laws passed in 1938 and 1939. During discussion in Hungary's Upper House of the first Anti-Jewish Law, Bishop László Ravasz, of the Reformed (i.e. Calvinist) Church, accepted the Bill, calling on the Jews to join in the fight against "man's Jewish complex"[58]. Bishop Sándor Raffay, of the Evangelical (i.e. Lutheran) Church, also supported the Bill subject only to minor modifications regarding definitional questions.[59] In the following year, during discussion of the draft Second Jewish Law in the Upper House, Cardinal Jusztinián Serédi, Archbishop of Esztergom, stated that the measures contemplated by the Bill were no more than "legitimate national self-defence" and that the Bill did not criminalise membership of the Jewish faith as such.[60] He went on to accuse a section of Hungary's Jews of having corrupted Hungarian society and mores:[61]

> ... in literature, in poetry, in the theatre, in the cinema, in music and in painting [they] cast doubt on, or discredited, practically everything which is holy to Christians, including God, the saints, religious faith, the Church, marriage, the family, etc.

Even when the plight of the country's Jews had become all too clear, particularly following the German occupation of Hungary, intercession by senior clerics on behalf of the Jews was both comparatively rare and notably restrained. Such intercession was also frequently focused on Jews who had converted to Christianity and who, in the eyes of the churches, if not of the law, were no longer even Jewish. For example, a petition to the pro-German Prime Minister, Döme Sztójay, from the Protestant Bishops of Hungary, dated 21 June 1944, had protested at the indiscriminate deportation of Hungarian Jews and had referred to the general conviction that "their journey led to a final annihilation".[62] The Bishops had emphasised that, while "the solution of the Jewish question is a political task" - note that the Bishops did not challenge the assumption that there was a "Jewish question" - they were obliged to speak out where the means

58 67th session (24 May 1938), 312, in *Az 1935. évi április hó 27-ére hirdetett Országgülés Felsöházának Naplója*, Vol. 3.

59 *Ibid.*, 306.

60 85th session (15 April 1939), 136, in *Az 1935. évi április hó 27-ére hirdetett Országgülés Felsöházának Naplója*, Vol. 4.

61 *Ibid.*

62 The letter is part of a series of documents reproduced in Z. Fürj, "Az evangélikus egyház és a Holocaust", (XXXII) *Világosság* 1991:12, 939, at 946.

for implementing such a solution "defied God's eternal laws". The Bishops were particularly indignant at the fact that:[63]

> ... devout members of our Churches, because from an ethnic viewpoint they qualify as Jewish, and without regard to the fact that their individual lives bear witness to their Christian spirit and morals, should be punished for the very Jewish mentality which they ... or in many cases their ancestors solemnly broke away from, and from which they kept aloof ...

The inability of Protestant and Catholic ecclesiastics to engage with the full horror of the genocidal campaign against the Jews - and their evident distaste for the individual Jews whom they came into contact with - is conveyed in a memorandum written by Bishop Ravasz at the end of June 1944 - after hundreds of thousands of Jews from the Hungarian provinces had been herded together and deported amidst inhuman conditions:[64]

> ... amongst the countless personal cases I have been involved with as a pastor, there has not been a single one where someone [a Jew] sought from the Church not a life-saving document, nor protection, nor intercession, but the Word of God, the Holy Ghost, the Sacraments, in one word, Christ himself.

The disappointment of the Bishop at the scarcity of genuine Jewish converts to Christianity in Nazi-occupied Hungary, and at the Jews' worldly concern with their physical survival, is all too revealing.

The Road to Genocide, 1932-1945: Hungary's Gypsies

While Hungary's Jews were subject to savage attacks in both Houses of Parliament and - from 1938 onwards - to a succession of ever more draconian statutes and decrees, the vast majority of Gypsies were spared institutionalised persecution until as late as October 1944. While a number of earlier laws and decrees had been directed at elements within the Gypsy community, these had concerned solely the small minority of Gypsies who had clung to an itinerant lifestyle and who had resisted integration into the economic fabric of Hungarian society.[65] By contrast, the overwhelming majority of Hungary's Gypsies lived in settled, albeit impoverished, communities and had work or skills of some kind. Crucially, every Jew was

63 *Ibid.*, 967.
64 Quoted in Pelle, *supra* n. 25, at 60.
65 Karsai, *supra* n.23, at 66.

the target of legal restrictions simply because he was a Jew; Gypsies were subject to punitive or coercive measures only if their individual lifestyle was considered undesirable.

The German occupation of Hungary, in March 1944, resulted in the deportation of hundreds of thousands of Jews from the provinces within the space of barely three months. By contrast, the German occupying authorities showed no interest in Hungary's Gypsies.[66] As late as September 1944, non-itinerant Gypsies were being conscripted into the Hungarian army on exactly the same terms as their Magyar peers.[67]

However, following a German-engineered coup in mid-October 1944, which brought the national socialist Arrow Cross to power (thereby averting a possible peace settlement with the Allies), Hungary's Gypsy community was subjected to mounting persecution. László Karsai, one of Hungary's foremost historians on the subject, estimates that several thousand Hungarian Gypsies were interned, deported or subjected to forced labour, of whom some hundreds died.[68] However, the implementation of the anti-Gypsy measures was done without the ideological fervour, administrative zeal or general callousness which had characterised the persecution of Hungary's Jews. In the final months of the War, provincial officials in certain parts of Hungary chose not to implement measures directed at the wholesale deportation of Gypsies.[69] In one instance, women accompanied by babies or young children were removed from a group of Gypsies that were being assembled for compulsory labour service in Germany.[70] No comparable instances of administrative discretion or common humanity can be found in the treatment of Hungary's Jews by state or local officials.

(Re)Building the Rule of Law in Hungary: Jewish and Gypsy Perspectives

Contemporary responses within Hungary to the enterprise of (re)building the rule of law have been shaped by historical, social, economic and other factors. The distinctive historical experience of Hungary's minority groups, particularly Gypsies and Jews, has invested the rule of law with peculiar

66 *Ibid.*, at 99.
67 *Ibid.*, at 102.
68 *Ibid.*, at 102-41. The comparatively "modest" scale of these fatalities has been challenged by some historians.
69 *Ibid.*, at 134-35.
70 *Ibid.*, at 126.

importance, particularly in the eyes of community leaders and amongst members of the Jewish and Gypsy intelligentsia. In essence, the rule of law is seen as a bulwark against discrimination, arbitrariness and abuse of discretion - the very features of the pre-Communist legal order of which Jews and Gypsies were conspicuous victims.

Nevertheless, despite the potential importance of the rule of law for such minority groups, there exists a striking scepticism about the new constitutional structures erected since the collapse of Communism, notably amongst elderly members of Hungary's Jewish community. The rule of law, democracy and human rights are seen as flimsy and potentially deceptive devices which could all too easily be swept away in times of social or political unrest. On this quintessentially Hobbesian view, Communism at least had the virtue of containing the potentially homicidal passions of the masses.

Fears concerning the impermanence of the new, liberal political settlement in East Central Europe may be unwarranted. Nevertheless, it is ironic that while the rule of law has been enshrined in the constitutional order inaugurated since the collapse of Communism,[71] there has been a noticeable increase in the expression of anti-Semitic and anti-Gypsy sentiment in Hungary, as in many other post-Communist states.[72] In recent years, anti-Gypsy sentiment has become particularly severe. In an article originally published in Hungary in 1994 the philosopher, Ferenc Fehér, suggested that, "in several countries the Gypsies have inherited the fate of the Jews".[73]

71 Article 2(1) of the revised Hungarian Constitution states that: "The Hungarian Republic is an independent, democratic state governed by the rule of law". For the consolidated text of the 1949 Hungarian Constitution, as amended through to 1990, see A.P. Blaustein and G.H. Flanz (Eds.), *Constitutions of the Countries of the World*, Binder VIII, issued October 1990, Dobbs Ferry, New York, Oceana Publications, 1990.

72 For an overview of antisemitic tendencies amongst the post-Communist states see Wasserstein, *supra* n.25, at 253-67. In 1992, István Csurka, then a Vice-President of the ruling Magyar Democratic Fórum, published a thinly veiled diatribe against Jewish influence in Hungary. See I. Csurka, "Néhány gondolat a rendszerváltozás két esztendeje és az MDF új programja kapcsán" ["Some Thoughts in Connection with the two Years of the Change of Political Orders and in Connection with the MDF's New Programme"], 20 August 1992, *Magyar Fórum*, 9. The influential Hungarian writer and public figure, Sándor Csoóri, wrote in October 1990 that, "Jews are trying to assimilate Hungarians. Of course, not in a biological sense ... but in terms of their consciousness". See, also, Sándor Csoóri, *Nappali Hold* ["The Moon by Day"], esp. at 339 (Budapest, Püski, 1991). For an overview of anti-Gypsy tendencies in Europe, including East Central and Eastern Europe, see Brearley, *supra* n.24, esp. at 14-35. On the current problems of the Gypsy minority in the Czech Republic see e.g. *The Observer*, 7 September 1997, at 31.

73 Fehér, *supra* n.24, at 108-09.

The continuing social, economic and political marginalisation of the bulk of the estimated 400,000 Gypsy population in present-day Hungary,[74] renders talk of building, or even of rebuilding, the rule of law as artificial and as irrelevant for most members of this minority as for the impoverished 'dwarf-holders' and agricultural labourers of pre-war, Horthyist Hungary. For Gypsies, as for certain other vulnerable groups in post-Communist societies (pensioners, the unemployed etc.), the collapse of Communist rule and the introduction of cherished constitutional precepts such as the rule of law has been accompanied by a significant deterioration of their relative and even absolute material conditions. For them, at least, perhaps that has been too high a price to pay.

74 Some statistics compiled by the Hungarian Statistical Office, in 1993, should serve to illustrate my point. According to these figures, only 12.6% of the Gypsy community have graduated from secondary school or obtained a degree, as against 44.6% of the non-Gypsy community. Similarly, unemployment is more than three times as high amongst Gypsies (35.8%), while the overwhelming majority of Gypsies who are working engage in manual work. Thus, only 17.6% of Gypsies who are in employment perform white collar or skilled work, as against 37.2% of employed persons from the non-Gypsy community. See *A Cigányság Helyzete, Életkörülményei 1993* [The Situation and Circumstances of Life of the Gypsies, 1993], Központi Statisztikai Hivatal, Budapest, 1994, at 8.

9 Socialist Welfare Schemes and Constitutional Adjudication in Hungary[1]

ANDRAS SAJO

In 1995 the governing socialist liberal coalition voted for a law reducing most of the welfare services in Hungary. The Act was part of a series of austerity measures named after the Minister of Finance, Mr Bokros. The Government claimed that the measures were made imperative by the forthcoming budgetary crisis. The Hungarian Constitutional Court found many provisions of the Act unconstitutional. As a consequence of the decision taxes were increased. The restructuring of the Hungarian welfare system was slowed down. The Court's decisions dramatically raised fundamental questions concerning society's post-communist welfare dependence. In order to understand what is at stake in these decisions, one must look at the role of welfare rights before and after 1989. Only in this framework can we explain the constitutional significance of the Court's decisions for the whole region. Indeed, a broader view reveals some perverse effects of the rule of law in a poorly designed separation of powers system. Against this background, moreover, the tension between constitutional rights protection and economic modernisation, under the specific circumstances of post-communism, becomes visible. Contrary to the pattern commonly observed in less developed countries making the transition to market economies, in a number of East European countries legal institutions introduce a new dimension to the process. The rule of law, generally associated with both democratisation and support for emerging markets, produces unexpected outcomes.

Welfare rights and welfare service provisions, as used in this chapter, refer to all social services and monetary support provided by the

1 An earlier version of this chapter appeared in *East European Constitutional Review*, Winter, 1996. The chapter discusses events until the end of 1995. In late 1996 the Hungarian Constitutional Court, reaffirming that it favours the long overdue reform of the welfare system, upheld a number of large welfare cuts quite similar to those which were held not to be constitutional in 1995.

government to individuals according to their social status. It includes pensions for the retired and the handicapped, sickness benefits (including the universal and free health care system), child, maternity and family support (both monetary supplements and special care), unemployment benefits, and free or subsidised housing-including low-interest loans. (Free education, subsidised cultural activities, and even communications are or were provided as free or heavily subsidised ["social"] government services; but they are not included here, although they too were intended to promote the general welfare.) All of this is generally referred to as the social insurance scheme. The scheme is administered with government-underwritten, non-voluntary "social insurance funds", governed by the 1975 Social Security Act which is used as a reference law in special benefits schemes (e.g., unemployment benefits).

The indiscriminate use of the expression "welfare rights" in post-communist Hungary reflects the indiscriminate provision of welfare during state socialism. Recent decisions of the Constitutional Court, which reflect its social welfare theories, represent the most elaborate effort so far to protect welfare rights and institutional services inherited from state socialism. The social and political consequences of its 1995 social welfare decisions indicate that the rule of law and constitutional arrangements indeed play an obstructionist role, preventing changes to the inherited welfare system. In the current stage of the transition process, the constitutional social-rights provisions help to perpetuate the inherited status quo, including state socialist institutional and organisational arrangements.

Welfare Rights and Transition (to What?): Hungary as an Example

An important debate is taking place in the West concerning (a) the affordability of maintaining welfare services, such as those provided under state-socialism, and the efficiency of the structures and institutions that provided these services; and (b) the wisdom of writing into the new constitutions these welfare entitlements as enforceable or vested rights, state goals, state promises or, for that matter, in any other form.

Cass Sunstein, in particular, has warned about the perils of such constitutionalisation. In his view, constitutionalising social rights at this stage of economic and social development may undermine private property rights and economic development itself.[2] Other authors emphasise the importance of local East European political realities and pragmatically invoke the political impossibility of omitting such rights. They argue that the majority will never endorse a constitution or support any political leadership that does not offer the social services and social security enjoyed under state socialism, or at least does not promise most of the traditional forms of social security. Without an adequate safety net, or simply because of growing economic inequality, increasing social discontent may permit populist or totalitarian groups to win the day. Others assert that social and economic rights are indeed fundamental human rights, heralded in the United Nations Universal Declaration of Human Rights. Socialists claim that such social rights were indeed provided under state socialism: they belong to the people, and therefore the people cannot be deprived of these services or of social security in general.

The counter-argument is that, by constitutionalising welfare rights and thus obliging the state to provide welfare services, the relatively poor countries of East Europe are destined either to stagnation and eventual economic collapse, or to a cavalier disregard of constitutional provisions. Such disregard will undermine the constitution's credibility. Actually, most East European constitutions promise a fair number of social rights that are unenforceable in court, mandating that the government maintain welfare institutions, particularly a social insurance scheme. Despite constitutional promises and political pledges, there has been a steady deterioration in the quality and quantity of these services.

The actual impact of constitutionalised social welfare provisions on society is not easy to determine. The welfare provisions of the East European constitutions force governments in their region to offer at least a minimum of services. Under conditions of early capitalist accumulation, a constitutionally required safety net may play a humane and even politically stabilising role, tempering a system of unlimited exploitation and rampant theft. After all, in these societies, private charity is ridiculed, social solidarity at the interpersonal level is on the verge of collapse, and a considerable percentage of the GNP escapes taxation (20 to 30 per cent of the market in Hungary is "black", and thus unreachable by the authorities).

In Russia, a substantial amount of private revenue simply leaves the country (two to ten fold the amount received annually in foreign loans),

2 C. Sunstein, "Against Positive Rights", (1993) 2 *East European Constitutional Review*.

without paying even a penny to the budget. Under these circumstances, what otherwise may be considered to be "excessive" welfare services may become a form of corrective "social justice". In Russia, for example, workers today seem more helpless and exploited than ever. Throughout most of the former Soviet Union, public-sector wages go unpaid. In the private sector, companies go deliberately bankrupt or simply disappear to avoid compensating employees and paying taxes. Everywhere in post-socialism, pensioners are the victims, paying an excessive price for having lived under state socialism. They are now at the mercy of state socialist pension schemes. And do not forget that it was prohibited during the communist period to accumulate personal wealth. With such a legacy, state welfare remains the only major form of compensation for lived injustices and, for many employees, particularly those with many children, the only chance to retrieve at least the crumbs of their earlier contributions to national wealth.

On the other hand, both the inherited bureaucracy and the clients or recipients of the welfare system insist on welfare spending that is excessive given deficit-riddled budgets and scant public resources. In 1993, for example, welfare spending in Hungary was 27.7 per cent of GDP, compared to 23.3 per cent in France (which the Juppé government in 1995 believed to be inhibiting growth even in France.) Welfare spending in Hungary is much higher than in most other countries with a comparable level of economic development.[3]

Losers in the market transition, in any case, may find that constitutional courts are ready to spring to their support. This help is somewhat unexpected, as constitutional courts are not designed to respond to special group interests. Nevertheless, some of these courts, notably the Hungarian and the Polish ones, seem prepared to give more protection to welfare entitlements than any political party in power. Of course, political parties in power are subject to relatively less pressure from welfare recipients than from fiscal bureaucracies, private entrepreneurs, and government employees. One cannot expect much social responsiveness from governments, unless it is extorted by strong trade unions or the direct action of powerful groups (e.g., railway engineers), especially before elections (consider Yeltsin's sudden pre-election attentiveness to pensions and wages). Constitutional courts, by contrast, are well-insulated from both pro-

3 Hungary: Structure reforms for sustainable growth. A World Bank Country Study, EBRD: Washington, 1995).

and anti-welfarist influences. The judges are therefore free to follow the ideological platform of the parties that elected them. Since Christian and social democratic parties played a crucial role in appointing these judges, they usually sympathise with the values of social solidarity and are less acutely concerned with fiscal responsibility. Judges are inclined to justify their decisions by invoking timeless values rather than economic calculations. Moreover, the language of the constitutions in Eastern Europe mandates (although not imperatively) the protection of social rights, while market development and deficit reduction are not constitutionalised aims. Creating market economies is an aspiration, while welfare is a requirement.

As a consequence, constitutional courts will assume the role of defending the poor, and even more, of the "respectable" impoverished classes, whatever the social costs. This attitude may result in a kind of judicial activism that destabilises the constitutionally mandated, although imperfect, separation of powers. To assume the role of "protector of ordinary people" is undoubtedly tempting. By defending entitlements against budget-cutting measures, constitutional courts may gain popularity and public authority, as happened after the Hungarian Court overturned certain legal amendments that would have reduced welfare spending.

The Inherited Welfare System

The erosion of welfare or "socio-economic" rights, together with rampant nationalism, have been the most important factors in shaping post-communist political developments. The mass pauperisation that has occurred during the "transition" is perceived by the public to result from price increases triggered by the end of state subsidies and by the reduction of welfare programs and government services in general. Perceived under-performance has resulted in mass discontent and surprising electoral support for "repentant" or "reformed" communist parties. A considerable number of the socialists' supporters expect them to re-introduce the social services that were provided (with increasing insufficiency) prior to 1989.

Due to the current shortfall in services (shortages of heating and electricity, inadequate health care, non-availability of prescription drugs, absence of affordable housing, etc.), the state socialist welfare system, in hindsight, looks attractive to most citizens, notwithstanding all the inadequacies and hidden inequalities in that system.

What nostalgic citizens seem to forget is that the former welfare system hampered genuine economic modernisation. There is probably no "iron law" concerning the relationship between the level of economic development and welfare expenditure, but the costs of social welfare services provided under late state socialism clearly exceeded available resources. Welfare overspending and non-productive incentives hampered economic reforms aimed at growth and social modernisation. The welfare system was based on the assumption of full employment. Social services quite often included free or below-cost in-kind benefits. In Russia, for example, food was heavily subsidised at the workplace canteen or in school meal programs. Childcare, housing, vacations, and many other services were provided by the employer. Most healthcare services were provided free of charge at the workplace. As long as the government welfare sector survives the collapse of communism, strong pressure to maintain these elements of "local welfare" will persist.

Under state socialism, ironically, and in a most distorted way, state-owned firms had to internalise perhaps even more than the full social costs of production. Although wages did not reflect real labour costs, firms had to employ (or at least pay wages to) those who would otherwise have been unemployed. Firms also provided at least part of the health care system on site. The heaviest burden on firms was that prices for goods and services were set more or less arbitrarily, following political and welfare considerations. Firms were therefore compelled to provide goods and services below real costs, turning their customers into welfare recipients. Electricity and heating (or "social apartments") were offered to the public below cost, while the national budget was used to subsidise the service providers.

The social insurance (pension and illness benefits) system operated largely without reference to individual contributions and were financed directly from the budget. Before 1989, pensions covered only a fraction of the cost of living, because basic commodities were subsidised. For example, rents were kept at a minimum, and rent controls were rigid and included special protection for the poorest. The same applied in a different way to child care (from housing to subsidised clothing and free school text books).

State socialism as an apparently egalitarian system officially distributed its rewards according to social status. Social status was assessed by quasi-biological characteristics (age, health, gender, maternity, and parental status). Thus, those dependent on rents derived from status (those unable or unwilling to adapt to a contract-based system) have a direct interest in maintaining the status quo, even when this is socially counterproductive and results in deteriorating living conditions for all.

The costs of reforming the welfare system are inhibiting the transformation. Restructuring the welfare system is expensive. It involves enormous economic losses, and generates substantial material and human sources of resistance. In addition, certain services were provided in a manner that is impossible to reproduce. (What can one do with social welfare provided at the workplace when the workplace has been shut down? Who would like to take over a factory-based kindergarten, especially if, say, heating at the kindergarten was provided by the factory's now defunct power station?) The inherited pension service is incapable of coping administratively with the problem of fund management, even if governments were to transfer assets to pension funds and if new contributions were allocated directly to those funds. Inefficient service providers, delivering now unaffordable services, resist changes and insist on continuing services. Hospitals and schools resist scaling down even where alternative, and more cost-effective, methods are available. Traditional welfare bureaucracies continue with their previous managerial practices.

Of course, bureaucratic and organisational resistance to change is commonplace. Obtuse institutional behaviour is widespread in all social systems. Such obduracy has quite serious consequences, however, when the performance and perhaps the very survival of the whole system depends upon institutions and bureaucracies being willing to change. This is the case with most post-communist social insurance systems.

Only against this background can we understand the "mystery" of the socialist electoral victories and resistance to welfare reform in general. It also helps us understand why, even where and when non-socialist parties were in power, inherited welfare services were not formally discontinued. Both Catholicism and nationalist solidarity favoured the perpetuation of welfare provisions. In Hungary, during the centre-right coalition government (1990 to 1994), social service entitlements were actually extended to new groups and made available to all citizens, and means-testing was not used. In most socialist countries, welfare spending was further increased as part of the effort to compensate for past (communist) injustices.

The importance of welfare provided in the form of special services increased gradually after 1990, along with the cost of living, due to the piecemeal abolition of direct service subsidies. Private and competing public firms sold their products and services at market prices, but these became less and less affordable to those depending on government welfare. Moreover, as prices were deregulated, the prices of basic products began to reflect their real costs.

In at least two respects, privatisation has contributed to increased reliance on government services and welfare spending. First, private owners are reluctant to bear the costs of social welfare for those they employ. Second, competitiveness requires new owners to undertake massive layoffs. After 1989, therefore, governments had to subsidise welfare recipients more directly. The pensioners and the unemployed (including the temporarily unemployed, such as the sick) needed more money to cover food, rent, and utility expenses. The free health-care system faced increased expenditures for pharmaceuticals and personnel.

To the extent that the state tried to meet the above requirements, at least where economic stagnation or depression did not allow high taxes, governments had to increase budget deficits. The financing of the public debt contributed to inflation, which then further contributed to an increase in the deficit and additionally undermined the position of the socially most vulnerable welfare-dependent groups. The initial under-financing of public services was further aggravated by inflation and these two factors resulted in a deterioration of the social services provided.

The Social Gospel according to the Constitutional Court

After 1989, having added to an already enormous internal and foreign debt, Hungary was particularly vulnerable to (since dependent on) foreign lending institutions. It had no choice but give serious consideration to the demands of Western lending organisations and to foreign and domestic investors. The conservative Antall government continued state socialist welfare spending practices, thereby increasing the budget deficit, which was financed in part by foreign loans. In 1995, servicing the debt risked plunging the country into bankruptcy. After considerable delay and numerous failed attempts, in February 1995, the socialist government agreed to an austerity package that included reduced welfare spending.

These measures primarily affected higher education (layoffs and a monthly tuition fee), health-care (contributions were required for certain services), family and child support (restricting child support and maternity support to the needy), and social insurance (limiting sick-leave benefits and apparently imposing more sick-leave costs on employers). The government also introduced measures to reduce tax evasion and other forms of cheating.

Although the austerity package was watered down to some extent in Parliament, the "Act on Economic Stabilisation" was adopted in May and promulgated in June 1995. The president of the Constitutional Court declared (while the act was still being debated prior to the president's promulgation) that the Court had received many complaints on this matter and that it would review the case with exceptional urgency. According to Court precedent, such speedy review of unsigned bills should have been granted only upon a presidential request.

On June 30, 1995, the Constitutional Court ruled: (a) that the welfare changes could not enter into force as of July 1 1995 because there was no "adequate adjustment period" granted; (b) that some of these restrictions were unconstitutional and therefore void per se, irrespective of their date of entry into force; and (c) that the Court would continue to examine the legislation after its summer recess.

In a series of additional decisions rendered during fall 1995, the Court refused a number of complaints challenging the bill but continued to strike down a number of its provisions not meeting the test established in the June decision. In response, cabinet members criticised the Court for exceeding its constitutional mandate. In the opinion of the Minister of Finance, half of the expected savings from the legislation were lost because of the Court's decisions. In order to maintain most of the social services and benefits, without further increasing the budget deficit, the socialist majority in Parliament increased personal income tax for the highest income bracket (48 per cent in the top bracket, which represents about 10 per cent of the taxpayers).

The Doctrinal Position of the Court

The Constitutional Court based its decisions on a number of principles that were developed around the concept of "legal certainty". The Court considered legal certainty the "most important conceptual element of a rule-of-law system". The Preamble to the Constitution states that it was created as a means of transition to a social market economy, and Art. 2.2 Constitution states that Hungary is a rule-of-law state.

In previous rulings, the Court often referred to legal certainty as a core element of the rule of law, particularly in the context of retroactivity. While in earlier pension cases legal certainty meant the "relative stability of the legal system" only,[4] in the 1995 context, the Court added that legal certainty was "of particular importance for the stability of the social [welfare] system as [it serves as] the theoretical foundation of the protection of acquired rights".[5]

The Constitution clearly states that Hungary is not a welfare state. Nevertheless, in the 1989 revision the language of the Universal Declaration has been transcribed into the text, promising "social security". In a dissenting opinion, Justice Geza Kilenyi argued that it is part of the right to social security "that the state should refrain from those legal interferences into citizens' material [financial] relations that would impose on large masses of the population disproportionate burdens which exceed their capacity to comply (in the domain of taxation, increased interest rates, housing rent, etc.) without compelling necessity".[6] In the pension value security decision, opinions were split: four of ten justices voting against, with one justice in the majority later resigning. In the past, the majority has refused to interpret social security as guaranteed social welfare and the Court was divided over pension indexation and similar issues, supporting the rather unrestrictive welfare-related legislation of the conservative government. But, even when the majority decided to uphold legislative solutions, it was not deferential. In each case it reaffirmed that there were constitutional limits, albeit not specified, to cut-backs in social rights.

Formally, the 1995 stabilisation decisions remain consistent with the earlier majority position. But the unanimous 1995 decisions were based on non-material concepts of legal certainty. Justice Imre Voros, who did not sign the June 30 decision, later wrote a resounding separate opinion, arguing that the Constitution provides only a right to social subsistence. The way the notion has now been extended amounts to material social certainty, as desired earlier by the minority. The concepts that are now classified as elements of legal security were originally used by the minority to justify

4 32/1991 (VI.6.) AB hat. ABH 1991. 158.
5 43/1995 (VI.30) AB hat.
6 24/1991 (V.18). ABH. 1991. 356

welfare rights based on a material concept of justice. The Hungarian Court has now gone beyond the position of the Constitutional Court of the rich German welfare state, which limits its own control over guaranteed welfare to securing a minimum level of subsistence.

In order to provide substantive social security, in the name of formal legal certainty, the Court relies on a number of doctrines.

Purchased rights

In earlier pension cases, the Court emphasised that a pension is, at least partly, a purchased right because employees actually contribute to their pension funds. As late as 1993, however, the Court recognised that the Hungarian pension system did not operate as an actual pension fund. Contributions were not managed separately, the actuarial principle did not apply, and the pension benefit provided to a person was largely unrelated to actual contributions and was paid out of the current budget. Before 1995, the Court recognised that social and insurance considerations were mixed in the pension system. In this regard, only the "arbitrary disregard" of the insurance element would be unconstitutional.[7]

In Hungarian law, the pension fund and pension claims are called *tarsadalombiztosites* (social security) and the 1975 Social Security Act regulates, among other benefits, pensions of the handicapped, sick leave, and work-related benefits. The 1995 "stabilisation" legislation was concerned with sick leave which was financed from a Sickness Insurance Fund, separate from the Pension Fund, and was based on ongoing employer and employee contributions. The employer contribution was in the range of 45 per cent of the employee's salary, while the employee contributed only about 1.5 per cent. The austerity legislation provided that the first five days of sick leave would not be paid, while an additional 20 days would be paid directly by the employer and not by the fund. (Previously, between 1990 and 1995, three days were unpaid and the employer had to cover the sixth to the fifteenth day of an illness.)

The Court ruled that sick-leave compensation was a social insurance service. The right to benefits under the law was a purchased right based on pension contributions. The Court stated that to disregard employer and employee contributions in determining the amount of services and benefits

7 ABH, 1993. 203.

under the scheme was arbitrarily excessive and therefore unconstitutional. The insured employer received less than half of his contribution's value and a reduction that exceeds 50 per cent is arbitrary, according to the classic legal notion of *laesio aenormis*.

The Court did not compare insurance contributions and the service delivered (which would have been extremely difficult, as contributions are used for more than sick leave wage compensation). The contribution serves, among other things, to finance part of the free health care system. The Court simply stated that, prior to the Stabilisation Act, 33 days of sick leave were paid, on average. Because of the reform, 25 days will now not be covered (more than half), without any corresponding decrease in contributions. Interestingly enough, employer contributors were granted the status of beneficiaries under the theory that it is simply a technical choice to impose on the employer 95 per cent of the contribution. In reality, according to the Court, this could be paid by the employee and, in that case, the amount earlier paid by the employee would figure on the employee's pay slip as an increase. This not only contradicts the Court's earlier position, but it is bad economic theory. There is no assurance that, once relieved of the burden, the employer will automatically transfer all the current contribution to the employee. As Richard Epstein, "the employer can capture some portion of the employees' gain by reducing wages".[8]

New Property

The identification of sick leave compensation with insurance-based social security allows the Court to grant it property-like protection. In order to do so, the Court developed its own "new property" theory of social security services.

The idea of a property-like protection of welfare rights was developed by Charles Reich. The US Supreme Court granted property-like protection to welfare recipients.[9] Given the fundamental textual differences between the US and the Hungarian constitutions, "property likeness" means opposite things in the two countries. In the United States, property-like protection in this context means due-process protection. Accordingly, an individual cannot be deprived of a welfare service without due process, meaning that

8 *Takings: Private Property and the Power of Eminent Domain* (1989) Cambridge, Mass, Harvard University Press, 1985.

9 *Goldberg* v. *Kelly* 397 US 254 (1970).

the beneficiary is entitled to some kind of hearing. In the Hungarian constitutional context, property protection means a flat prohibition on takings. The purely procedural-individual new property of the Supreme Court has thus been transformed in Hungary into a substantive property protection against legislation. The Hungarian Court considers the non-contribution-related pension benefits (and as mentioned above, by extension, all contributions presupposing social security benefits) to be constitutionally secured against legislative alteration. Today's legislation cannot change in a fundamental way social benefits promised by earlier legislation, unless the legislature can prove to the Court that the taking serves the public interest and only if there is full and immediate compensation. Such compensation is highly unlikely, although the ongoing reform contains an element of institutional compensation, namely, the government is supposed to transfer assets to the funds in order to guarantee their independence.

In a 1993 concurring opinion, Chief Justice Laszlo Solyom argued that the communists took away private property, which is an important guarantee of personal autonomy. In order to assure the autonomy-granting function of property, the functional equivalent of property, namely, welfare entitlement, should also receive property-like protection. In other words, the autonomous citizen of post-communism will be independent of government if government cannot deprive him of government-provided services and benefits. If citizens take for granted that they will receive benefits irrespective of their contributions, their decisions will not depend on the attitude of the state in this or any other matter. This is not socialism. This is communism, pure and simple. It presupposes that the communist abundance of goods will satisfy all needs. It also presupposes that the social welfare *status quo* is financially affordable.

But what if the Hungarian welfare system is bankrupt and administratively incapable or corrupt? What kind of autonomy do we have if the beneficiaries, as political (voting) actors, depend on the survival of the *status quo ante*? They will insist, by democratic means, on channelling more and more resources into the system (or the "system" itself will do so, following its autopoetic-Solyomian program). Autonomy has become dependency in this brave new post-communist world. In the end, the noble attempt to create autonomy by tying the state to social rights and constitutional promises has obstructed the dismantling of the socialist-bureaucratic, red-tape state.

Acquired Rights

The Hungarian Court has extended the legislative irrevocability of property-like social rights (in case of contributions) to other welfare rights, even where there is no contributory element. It carried out this extension on the basis of the theory of acquired rights. It has granted constitutional protection to various forms of status-related family support (child and maternity support) against legislative attempts to turn these supports into means-tested allowances.

The concept of acquired rights is one of the vaguest in legal history. Its legitimating power is therefore limited, but its very nebulousness has made it the best argument for winning general public recognition. Its congenial obscurity has found resonance in the suppressed collective consciousness, haunted by ghosts of outdated social democratic slogans. The layman might even assume that these benefits are based on a specific legal doctrine. At the same time, he will believe the doctrine wholly legitimate, because he was indoctrinated to respect workers' social rights, which were irrevocable promises, acquired in the class struggle. "What? This new socialist government would like to deprive us of what even the communist government had to respect as an irrevocable achievement of the class struggle?" So asks the socialist voter. Under state socialism a "natural expectation" of paternalism developed: the state must feed us.

It should be noted that the Hungarian Court has avoided the simple language of constitutional welfare rights. To have struck down the Stabilisation Act's provision on the grounds that it directly violates social rights granted by the Constitution, would have been inconsistent with the majority's view. In the earlier cases, the Constitutional Court ruled (in conformity with the text of the Constitution) that, without further legislative steps, social security rights guarantee only subsistence-level care. Subsistence-level protection was not challenged under the Stabilisation Act. In order to protect entitlements above the level of subsistence, the Court had to rely on non-subsistence based rights. Some of these rights are not even in the Constitution, such as a mother's right to self-determination, a concept developed in the context of the Court's abortion decision.

According to the theory of positive (affirmative) rights protection, the material conditions guaranteed by the state should enable such self-determination. Restrictions on these entitlements would therefore undermine those claims apparently related to civil status, such as the protection of motherhood, which are directly related to human dignity, the core value of the constitutional system. The key concept is that there are legitimate expectations, based on constitutional promises made good by legislation. But legitimate expectations of welfare support are based on personal contribution or sacrifice. But what kind of personal contribution can there be in a welfare system that is not based on need? What are the personal contribution-generating expectations in the case of maternity benefits and child support (and here the beneficiaries include the unborn foetus)? Is procreation a sacrifice, generating legitimate expectations? The last time that people were rewarded by the state for procreating was when the Romans granted benefits to the mob because they were providing proles. Is the Court saying or intending to say that people should be rewarded for reproduction simply because they expected the state to give financial support once they produced babies? Is there an implicit contract between parents and the state whereby the baby is delivered in consideration of a welfare package? The Court's reasoning implies that, wherever there is a constitutional task for the state, legislation cannot deprive rights-holding beneficiaries of what was once promised by law because, in the case of constitutional welfare tasks, the legislatively generated expectations of the beneficiaries result in acquired rights.

The ratchet effect of rights-promoting legislation is not completely unknown. The French Conseil Constitutionnel came close to it, although mostly in regard to public liberties expressly mentioned in the French Constitution.[10] Restrictions on liberties, compared to previous legislatively guaranteed situations, are admissible only if circumstances change and make them imperative. In another context, the Conseil stated that "claims of constitutional nature cannot be deprived of their legislative safeguards" by repealing legislation. The German Court's jurisprudence, which the Hungarian Court has followed in other cases with remarkable sympathy, leads to a very different conclusion. As one leading commentator summarised the German position: "one cannot deduce from the concept of a social welfare state the general prohibition of irrevocability (Rückschrittsverbot)". The Hungarian Court refused to accept or even consider the government's position as to the imperativeness of the new circumstances that would allow, under French doctrine, a restriction of rights.

10 Conseil Constitutionnel Décision 84-181 DC, 10, 11 Oct. 1984, upholding a law designed to promote pluralism in the press.

In the context of low-interest housing loans, where the difference between the market interest rate and the actual preferential rate is paid from the budget, the Hungarian Constitutional Court argued that a regulatory increase in the interest rate (basically an adjustment reflecting the increase in inflation) cannot be justified as an amendment to the loan contract. Such legislative amendment of private contracts is expressly authorised by Art. 226.2 of the Civil Code under "exceptional circumstances". The Court declared in a 1991 case that Art. 226 is constitutional so long as the Court has final jurisdiction to determine whether "exceptionality" exists. In 1991, the increase in interest rates mandated by Parliament on the same housing loans was held constitutional. Using the principles applied in the 1991 decision, the Court ruled in 1995 that the exceptional circumstances of the régime change, which legitimated an increase in interest rates under the conservative government, were not present in 1995. As a result, the austerity measure was not constitutional. In 1995, there was an additional 10 per cent increase in inflation compared to 1993 (when the interest rate fell) and the interest service burden on the budget nearly doubled between 1993 and 1995. In the Court's mind, however, this did not amount to an exceptional, i.e. unforeseeable, situation. Implicitly, the Court was rejecting the government's argument that the austerity package had been enacted during an economic crisis. In short, the Court challenged the government's position, that it is the privilege of the legislative branch, not the judiciary, to decide when such emergencies occur.

In order to balance the government's powers, the Court holds up constitutional rights that need protection. The more fundamental rights citizens have, the more there is to be protected and, therefore, the regulatory domain becomes increasingly constitutionalised, i.e., subject to constitutional review. Every time the Court is perceived to be the protector of additional rights, it gains additional power of review over both legislative and executive branches.

This non-deferentialism has serious doctrinal consequences. In order to maintain its permanent control over legislation, the Court may undermine the very value it claims to be upholding, namely, the predictability and stability of legal relations. While the Hungarian Court strongly emphasises its reliance on earlier decisions in politically sensitive cases, unfortunately, these precedents are often only two weeks old. The Court, as was predicted by Max Weber, has to disregard the binding power of its own precedents. With more rigid rules, the Court's power to manipulate would disappear.

Deference to the legislative branch, in any case, is not the Constitutional Court's guiding consideration. The Court recognised in principle that the welfare system can be, and even should be, transformed. These changes cannot, however, have a destabilising or expectation-annihilating effect on the actual beneficiaries of the system and a "sufficient" transition period is needed. It is not clear from the Court's decision how long expectations are to be respected. The six months expressly provided for in the Stabilisation Act was not enough time in the Judges' eyes, although those who would qualify under a subsistence-income test for support were still to receive benefits at a slightly lower level.

As for the maternity-leave system (270 days plus three years after birth), it seems that everyone who has a claim will receive all actual or comparable benefits. In the case of child support, the Court allows adjustments, although only after a non-specified period of preparation. The Court stated that, with respect to immutability, child support is different. In this case, the service is provided for a very long period of time (up to age 18 and 25 for students). It is therefore legitimate or reasonable to expect that there will be changes in the benefits. There can be no legitimate expectation that the benefit will be provided without significant changes throughout the whole period. It is not clear whether a significant reduction in the amount of support or its restriction in time (for example, child support only until the age of 14) will be held constitutional.

From the Formal Rationality of the Market to Populist Material Justice

The Hungarian Court attempted to ground its decisions on strictly neutral and formal rule-of-law concepts. But it usually employs these formal rule-of-law criteria without heeding their generally held meaning, and in a way that has systematically extended the review powers of the Court over legislation. As the Court tried to argue on neutral grounds, it could afford not to look at the socio-economic consequences of its decisions. In practical terms, the social and economic consequences of the Constitutional Court's Stabilisation Act decisions support the social status quo. The effects are in line with populist reasoning, which claims that "ordinary people" are entitled to currently enjoyed gratuities. The people deserve it, simply because they are the people. Or, as was openly stated in a concurring opinion by Justice Janos Zlinszky, the state should support those groups that undertake the reproduction of society. Such support should be granted by the whole of society. In practical terms, this means a redistribution at the expense of those whom the state can most easily tax. As mentioned above, the government was constrained to increase further taxes for the highest income bracket.

Moreover, as most people feel that they have a vested interest in the current system, and because this feeling received constitutional status in the Court's reasoning, the Hungarian social welfare system will continue to deteriorate and offer deteriorating services to all. The inflation of social services (as well as the inflation generated by an unrestricted financing of these services) is the least efficient and, in terms of its distributive effects, probably the most unfair way to reshape and streamline the social service and welfare systems. The price will be paid even by those now believed to be the principal beneficiaries of welfare services.

The Court's formalistic approach is based on a series of doctrines and notions, all interpreted in a singular and dogmatically distorted way. The interpretation is systematically biased towards the *status quo*. What was intended to be a formal doctrine of the rule of law turns out to be a series of non-neutral concepts with a clear material (substantive) or natural law orientation (acquired rights, legitimate expectations without contribution, new property and the injustice of *laesio aenormis*). These concepts help to give formal support to specific non-positive claims that belong to natural law (substantive conditions or material guarantees of the right to self-determination).

It is tempting to see a certain parallel between the disguised aspirations of the Court to material justice (in the Weberian sense) and the prevailing populist attitude of the welfare-dependent masses under post-communism. Many Hungarians believe that the state should take care of them irrespective of their efforts, as was customary under state socialism. People expected that, in exchange for their political loyalty and docility, the government would provide services. The welfare provided by the state as a monopoly provider developed a dependency on the state. If they were non-compliant or disloyal, people deprived of their means of independent subsistence could be brought "into line" under this system of dependency. To receive housing or housing support from your employer was a matter of discretionary choice, based on micro-loyalty (loyalty within the workplace or party cell). Of course both the oppressors and the oppressed cheated.

People thought that they were exploited, and many felt that they were robbed (by nationalisation, lack of opportunities, censorship, etc.), and therefore whatever they got back surreptitiously was less than what they deserved. People believed they were entitled to all free social services regardless of their performance and contribution. Their loyalty was limited. In those days, the social compact was based on the assumption that there could be no open resistance or challenge to the regime while a certain amount of cheating, black market activity etc., was more or less "legitimate" in everyday thinking. "One has to make a living under hardship." This is the mentality of petty survivalism. It is reproduced today in the general welfare expectancy of the public. People feel that formal restrictions concerning these services are unfair, irrespective of their needs, and access to those services by mass cheating is legitimate.

Socialist entitlement is a public sentiment. It is echoed in the Court's decisions, even in their striking down of provisions against welfare cheating. The Court has become the defender of popular expectations, simply because people think that way. Using abstruse and formal terms, the justices apparently deferred to those obscure concepts of equity that prevail in the mentality of the majority. It is a phenomenon already well described by Max Weber.

The Hungarian Constitutional Court, in its earlier decisions, declared that its mission was to restore the rule of law. Ironically, it ended up propounding a concept of material justice, the sworn enemy of the formal rationality of the rule of law. Material justice will undermine the market economy and limit freedom of contract. In our case, the anti-market effects of material justice are exacerbated because of the existence of the inherited, premature welfare state. Material justice in Hungary jeopardises the efficiency of the social, formal rationality of the budget, hence it threatens the financing of state activities and even macro-economic stability itself.

PART IV

POLAND

10 The Rule of Law in Poland

JACEK KURCZEWSKI

Introduction

The summer of 1997 seemed an ideal point to choose for summing up the Polish experience of transformation. Whatever happens in the future, seven years had already passed. In this time, communist power was first, changed, then abolished after the 1989 Round Table talks and subsequent half-free elections. A series of elections for the presidency and Parliament resulted in changes of government, from the communist-opposition truce government to the full Solidarity-supported government, to post-Solidarity coalition governments, to a post-communist coalition government based upon free elections for the first time in Polish history. The reform of the Constitution that started in 1989 was finally completed in 1997. The new Constitution may not withstand the pressure of future circumstances, but it has been constructed as the normative project for the Republic, with all the inconsistencies, gaps and ambiguities that characterise any text, and even an "unwritten" Constitution. The document seeks to influence future acts and expresses past experience as understood, negotiated and agreed in the year 1997. It is in this context that the issue of the Rule of Law in Poland will be reconsidered. My approach is to identify problems in last seven years as they are expressed in or inhibited by Polish law. This particular perspective somewhat limits the scope of the study and leaves room for a subjective interpretation of the experience of these years.

Frame of Reference

A paper by Roger Cotterrell will serve as one point of reference. His paper was written in the broader British and European context exploring problems concerning the rule of law, interest in which has been revived by the experiences of the new Central and Eastern European democracies. As another reference point, I shall refer to my earlier paper on the Rule of Law dating from 1989, formulated at the beginning of the process of transformation in Poland. In this way both external and internal perspectives may be combined. The internal viewpoint is how, from within the new democracies, those more established democracies acting within a

Rule of Law environment are perceived. The external perspective is represented by Cotterrell, according to which the view from within the new democracies at least over-estimates the degree of success of the Rule of Law elsewhere. Prior to the 1980s the Rule of Law was a suspect concept for critically inclined legal and social scholars in the West, partly at least because they assumed that, from the perspective of the East, the West's performance was seen as the ideal level. The decay, resistance, overthrow, and, maybe, even more the self-dissolving of the self-styled socialist regimes, was evidence that the West-East gap was acute. Even self-confessed critical legal scholars, on missions to ascertain the role, if not the rule, of law in an ex-Communist environment, acknowledged the existence of this gap. Whether critical legal and social scholars of the East, who have been busy pushing their societies up to a western level of performance, are satisfied with this level of performance as the frame of reference for their own societies seems more important than how satisfied they are with the progress made. Nevertheless, this progress has to be examined and assessed. And that is a third point of reference in the complex triangulation of the issue of this essay and volume - the functioning of law in post-communist Central Europe. Only by taking all three points into consideration, may one understand the progress made since 1989 and the role of law in a given country, while at the same time forming a judgement as to whether that progress has been satisfactory or that role unsatisfactory in any particular country.

Prospects in 1989

Written in January 1989 and published in *Res Publica* when the Round Table started, the first of the formerly underground journals licensed by the State, my article was probably the first one to introduce the concept of the "Rule of Law" ("rządy prawa"), into everyday Polish political discourse.[1] The choice of words was deliberate, since I discussed whether Hitler's or Stalin's legality were examples of the Rule of Law, and, generally rejecting the positivist notion of law, I explicitly discarded definitions that would include these two historical examples.

English law seemed to me to be more general than legislation which is the basic point of reference for continental jurisprudence and which is linked with law as the decision of the supreme power, whether elected or not. Old Polish law from pre-1798 times was, like the common law, based

1 J. Kurczewski, "Rządy prawa" [The Rule of Law] in Res Publica, 3 (March) 1989.

upon the notion of procedural justice. So A.V.Dicey's linking the Rule of Law with due process before the common courts of the country fits the First Republic (as the Polish-Lithuanian *Res Publica* with its elected monarchy and nobles' parliamentary democracy is called nowadays) as well. "Law is the lord in the free Kingdom", observed one of the most influential political writers of the day, Stanisław Orzechowski, in 1543, while the maxim, *non Rex regnat sed lex*, was the basic principle of political culture from the 16th century on, though, with time, the stress on the limits to royal power became stronger at the expense of public order and respect for the law. Yet, we cannot naively assume that it is enough to import into Polish translated conceptions elaborated somewhere else, in accordance with alien traditions and in answer to different challenges.

While agreeing that there is a certain common pool of basic rights, entitlements and duties innate in humans both as a species and in their particular social environment, we may acknowledge that the content of this normative structure appears in various ways in different situations. It is likely that rights are both discovered and then exercised, like other human faculties. The American and French Revolutions are the next stage, after the discoveries made by 16th and 17th century English and Polish thought. In the context of a trial and error approach we must also refer to the Russian revolutions of the 20th century and the whole gruesome chain of events that followed. This was another tragic and important step in the process through which mankind collectively approaches the truth about itself.[2] Such a concept of the Rule of Law, as based upon the basic rights in the process of being collectively discovered throughout history, is, indeed, different from "Rechtsstaat", "l'Etat legal" and the "State of Law", as well as from the Polish version of it - "państwo prawne", which, perhaps at the suggestion of Professor M. Wyrzykowski, was introduced into the amended Constitution immediately after the 1989 elections.

After decades of Stalinism and the official (Marxist) theory of State and law, I argued that the term "legality" has been abused so much that it amounts to identifying any law with positive law. Friedrich A. Hayek, in contrast, rightly linked the notion of the Rule of Law with *nomoi* as opposed to the *thesei*. The controversy over the origins of unconditional human rights may be abandoned.

It should suffice to observe the contradiction into which one falls when trying to speak about justice and legality while at the same time allowing for relativism. It should suffice for us to observe that agreement on human rights is achieved in free and unconstrained dialogue between equals,

2 *Idem*, p.9.

whether private individuals or people acting as representatives of political associations. From these two facts follows the recognition of a natural order of human affairs. Such recognition does not mean that this order will be always and everywhere the same. *E pluribus unum*! Such an order presents itself in different ways to different people, differently to Athenian slave-owners, calmly debating nomoi and thesei, to Polish nobility engaged in the parliamentarianism of various Seyms under the Rule of Law, and to participants in a United Nations debate. But the general tendencies are sufficiently visible that ignoring the basic structure hidden behind these variations would be due to blindness or bad faith. The debate on just law does take place in the opposition between legislation and a social sense of justice, but within a triangle that includes the Law manifesting itself as a normative structure of social life.[3]

From this, some practical recommendations followed:

(1) The minimum minimorum for the new Constitution was the inclusion of the Universal Declaration of Human Rights as a Bill of Rights.

(2) The tradition of the separation of powers with organisational and substantive safeguards of the independence of the judiciary should be re-established.

(3) A Constitutional Tribunal should have the last say on the constitutionality of legislation and should be accessible to all citizens, who should also have access to the European Commission of Human Rights.

(4) While the Bill of Rights should be irrevocable, the Seym should be democratised enough to guarantee the expression of majority public opinion in legislation passed within the limits established by the Bill and the Constitution.

(5) Judicial remedies should be available to citizens whenever they are dissatisfied with actions taken by State bodies.

(6) Procedural safeguards of human rights should be developed, including judicial control of criminal proceedings from the very first stages onwards, the elimination from civil procedure of the vestiges of State interventionism and the reconstruction of a fully independent bar.[4]

(7) Civic participation in justice should be secured through introducing, *à la mode Americaine*, the jury which existed to a limited extent until 1938 as well as popularly elected justices of the peace which only existed in books in the pre-war Polish legal system.

3 *Idem*, p.16.

4 On this, somewhat neglected aspect of the transition, cf. my "Legal professions in transformation in Poland", (1994) 1 *International Journal of the Legal Profession*.

(8) In case the reintroduction of democracy might mean the strengthening of the Seym at the expense of executive power, the possibility of a directly elected supreme executive body should be considered, as should be the transformation of local councils into instruments for democratising executive power.
(9) Freedom of speech, association, and assembly safeguarding the expression of public opinion and its organisation independently of the Government.
(10) The above-mentioned institutional guarantees such as free association, assembly and freedom of expression will become illusory if institutional and normative structures are not accompanied by the appropriate social structure. Aristotle first formulated the thought, self-evident in the context of the experience of the ancient republics, that stable democracy functions best when there is a relatively strong middle class within society.

Since then the Aristotelian thesis has been corroborated by dozens of historical examples and became the foundation of contemporary democratic theory. A relatively high level of prosperity and relatively equalised distribution of property is needed in society to enable the average citizen to feel materially safe and to have an interest in preserving the existing state of affairs. Short periods of stability in post-war Poland indicated that even simply the chance of prosperity, if generally considered to be rational, may lead to people giving mental approval to the political system. Citizens' material independence from the State's power is, however, a condition of the stability of the Rule of Law and parliamentary democracy. This independence is absent today as the whole Marxist doctrine, not only of Stalinism, aimed at collectivising social life, turning private property into partial and conditional individual use, and with the State's interest taking priority over the interests of citizens. Without reconstructing civil society in the economic sphere, which certainly should not lead to the return of the 19th century capitalist economy, the introduction of the Rule of Law seems in the long run impossible.[5] But the economy was changed, and after a painful but short shock the GNP is permanently rising, so what happened to the ideal itself?

Five Reasons for Satisfaction

When attempting a few years ago to assess the degree of success with

5 *Idem*, p.19.

which Poland after 1989 was following the ideal of the Rule of Law, I was torn between two opposing tendencies. One was to express my and others' dissatisfaction with the way in which we were dealing with the issue; the other was to acknowledge the refreshing feeling of freedom which, fortunately, according to all sociological wisdom, was not limited to the new or old top-dogs and intellectuals. This positive assessment was based upon the following observations that do not include cleansing from the law the various totalitarian elements introduced during the decades of the Communist rule in Poland.[6]

(1) Legal form was everything as no aspect of the changes that followed 1989 was left without proper legal articulation and legitimacy, although, on the other side of the coin, that has delayed many needed changes such as the re-privatisation of property expropriated illegally after 1945.

(2) The "inner morality of law"- to use Lon L. Fuller's words[7] - was preserved throughout the transition, to a degree found by some critics to be exaggerated. For example, all the laws passed in the past are considered valid and the *lex retro non agit* principle is fully accepted, so that, not only are police informers left untouched, but even the judiciary that was involved in the past regime's mixture of justice and injustice is held unaccountable.

(3) Political control of the judiciary was eliminated, and self-regulation established, with a panoply of courts that review legislation as well as administrative decisions. The latter, already started under the Communists, had been an empty institution until the independence of judiciary was reintroduced.

(4) Constitutional norms were accorded supreme importance and mutual relations between various powers and branches of government, as well as between the citizens and government are judged according to constitutional norms, however imperfect.

(5) Most significantly, internationally recognised human rights became the normative standard applied within the courts, and, since 1992, are binding norms, the violation of which by any branch of government entitles a person to take a case to the European Commission in Strasbourg.

6 J. Kurczewski, "Democracy and the Rule of Law: Poland After 1989" in Irena Grudzinska-Gross (ed), *Constitutionalism and Politics, IV Bratislava Symposium 1993*, Slovak Committee of the European Cultural Foundation, 1994.

7 L. Fuller, *The Morality of Law*, New Haven, Yale University Press, 1964.

Ombudsperson's Critical Review

This evaluation is in apparent contradiction with judgments of those who are dealing directly with the position of law in the new Polish democracy. Professor Adam Zieliński, the third Polish Ombudsperson (officially, the Spokesperson for Civic Rights) since the office was introduced by Law of 15th July 1987, concluded his annual report by answering the same questions that are of concern here:

> The fundamental question about which Ombudsman is most often asked may be reduced to whether Poland can already be recognised as a State of Law. It follows from the present report that, albeit that the Polish transformation has developed since 1989 in the right direction, the full realisation of the principle of the Legal State will require hard work.[8]

Professor Zieliński lists several obstacles to this objective. First, the constitutional catalogue of rights and freedoms has not been adequately reformulated. This was remedied in practice by reference to Art. 1 of the Constitution that Poland is "a democratic State of Law fulfilling the principles of social justice". This was interpreted by him, as well as by the Constitutional Court, as embracing all the rights and freedoms listed in the European Convention on Human Rights to which Poland is a party. Article 1 of the Constitution was also interpreted as meaning that Poland in its internal law is directly bound by the ECHR even if no constitutional law expressly acknowledged this rule in the writing. Secondly, the content of the law is still not accessible to citizens at large, as the law often enters into force before the addressees, both civil servants and citizens at large, have the chance to learn of it. Moreover, the administration continues the old regime's practice of in-house rules and directions interpreting the law, which are not examined as to their consistency with the law and are unknown to the citizen. Third, the administration of justice is malfunctioning, in some areas - like the fiscal one - judicial decisions are inaccessible, and execution of the court's decision is often impossible.

After this list, a second one follows which is linked with three major threats to civic rights and freedoms. Several categories such as the poor, unemployed, chronically ill, etc., are unable to enjoy fully these rights and freedoms while the Administration is acting "improperly", even within its

8 *Sprawozdanie Rzecznika Praw Obywatelskich prof. Adama Zielinskiego za okres od 8 maja 1996 r. do 7 maja 1997 r.* [Report by Prof. Adam Zielinski, Spokeperson for Civic Rights on Period From May 8th 1996 To May 7th 1997], RPO-MAT.Nr 33, Warsaw, Biuro Rzecznika Praw Obywatelskich, 1997, p.348.

tight budgetary limits. Secondly, the need to fight social disorder, especially new forms of crime, often leads to empowering State bodies with additional means and rights, to develop a system of policing and to increase the State's control of citizens' lives. Professor Zieliński has repeatedly emphasised that though the State cannot be left without the means to fight social disorder, this struggle must be conducted with full respect for civic rights and freedoms. Specifically, he refers to concentrating the powers to encroach upon the citizen's private life only within adequately skilled bodies, the need for independent review of the exercise of police powers, in the first instance by the courts, publication of the results of any review, and adequate safeguards for those whose rights have been infringed, with adequate means to defend themselves. These principles are not always followed.[9] Thirdly, the old regime's tendency to give priority to the immediate concerns of the moment, at the expense of individual rights, continues within the ranks of the State's administration as well as within the judiciary, while the civil servants who have infringed the citizen's rights are left unpunished.

In this context it is necessary to stress the importance of the Ombudsperson as a mechanism to safeguard the Rule of Law in Poland.[10] The office was introduced in 1987 in the last years of General Jaruzelski's rule, after decades of refusing to acknowledge the need for this institution, under the doctrinal pretence that the socialist Prokuratura already served the purpose of defending citizens rights.[11] It was conceived as part of the wider agenda to promote the socialist State of Law as advocated by then Prime Minister Rakowski. Greeted with understandable suspicion on the part of the opposition and criticised for neglecting the most important cause of the outlawed "Solidarity", the first Ombudsman, Professor Ewa Łetowska slowly gained respect by focusing on important areas of administrative abuse of the legal order. So, after 1989, the office was able to flourish both in terms of its activity and popular respect. It should be observed that the Polish Ombudswoman was, from the very beginning, equipped with strong powers, as she might directly refer a case to the Constitutional Court, request extraordinary revision by the Supreme Court and the Supreme Administrative Tribunal. These powers were in addition to those of making

9 *Idem*, p.347.

10 J. Kurczewski, "The Politics of Human Rights in Post-communist Poland" in I. Pogany (ed), *Human Rights in Eastern Europe*, Aldershot, Edward Elgar, 1995, p.132.

11 Such was argument given by Prof. Sylwester Zawadzki, later Communist Minister of Justice, in answering the memorandum I have dispatched to authorities on behalf of the Sociology of Law Section of Polish Sociological Society in the mid-1970s when the new law on social control was subject to routinely censored "social consultation".

legislative recommendations to the Government, presenting information and recommendations to the Parliament and making them available to the public. Within ten years the Polish Ombudspersons dealt with more than 250,000 cases, the majority of which was found ungrounded (57% of cases in the last year). Yet 22% of cases in 1996 were settled to the satisfaction of the claimant, while in 18% of cases the lapse of time or lack of evidence made investigation impossible. In 3% of cases the Ombudsman's requests have not been respected by the administration.

The New Constitution as a Remedy

One of the major obstacles to the Rule of Law as mentioned by Professor Zieliński has, in the meantime, been abolished. After seven years of work and seven drafts, the National Assembly passed the new Constitution which was subsequently approved in a nation-wide referendum on April 25th 1997. This is the legal fact. The sociological truth lies behind the figures. Only 42%. of the public turned out at the polls, despite the declared conviction of the majority that the new constitution is of importance to the country. Of those who did vote only 53%. voted in favour of the new constitution, while 46%. were against. The referendum was preceded by a bitter political debate between the supporters of the National Assembly's draft - including the ruling coalition and part of the opposition - and "Solidarity", backed by the Catholic Church and almost one million people who signed the "Civic Draft" as it was officially called following the special Act on the procedure of the Constitution-making passed by the National Assembly, that is both houses meeting jointly for that purpose. Both sides subsequently declared their satisfaction with the volume of public support, though on both sides a feeling of frustration was common. Post-communists included in their 1997 electoral platform the boast that, after four years of crisis from 1990 to 1993, their arrival in power provided new stability and constitutional safeguards for democracy. "Solidarity" leader Krzaklewski confirmed the intention to alter the Constitution once in Parliament, not unlikely if the electoral forecasts in 1997 are taken into consideration. It does seem, however, that it is not the general civil rights and freedoms but rather specifically the right to life which is under consideration.[12] The way in which civic rights have been listed and safeguarded in the new Constitution seems to be safely distanced from the

12 On this see my article on "Family As the Institution of Civil Society in Poland", (1996) *Polish Sociological Review*, 4.

main lines of the ideological debates of Polish politics. This seems to be proven by the development until today with "Solidarity" as the ruling force in Parliament and coalition Government in Poland since the 1997 elections. The new Polish constitution of 1997 replicates in Article 2 the post-1989 formula that Poland is "a democratic State of Law fulfilling the principles of social justice", which facilitates continuity in judicial interpretation, although the "social justice" part of the formula has been the subject of some marginal criticism. Chapter Two of the Constitution is devoted to the Freedoms, Rights and Duties of Man[13] and the Citizen and is composed of 56 articles that, apart from listing rights such as those in the ECHR and economic, social, and cultural rights, lists instruments for the defence of those rights. The most important innovation is the general accessibility of constitutional review, though review is limited to the normative basis of the administrative or judicial decision challenged. Art. 79 of the Constitution proclaims that anybody whose constitutional rights and freedoms have been injured has a right to apply to the Constitutional Court, in accordance with the law, requesting a ruling as to the constitutionality of the law or other normative act that served as basis for the administrative or judicial decision. This right has been postponed in practice not only by the need to pass the relevant procedural legislation (still badly needed), but also because of the notorious self-idolatry of Polish parliamentarians which delayed for two years the acknowledgement that the Constitutional Court's review of the constitutionality of parliamentary legislation was binding and final. Though limited, universal access to constitutional judicial review of national legislation and other normative acts may substantially enhance the rule of law, especially, when the issue of the so-called "xerox-legislation", made everyday within the administration mentioned in Ombudsman's report is taken into consideration. Exactly this type of the norm-making discretion enjoyed in practice by the administration might be curtailed through the Constitutional Court's review and its deterrent effect. It is also here that Article 77.1, granting everybody the right to compensation from State body that harmed him or her through illegal action, becomes of crucial significance. It remains to be seen whether the new mechanism of implementing rights will diminish somewhat the role played by the Ombudsman which is one of the constitutional institutions of the Republic (Articles 208-212).

The new Constitution deals also with another obstacle to the Rule of Law mentioned by the Ombudsman, that some areas of rights may beyond the

13 N.B. Polish "czlowiek" is customarily rendered in translation as "Man", though in this as in the other Slavic languages the term is gender neutral.

scope of the judicial review. Article 77.2 provides that "the law cannot prevent anybody from pursuing seeking a judicial remedy for the infringement of freedoms or rights." International agreements, such as the ECHR, after promulgation in the *Law Journal* automatically become part of Polish law and are directly applicable, taking precedence over national legislation (Art. 91.1). Finally, the important ECHR formula is repeated in the art. 31.3 of Polish Constitution to the effect that:

> Any limitation upon the exercise of constitutional freedoms and rights may by imposed only by law, and only when necessary in a democratic state for the protection of its security or public order, or to protect the natural environment, health or public morals, or the freedoms and rights of others. Such limitations shall not violate the essence of freedoms and rights.

Considering the fact that the content of the ECHR has been directly absorbed by the new Polish Constitution the country has gained a much better legal framework independently of the international system, though in fact it is necessary to realise that Poland now accepts the ECHR Strasbourg jurisdiction which seems to safeguard at least the lowest acceptable European level of the respect for the Rule of Law and Human Rights.

Cotterrell's Concept of the Rule of Law

Roger Cotterrell in his recent article accepts the Rule of Law as a legitimate subject for the socially concerned sociolegal scholar. His essay, occasioned by the tenth anniversary of English publication of Franz Neumann's book from the 1930s,[14] is to be seen as the attempt to dig the Rule of Law out of its historical context, for which Neumann has condemned it. Although the rise of the "State of Law" might rightly be linked by Neumann, as well as earlier by Max Weber, to the development of entrepreneurial capitalism, the corporate capitalism, which in Neumann's opinion undermined the emancipatory mission of the Rule of Law for the sake of the corporate interests dominating society, is no longer the same as it was sixty years ago. The tendencies might be the same, however, as "[t]he seemingly atomistic society of individual consumers [...] exists alongside - indeed, as the other side of the coin from - the vast extension of Neumann's society of corporate interests".[15] However endangered the Rule of Law under such

14 Franz L. Neumann, *The Rule of Law*, Leamington Spa, Berg, 1986.

15 Roger Cotterrell, "The Rule of Law in Transition: Revisiting Franz Neumann's Sociology of Legality", (1996) 5 *Social and Legal Studies*,.458.

circumstances may seem to be, Cotterrell, nevertheless, attaches great importance to it as a contemporary project. Cotterrell refers to Lon Fuller's idea of the relationship of reciprocity between the rulers and ruled that includes the idea of the former being subject to the laws they make as well as the latter, this idea being a "powerful component" of the mutual trust at the foundation of the reciprocity. The Montesquieu-derived conception of the Rule of Law meant that the protection of all by the law is incompatible with the present-day exclusion of the "underclass" by the bureaucracy in power. But individual autonomy, which is the aim of the Rule of Law, can be defended only if the law is used to safeguard "civil society" against corporations and bureaucracies.

Hence the fulfilment of the promise of the Rule of Law requires not only the universal protection of the rights of all citizens to participate as members of the polity as a whole but also the specific protection of degrees of autonomy of groupings of citizens in partially self-regulating communities of many different kinds. The possibility for citizens to take more control, but only insofar as law ensures possibilities for all members to participate as full members of the communities to which they belong. Equally, government and law need to guarantee the minimum conditions of material life for individuals that make this participation worthwhile and that give them a serious stake in the various communities with which they may associate.[16]

This requires that regulating bodies be brought closer to local contexts, making self-regulation as well as democratic monitoring of imposed regulation much easier. Moreover, the particularistic, if not unequal treatment of vast corporate structures, undermining their security and autonomy is needed in order to safeguard the autonomy of individual citizens at large, and their opportunities for engaging in pluralistic communal activities. "The society of freely interacting individuals, presupposed in much traditional thinking about the Rule of Law should be seen as a dynamic project and not static doctrine" - concludes Cotterrell, and then adds that "[t]reated in this way much of its promise remains to be fulfilled".[17]

While thinking on the Rule of Law from capitalist and socialist perspectives seem to counteract each other, there is an intriguing parallel between them. Cotterrell is against the abuse of the citizen's individual autonomy by the forces of corporate capitalism and the modern State's bureaucracy, and therefore aims at strengthening civil society through the

16 *Idem*, pp.464-465.
17 *Idem*, p.466.

law. Looking at socialist society as practised by the Communists one was appalled by the predominance of the Party corporate interests secured through direct control over the State's bureaucracy. The answer was sought in the reintroduction of private property and a market economy - not meant as ends in themselves but as the instruments to help to secure once again the individual autonomy of the citizen. It might be therefore, that the problems were structurally similar - the lack of symmetry whether in the market or in the public forum holds for both cases, corporate Capitalism as well as corporate Socialism.

Another striking element in Cotterrell's idea is the immediate link between the Rule of Law, seen as a developing project and the view that "much of its promise remains to be fulfilled". For myself, I would be at once more optimistic and of a more pessimist humour in the long run. If the project is dynamic, there is no reason to assume that it is an ever-ending one. Let it be repeated, what was quite a satisfactory level of the Rule of Law for an Athenian slave-owner or Polish noble of the 16th century does not fit our contemporary notions of universal citizenship and human equality. There is no need to assume that the process will suddenly stop, if it is, as I would suggest the process of permanently discovering and reinterpreting the rights and dues determined by the general idea of the good life which might be common to Aristotle, Montesquieu, Neumann and others. The dynamic character of the project on the other hand means that one is deemed to remain fundamentally ambivalent about the assessment of the actual performance of the Rule of Law. Even at its best, it needs to be improved, this is the trick that makes Sisyphus' task productive. However, if it needs to be improved, it does not mean that actual realisations cannot be ranked as closer or farther towards the ideal. The static concept of the Rule of Law about which Cotterrell writes is yet another thing. It is the legal form of the Rule of Law. One needs to deal with this concept briefly in order to transcend the difficulties encountered when assessing the state of the Rule of Law in Poland.

Social Rights as Problematic

First, however, one should move to the issue of social rights which until now had been left beyond the scope of the discussion. For Vilhelm Aubert, the lengthy Norwegian experience of the development of a welfare state within the framework of a well-established "State of Law", it was obvious that:

> ... the rule of law was of more assistance to the business community than to underprivileged groups. This can be explained quite simply by the fact that those who possess extensive rights have more to gain from mechanisms that protect rights than do those who hope to gain new rights. New rights are established by political means, means that are less accessible to underprivileged groups than to others. In spite of this, marginal groups (the unemployed, the disabled, old people, etc.) have acquired minimum rights in the welfare states [...] Modern West European states are simultaneously welfare states and law states. The welfare state may favour underprivileged groups, while the law state favours those with privileges [...] Inequalities persist, albeit on a higher level than in the old law state.[18]

The Polish Ombudsman, Professor Zieliński, has already been quoted as saying that there is no "law state" in practice unless underprivileged groups do not fully participate. Cotterrell advocating the abolition of the "dual state" divided into the ordinary citizenry and the "underclass", made up of those defined by the bureaucracy as a social problem, continued along the same line. Interestingly enough, Aubert makes the distinction between the "law state" and the "welfare state", limiting the first to the more narrowly defined area of the due process of law, civil and political rights and equality of rulers and the ruled before the law, while both Polish and British authors assume that they are inevitably linked. For Aubert, historically the rule of law preceded the welfare state as the natural next stage in the development, Zieliński sees an inextricable link, while Cotterrell historically sees the abolition of the "dual state" as the prerequisite to further the rule of law under the modern corporate/atomistic conditions.

In Poland the historical development was in a sense exactly the opposite to that in Norway. More than fifty years ago, a new regime was created which abandoned any pretence of realising the rule of law, except for "legality" understood in the narrow sense as the citizens' duty to obey the will of the Sovereign, that is the Party took upon itself the role of the representative of the proletariat in the process of class, and then universal emancipation. Marx ridiculed formal equality before the law and argued strongly for the need to have material equality. Here the delicate problem arose that divided his followers. Does it mean that equality of life should be the goal, or rather the equalisation of opportunity before the law? And, secondly, if there is inequality in fact behind the formal equality before the law, should one surrender the latter, even if the former cannot be achieved?

18 Vilhelm Aubert, *Continuity and Development In Law and Society*, Oslo, Norwegian University Press, 1989, p.86.

Communists proclaimed that their goal is the achievement of actual equality, and abolished the ideal of the rule of law altogether. There was also another, reformist approach that claimed the need to upgrade social conditions to fit more closely the ideal of the rule of law, and that instead of overall equality, the equilibration of the social positions of citizens is needed in order to secure as far as possible equality before the law.

The revolution created an economically fragile and militarily very strong social system in which social and economic rights were proclaimed, but distributed at the free discretion of the ruling elite. These rights could not be claimed by recourse to any body independent of those people who were distributing coupons or more abstract entitlements. The opening-up of the economic system and the surrender of an arbitrary power to use physical and other coercion has not prevented the recognition of social and economic rights, but has put them into the critical position of not being justiciable. With the right to work, for instance, the court hypothetically can order the manager to re-employ the fired employer or the state agency to pay unemployment benefit, but cannot order the company to re-establish itself from bankruptcy or require the bank to provide the credit to allow the previous level of employment. Not surprisingly in the new Polish Constitution the right to work has given way to the much more restricted clauses of Art. 24 ("The Polish Republic protects the work. The State supervises working conditions"), Article 65.1 ("Everybody has freedom in the choice and exercise of an occupation as well as in the choice of work place"); 65.2 ("The duty to work can be imposed by the law only"), and 65.5 ("Public authorities propose policies aiming at full and productive employment through implementing projects to combat unemployment, including organising and supporting occupational advice and education, public works and intervention works"). The Constitution goes as far as to call this last (Art. 65.5) a right, but adds defensively another Art. 81, whereby this right can be claimed only as provided by the (as yet non-existent) law.

This illustrates the problem facing the constitution-makers. While instituting proper judicial recourse for the infringement of civil, political and human rights, they were aware that this is not easily applicable to social, economic, and cultural rights. On the other hand, it was obvious that most of society expected these rights to be secured.[19] In effect, the relevant

19 In my bi-annual nation-wide representative surveys since 1988 the acceptance of the duty of the State to guarantee such rights has remained basically at the unchanged level, except for the duty to guarantee to everybody the welfare which became less supported by the public opinion.

chapter contains three sorts of rights: (a) a few general ones which apparently are directly justiciable, as, for instance, the freedom of artistic creativity (Art. 73) or the right of the family in social and economic hardship to special assistance from the authorities (Art. 71);(b) an abundance of more narrowly defined rights which remain to be implemented by legislation, as in the articles relating to work or the right to social assistance in case of the involuntary unemployment of someone who does not have other means of support (Art. 67.2); (c) rights following from the duties imposed upon public authorities, such as in Art. 68.5 ("Public authorities shall support the development of physical education, especially among children and youth") or Art. 74.1 ("Public authorities lead policy safeguarding ecological safety of the contemporary and future generations").

As, contrary to an earlier draft presented by the former President Lech Wałęsa, no mechanism is directly prescribed for pursuing related claims, one is left with expectation that it will be left up to the Constitutional Court to decide in case of dealing with constitutionality of particular normative acts or to the Tribunal of the State, the special court which in Poland is deciding on the constitutional liability of the supreme public office holders, including also the criminal responsibility in the case of the President of the Republic.

The issue was not clarified during the debate, while the doctrine of the programmatic constitutional statements was invoked to make a compromise between the procedurally understood Rule of Law and the wish to appease the public expectations of the public. This was an expectation not so much that the socialist welfare state would continue, but rather that it would be elevated to the pure "law state" form. Inevitably, in the coming years this will create a point of friction within a society that is between two systems, one socialist the other capitalist, and which, while embracing the market economy, wants to retain the welfare protection that has hitherto been provided.

Krygier's Test, or Does the Law Rule the Rulers?

Martin Krygier, an Australian scholar with a deep insight into the problems of Polish society in particular, and post-communist societies in general, observed that the rule of law is based upon two principles: rule through law and the limitation of the rulers by law, so the authorities implement their power by applying the law and at the same time are bound by the law.[20] He contrasts two cases. In 1975 Australian PM Gough Whitlam was dismissed by Sir John Kerr, then the Governor General. Whitlam as well as all others could debate the legality of this decision but once the telephone to the Queen had confirmed that the decision had already been made, there was nothing left but to surrender office and to run in the new elections. This is opposed to the 1979 case in Afghanistan, when the Soviet government applied to PM Mohammed Taraki to remove his deputy from the office. At the cabinet meeting the deputy known as Hafizullah Amin shot the Prime Minister and started a purge and later invited in the Soviet Army which killed him as soon as they entered the country. These two cases serve Krygier to explain the test for the rule of law, and more significantly to substantiate E.P.Thompson's claim that the rule of law is a precious cultural achievement. Krygier is far from underestimating the role of various institutional aspects of the rule of law, such as independence of the judiciary and of the bar, aspects that have already been discussed in this chapter. All this would not, according to him, explain the Mr Whitlam's readiness to follow the decision with which he was by no means in agreement. In order to understand one must take into account something less tangible but far more important than the institutions, that is "the rooted conviction that law really matters".

Although I have myself attempted to operationalise the rule of law by pointing to various institutional and extra-institutional aspects, I am in full agreement with Krygier on the issue of the essence of the thing in question. When tackled directly, it is difficult, of course, to answer. Do we have the Rule of Law in Poland? Does the law really matter?

The answer may be sought in two ways. One will follow tradition of Polish sociology of law and will refer to public opinion on the issue. Adam Podgórecki asked in 1964[21] whether one should always obey the law, even if one believes it is unjust, or whether one should either pretend to obey it, but bypass it in practice, or whether one should never obey a law which one believes is unjust. Assuming that Mr. Whitlam obeyed the law albeit thought it unjust, this seems a pretty good question to ask about the rule of law. In 1964, which was a relatively peaceful year under the somewhat stagnated rule of First Secretary Gomułka, about 45% of the nation-wide representative sample were for abiding by the law, while only 18% were

20 Martin Krygier, "Rządy prawa: kulturowe osiagniecie o znaczeniu uniwersalnym" [Rule of Law: Cultural Achievement of Universal Significance", 1990 *Res Publica*, 12.

21 Adam Podgórecki, *Prestiz prawa* [The Prestige of Law], Warsaw Ksiazka i Wiedza, 1966.

against it openly, and 23% in the practice. To Andrzej Kojder's dismay, almost the same results were found in 1995 when survey was replicated, leading him to conclude that "[t]he socio-legal awareness of Poles living in the Third Republic has apparently not changed since the years of the communist regime".[22] He then lists several factors that may explain this apparent continuity, such as the increase in crime, the lack of substantial change in the legal system, the widening of the social gap, the alienation of the new political class, the lack of a clear vision for the future, the State's withdrawal from its welfare functions, the emergence of high unemployment and the effective destruction of "normativeness" in Polish society during the last fifty years. All these factors seem significant, though at the same time the picture is not as simple as Kojder thinks. He does seem to underestimate the degree to which the "normativeness", or better normativity was destroyed in Poland in the last decade of the Communist rule. When studying the systematic biannual survey of a nation-wide representative sample which I have carrying out through the OBOP polling centre since 1988, the apparent stability of views turns into a *return* to the 1964 level, which is by no means easy to explain

Percentage of those answering that law should always be obeyed, even if unjust

	1964*	1988#	1990	1992	1993	1994	1995	1996
	45	27	28	33	43	43	49	42
100%	2820	926	898	1319	1111	983	N.D.	1116

All data from my surveys except *A.Podgórecki's data; #A.Kojder's data

Gomułka's Poland should certainly not be defined as a rule of law state. The problem of comparisons, however, is acute. Poles of 1964 could still favourably compare the system of "organised injustice" under Gomułka with the Stalinist terror of the early fifties that preceded his coming to power in 1956. It was two years after the 1964 survey that the first public confrontation blew up between the Party and the public on the occasion of the millennial anniversary of Christianity in Poland. Four years were to elapse before the still marginal clashes with students, and six years before the bloody confrontation with workers, the first of its kind since 1956. The

22 Andrzej Kojder, "The Prestige of Law. Thirty Years After", (1996) 4 *Polish Sociological Review*, 116.

decay of communism in Poland has its own long and complex history and the surveys teach us that the historical context needs to be seriously considered. The years after 1989 have witnessed a slow increase in the prestige of law amongst ordinary citizens, and as with economic growth, it still has not surpassed previous records, but the increase since the confrontations of the 1980s is unquestionable.

This is much more remarkable when the ruling elite is taking into consideration as in Krygier's test. Instead of comparing Afghanistan and Australia in the 1970s, it may suffice to compare the transfer of power before and after 1989. Gomulka was deposed in 1970 against his will in a closed meeting of the Party's leading group. The change of loyalty by the General Jaruzelski, commander-in-chief of the army in 1970 and in 1980, that is in both moments of popular riots, resulting political crisis, and the change of power was a crucial factor behind this. When Jaruzelski lost his office in 1990 to the newly elected President Wałesa, not a word was murmured about the possibility of military coup this time, though Jaruzelski in 1981 introduced martial law unconstitutionally. More interesting was how Kwaśniewski became President after he beat Wałesa in the 1995 election. The result was contested on the basis that false information was given to the electorate about Kwaśniewski's educational qualifications. Though sociologists have been asked whether this could have won votes for Kwaśniewski, the question was asked by the court, and the Supreme Court upheld the validity of the election. Apart from whistles of disapproval, nobody opposed the verdict that settled the issue once and for all. The judicial settlement of the case seems to embody the rule of law principle even better than the resignation of Mr. Whitlam invoked by Krygier.

The Meaning of the Rule of Law in Democracy as Context

The legal form exists. As Krygier rightly observes the form is not enough. More specifically, three separate issues are important here. Are the institutions described in books really working? Is the legal machinery in operation sufficient to allow us to speak about the rule of law in action. Is the rule of law independent of other principles of social life?

The first question is that of the efficacy of law. Professor A. Zieliński remarked that the inefficiency of the machinery of justice is a great obstacle to establishing the State of Law in Poland. The report by the Research Institute at the Ministry of Justice makes it clear that, "In recent years the functioning of the common courts is in systematically deteriorating. The present situation is critical, and the causes are difficult to eliminate".[23] In the last 6 years the volume of cases increased by 150%, the number of cases settled is on increase, but the congestion results prolonging the time that proceedings take - 7.1 months in criminal cases, 9.3 months in civil disputes, and 16.4 months in non-contentious civil cases (!) in 1995.[24] The delay in registration of the property deals is rising (5.9 months in 1995), and the estimated effectiveness of the execution orders amounts to about 30%, as compared with at least 70% in Western Europe.[25] There is a lack of judicial skills, an inadequate technical infrastructure, and insufficient expenditure on the machinery of justice at a time when the system faces a new task due to the rapid rise in the number of civil cases. This increase is related to the abolition of the State system of compulsory arbitration, the legal autonomy of the public companies and the explosion of private firms of various size. It is worth quoting Boaventura de Sousa Santos' remark, made during the 1997 Summer Course in Onati, that the inefficiency of justice in post-communist societies leads to the development of a "mafia" to meet the need for the quick and efficient execution of financial obligations. According to our studies in the 1970s,[26] the private unlicensed business in Poland already used the withdrawal or self-help. This has intensified with the legalisation of the private economy which is, on a massive scale, in the hands of individuals or small-scale joint companies that do not have the financial means to be able to rely on banks in order to survive the economic crises resulting from the unpaid debts. It is not necessarily the Mafia which is used, for this still seems to be more of a foreign than local phenomenon in Poland. Instead it is by armed self-help - the access to firearms having been liberalised - and the thousands of legal private armed protection agencies, which seem to be used for purpose of securing the payment of these sorts of debt. Thus in general, while the struggle against crime seems to induce the public authorities to violate strict human rights standards, the inefficiency of the public justice leads to small scale mass crime and abuse of human rights by private individuals and agencies.

The last point leads us to the second question, which in fact is that of the content. Rule of Law is not only the set of juridical institutions. Though historically the stress was on the procedure, at the base of this stress was the concern about the rights of the individual. As Cotterrell reminds us,

23 Andrzej Siemaszko (ed), *Quo Vadis Iustitia*, Warsaw Instytut Wymiaru Sprawiedliwosci, 1996, p.4.

24 *Idem*, p.6.

25 *Idem*, p.18.

26 J. Kurczewski, *Spór i sady* [Dispute and Courts], Warsaw IPSiR, 1982.

following Judith Shklar, two traditions meet here - the post-Aristotelian tradition of the rule of reason and the post-Montesquieu tradition of law for all. It is evident that, due to experience of communism, the stress on rights is fundamental. Polish legal culture - by this I mean not the official but popular culture - inherited from the noble past a concern with the rights of the individual, somewhat anarchistic, one may say, as the focus is on one's own rights and not on the rights of others. The "Solidarity" Movement resulted from a concern about rights, and was legally formulated - this is politics through law, though the politics of those who oppose the rulers - in terms of international standards of human rights, or more specifically the freedom of trade unions as safeguarded by ILO. This brings together human rights and the rule of law. Though juridical definitions of the rule of law traditionally pay attention to local institutions, Vilhelm Aubert already drew attention to the fact that with passage of time international human rights become more and more involved.[27] As I have put it in my previous publications, the third generation of the rule of law is the rule of law understood as the rule of human rights, with an international system of conventions and institutions transcending nation states. This is, by the way, why the term "legal state" or "law state" seems to me so anachronistic, and even dangerous, as justifying the neglect of rights by politicians running new democracies today.

As to the third question, it is worth mentioning that though the Rule of Law, especially in its State of Law edition historically preceded democracy, they seem intimately interlinked in the Polish case. Although at the beginning of transformation post-communists-to-be and some anti-communists expressed doubts about the possibility of economic transformation under conditions of democracy, and looked with envy at the strong-hand states of the Far East, this authoritarian diversion was simply unrealistic, due to external and internal expectations. The desire for democracy was great, and remains. Some people may still think that in economic terms they might have been better off in the old days of Communist rule, as with early Gierek or middle Gomulka, but the majority agrees that there has been an indisputable net gain in the establishment of various freedoms and democracy. To this one may add the role of "Solidarity" which helps all other trade unions to play a decisive role in Polish politics. This is an organised, though by no means politically innocent way of supplementing the official political structures with mass participation. The rule of law is linked with Polish democracy and its fate, and so major threats to the rule of law amount to threats to Polish

27 V. Aubert, *op. cit.*,n 18 Chapter 19.

democracy in general. I have listed some of them already in a book on that part of Polish history which ended in 1989.[28] While presenting the dark scenario in which the political class would turn into the democratically elected oligarchy far from the feelings of the average citizen, I pointed to pluralism in public life as the necessary counterforce to this possible development which might occur despite pluralism in the political and economic market.

> The third stage in the construction of democracy, after the abolition of communism and the introduction of parliamentary pluralistic representation, is to fill the social void between state and citizen through thousands of openly and legally active voluntary associations that would in daily life, in-between parliamentary elections, control the representatives, and precede the assumption into political Heaven that, as the beginnings of the new democracies show, seems to be miraculously easy to attain.[29]

After seven years of experience, the above warning should perhaps be more detailed. The trouble is that the transformation of the economy has not been completed yet. The integration with European Union, if effected as is hoped, will inevitably create new turbulence. The degree to which social aspirations may be harmed or satisfied is difficult to predict. And all this seems important in the context of the social aspect of the rule of law which is usually the most neglected. While a plea for more participatory democracy seems to be unsubstantiated by the low turnout at the referenda and elections, one should take into account that Poland has had at its disposal the great instrument of mass mobilisation and participation of the syndicalism without parallel in the Central and Eastern Europe. "Solidarity", notorious for setting up and putting down the governments not on the streets but within the Seym, acting according to the rule of law through its own members of parliament, is not the only such organisation. Other post-communist trade unions also play an important part in the parliamentary politics of the country. It remains to be seen whether the strength of syndicalism in Poland will continue after the much- awaited further privatisation of the economy. What may be sound from the economic perspective, may also be harmful socially. It seems therefore that the inevitable further privatisation and the very likely decrease in the importance of trade unions, needs to be counterbalanced by making political life more transparent and public life more accessible to citizens at large. Thus it seems that the question of the rule of law needs to be tackled

28 J. Kurczewski, *The Resurrection of Rights in Poland*, , Oxford, Clarendon Press 1993.
29 *Idem*, p.451.

in its direct relationship with the fundamental question of democracy, that is the quality of representation.

11 Between "Civil Society" and "Europe": Post-Classical Constitutionalism after the Collapse of Communism in a Socio-Legal Perspective[1]

GRAŻYNA SKĄPSKA

Introduction

The crowning achievement of democratic change is the formation of a new constitution: the emerging new, constitutional order, signals the consolidation of democracy, and generates further processes of the new polity, self-reflection and self-organisation. Yet, this stage in post-1989 Central and Eastern Europe has proved to be difficult and problematic. In most countries in the region new constitutions were duly framed, and institutions, important for the functioning of the liberal constitutional order such as constitutional courts or tribunals, were successfully established. Yet the newly framed constitutions are often accused of syncretism, (incompatibility with the challenges brought about by the transformation, first and foremost, liberalisation of the economy and reform of the dysfunctional welfare system), lack of clarity and simultaneous casuistry. They seem to legalise the immense scope of social life in a casuistic, if otherwise incoherent and unclear manner, leaving many fundamental questions unresolved.[2] In some cases, as in Belarus or Slovakia, democratic constitutions are either changed, or not observed.

Critical remarks about the constitutions that remain democratic are directed principally against the promotion of the "welfare state" in the new constitutions, against the abundance of positive economic rights. These often have a purely declaratory character, but nevertheless may pose serious

1 This article was written while I was a fellow at Collegium Budapest, Institute for Advanced Study. It forms a part of my broader project on the constitutionalism in post-communist societies.

2 For example, nearly half of the articles of the new Polish constitution, which has more than 250 articles, refer to statutes and bills, which are not yet passed.

obstacles to the reform of the dysfunctional welfare system, and sometimes could even have corruptive political consequences.[3] In this way the new constitutions are blamed for contributing to preservation of citizens' state-dependence.[4] Criticism is also directed at the nationalistic provisions in some of the new basic laws for a violation of minority rights, and the conceptualisation of citizenship and nation according to purely ethnic criteria.[5] More generally, post-1989 constitutionalism has been characterised as only "transitional" and the command "Back to the Drawing Board" was formulated to indicate the author's clear dissatisfaction with the framing of the new constitutions and the need to define clearer principles pointing the way to the future for post-communist societies.[6]

In trying to explain the difficult process of new, post-communist constitutionalism, one must stress that the events after 1989 proved to be full of internal tensions and contradictions, "ontological", conceptual and epistemological. Observers of those events underline the necessity of

3 Such consequences of welfare rights are visible in formation of an easy-rider attitude which in Poland is also known as a "thieving-begging" syndrome. The syndrome is also correlated with the general attitude towards the state. On the one hand, one feels totally justified when cheating the state, for instance in not paying taxes or custom duties, on the other, one uses without shame state support by every opportunity. C. Sunstein, "Something Old, Something New", in A.Sajo (ed), *Western Rights? Post-Communist Application*, London, Kluwer, 1996; J. Kornai, "Paying the Bill for Goulash Communism. Hungarian Development and Macro Stabilization in a Political-Economy Perspective", *Collegium Budapest Discussion Paper Series*, Discussion paper No. 33. March 1996; Sajo, ch. 9, *supra*.

4 State dependence of citizens because of the vast protection of social welfare rights is stressed, among others, by Cass Sunstein, according to whom removing of socio-economic rights beyond constitutional entrenchment may be beneficial to those states which wish to undo "the culture of dependency". C. Sunstein, "Against Positive Rights", (1993) 2(1) *East European Constitutional Review*, 35; J. Ciemniewski, "Sejm i Senat w projekcie Konstytucji RP", in J.Krukowski (ed) *Ocena projektu Konstytucji RP*, Lublin, Towarzystwo Naukowe Katolickiego Uniwersytetu Lubelskiego, 1996; W. Osiatynski, "Social and Economic Rights in the New Constitution for Poland", in A. Sajo (ed), *op. cit., supra* n. 3, at p. 262; M. Gintowt-Jankowicz, Panel Discussion, (in:) J. Krukowski (ed), *op. cit, supra*, n., 184, at p. 186.

5 The new Central and Eastern European democracies are usually blamed of excessive nationalism. One may refer here first and foremost to the "ethnic cleansing" in former Yugoslavia, but also to the constitutional definitions of citizenship in Estonia, the "velvet divorce" of the Czechs and Slovaks, the limits of citizenship rights of the Turkish minority in Bulgaria, the difficult questions concerning the political and cultural status of ethnic minorities in Slovakia, Romania, and the situation of the *Roma* everywhere. However, the ethnic concerns and problems characteristic of each of those separate societies are not comparable, and the methods of dealing with those problems and constitutional regulations of them are quite different.

6 S. Holmes, "Back To the Drawing Board", (1993) 2 *East European Constituional Review*, 21.

simultaneous economic, political, and social change, which makes the constitution-making so difficult.[7] Others point to the specific tensions and contradictions between the introduction of an efficient economy, and democratisation;[8] between the introduction of liberal, individualistic principles and the necessity of protecting group rights and solidarity; between the shaping of a national identity and the processes of internationalisation and globalisation that contribute to the complexity and unforeseen consequences of post-communist transformation.[9]

The disappointments expressed are very critical evaluations, which sometimes have the character of lecturing the new democracies, or disappointments with one's own society or its representatives. Together with those tensions and contradictions, these disappointments suggest that we are dealing with the specific processes of establishing constitutional orders, which are quite different from those in the past. In this chapter I will argue that indeed, the new processes of creating constitutions are different from the classical ones, upon which the concept of liberal constitutionalism was built; and that the new, post-classical constitutionalism in Eastern and Central Europe reflects not only the tensions and contradictions characteristic of post-communist societies, but also those which characterise the epistemological and ontological conflicts of late modern polities. As has been observed, post-totalitarian constitutional order formation is occurring in an environment, characterised by deep and overwhelming change, involving the decomposition of traditional values, the growing "disembeddedness" of political and legal institutions, globalisation and simultaneous fragmentation,[10] growing uncertainty and undefined risks.[11] The changes characteristic of the modern world are reflected in recent normative theories of constitutionalism. According to the first, known as the theory of "societal", or the "reflexive" constitutionalism, constitutional orders take the form of informal quasi-legal arrangements, and reflect complex structures of civil society.[12] According to the second, modern constitutionalism is closely related to the international

7 C. Offe, *Der Tunnel am Ende des Lichts*, Frankfurt, Campus, 1994.

8 J. Elster, *Rebuilding the Boat in the Open Sea. Constitution-Making in Eastern Europe*, Centre For European Studies, Nuffield College Oxford, Discussion Paper No 24, February 1993.

9 R. Bellamy & D. Castiglione, *Constitutionalism in transformation: European and theoretical perspectives*, Oxford, Blackwell, 1996.

10 U. Beck, A. Giddens, S. Lash, *Reflexive Modernisation*, Cambridge, Polity Press, 1994; Z.Baumann, *Life in Fragments*, Blackwell, Oxford, 1995.

11 U. Beck, "The Reinvention of Politics: Toward a Theory of Reflexive Modernisation", in U. Beck, A. Giddens, S. Lash, *op. cit.*

12 D. Sciulli, *Theory of Societal Constitutionalism: Foundations of Non-Marxist Critical Theory*, Cambridge, Cambridge University Press, 1992.

legal order, especially, but not uniquely, in the domain of civil rights. Both of those propositions, and the underlying theories of modern constitutionalism, are very important. Inspired by those theories, I will try to outline a theory of post-classical constitutionalism, and consider the emerging complex and overlapping structure of constitutional orders that are forming themselves around differentiated "tiers".

My short analysis will focus on the predominantly socio-legal aspects of the processes of building a constitutional order after the collapse of communism. In the first part I will briefly present the characteristic features of the socio-legal context of post-communist constitutionalism. This includes the peculiarity of the events leading to formation of the new constitutions, the characteristics of the main actors, the socio-philosophical contradictions of the concept of law and the rule of law, and the main ideas, which underpin the foundation of the constitutional orders. In the second part, I give a broader analysis of the tensions and contradictions, the characteristics of "civil society" and "Europe" as the main ideas in shaping the constitutional orders in Central Europe. In the concluding section I return to the conceptualisation of post-totalitarian and post-classical constitutionalism. This is based predominantly on the analysis of the processes which led to the formation of the Polish constitution, but I refer also to the broader events and phenomena.

Socio-Legal Context of New Constitutions Formation

The route to constitutionalism at the end of the twentieth century reveals some specific and unique features. First, in contrast to the liberal revolutions of the seventeenth and eighteenth century (the wars in England, the French Revolution, the American War of Independence), the events of 1989, which eventually led to the formation of new constitutions, were "velvet", and even "lawful", in other words: "civil". Their participants did not have very inventive political imaginations. They wanted their societies to be relatively prosperous, peaceful, democratic and law-governed. The peacefulness of changes was widely applauded and the importance of international opinion was clearly stressed by representatives of the ruling, communist parties, as well as by members of the democratic opposition. This process of the constant mirroring of the events in post-communist Europe - the role of "one's own picture in the other's eyes" for the framers of the new constitutions, justices of the constitutional courts and tribunals, politicians and activists - was a factor of substantial importance in the whole constitution-making process.

The events of 1989 were "civil" in yet another meaning, since with the one (problematic) exception (of Romania), they were particularly peaceful. In that respect, those events, also called "peaceful revolutions", were decisively different from the events which led to the formation of classical constitutions and bills of rights - the French revolution in which hundreds of thousands were exterminated, the English Glorious Revolution, preceded by the English Civil War, and the American struggle for independence.

The main characteristic feature of the "peaceful revolutions" consists in the rather unusual fact that they were conducted through negotiations. These negotiations by "round tables" resulted in pacts and agreements concluded between the main adversaries - the communist authorities and representatives of the democratic opposition. The peacefulness of the processes leading to the formation of new constitutional orders is characteristic not only of post-communist Europe round table agreements, but also pacts initiating democratic change in Spain and in South Africa, where "round tables" led to democratisation in some Latin American countries. In effect, "round tables" were initially an important source of post-totalitarian and post-authoritarian constitutionalism, preceding the legislation by democratic representatives.

In Poland, the concept of a "social constitution" was used to describe the Gdansk Agreement of 1981. In Hungary, the "round table" of 1990 was considered as the event contributing to the legitimacy of transformation and its constitutional character, its conformity with the postulate of the "rule of law".[13] In Poland, as elsewhere, the "constitutionality" of change was on the agenda of the democratic opposition. In consequence, the law proclaimed by the *ancien régime*, popularly accused of being "bad law", legitimised the overthrow and transformation of the regime itself and the establishment of a new order, which claimed to promote new principles and new values, contradictory to those, which were incorporated in the old law. In effect, in the new situations which emerged, together with the economic transformation, democratisation of the political system and cultural changes, the lack of clear guidelines became visible. The constitutional order was faced with gaps and "dead locks", to use the terminology of systems theory, when dealing with the past (issues of restitution of nationalised property/re-privatisation, lustration and decommunisation), and the future (privatisation of the state-owned economy, internationalisation of the economy, globalisation of the market). The "lawfulness" of the overthrow of the system and the legitimation of the new system by the old law make it extremely difficult to deal with past injustices. They put in question the restitutive and retributive concept of justice, and pose a serious obstacle for the future. The most telling example is

13 J. Kis, "Between Reform and Revolution: Three Hypotheses About the Nature of the Regime Change", in: B.K. Király and A. Bozóki (ed) *Lawful Revolutions in Hungary 1989-94*, Boulder, Colorado: Atlantic Research and Publications, 1995.

the restitution of property which was unlawfully, i.e. in disregard of the laws issued by the communist authorities, expropriated or confiscated. In the past forty years, however, but especially shortly before 1989, that property often became the subject of legal transactions, contributing to the complexity of individual property protection, declared in all post-communist constitutions to be a fundamental civil right. Another difficult problem is presented by welfare rights, in particular privileges granted to the functionaries and beneficiaries of the overthrown regime, the legality of which cannot be challenged because of the declared constitutionality of the changes. Yet another, and for the same reasons difficult, problem is posed by the retribution undertaken against the functionaries of the old regime, especially members of the party apparatus or the secret police, known as lustration and decommunisation.

Nevertheless, the "agreements" and "round tables" enabled that active part of society, excluded from official politics because of its opposition to the system, to participate in the framing of the new constitutional order. Pacts and agreements between these active social groups also provided a model for future conflict resolution and reaching agreement on principles for the establishment of new constitutional orders.

The revolutions of 1989 were led in the name of the whole society. They were promoted either by large-scale social movements (as the 10 million Solidarnosc movement in Poland, ecological movements, peace movements), across ethnic, class, professional and gender boundaries, or by the democratic opposition, who claimed to represent the whole of "civil society" and to protect civil and human rights, conceptualised as universal rights. The main enemy of the revolutions was the "system", and not the people. This was probably the most clearly expressed by Václav Havel, in his essays on the "power of the powerless".[14]

In the round table proceedings, as in the peaceful events which led to negotiations, the impact of the international community was unavoidable. The main demands of the democratic opposition included the observance of the ratified covenants on human and civil rights. In Poland, implementation of rights of association and to form trade unions, derived from the International Labour Office Convention, was stressed in the "Gdansk Agreement". International pacts and covenants were also important for the communists, since their observance was considered to lend support to the legitimacy of the regime.

The normative consequences of the negotiated pacts and agreements as the sources of constitutional order are closely related to the general concepts of procedural democracy and deliberative constitutionalism, to which I return in

14 V. Havel, *The Power of the Powerless*, (ed. J.Keane), New York, M.E.Sharpe 1990.

the concluding part of this chapter.

The second feature of events leading to the framing of new constitutions in post-communist Europe consists in the characteristic lack of clear and visible economic interests of the main democratic proponents of change. In Poland, the Czechoslovakia, Hungary, Bulgaria, Slovenia, the former Soviet Republics, it was not a struggle for fair taxes, tariffs, custom duties, protection of property rights, economic freedoms and liberties which provided the focus of the efforts of democratic opposition. This is in obvious contrast to events that led to the founding of liberal constitutions in France and the United States, and the establishment of the constitutional order in the United Kingdom. The revolutions had strong moral undertone, and consequently, moral concerns occupied the minds of the participants, who called themselves representatives of civil society. Indeed, as a Polish historian of ideas remarked, a member of civil society in that region was at that time by no means a *homo economicus,* but a moral entity "living in truth".[15]

Lacking a clearly defined enemy apart from the "system", revolutions of 1989 lacked then also a clearly defined economic agent interested in formation of such constitution that would defend his or her vested economic interests. The classical revolutions were led in the name of, and by, the "third estate", by people deprived of civil rights, though predominantly of property rights and rights to free economic activity, or by the merchants and entrepreneurs, whose vested interests were focused on taxes, customs duties, and the limitation of state power, which albeit limited, still had to be strong. In contrast, the interests of civil society in Central and Eastern Europe, apart from moral concerns, were concentrated on social welfare rights and services provided by the state. The importance of a good and rational constitution and constitutional law for economic transformation and the daily operations of the market was initially not on the civil society agenda. Equally lacking were the concerns with customs related to the commerce, entrepreneurial activity, functioning of individual and collective economic actors, compatible with the free economy.

The agents of the "peaceful revolutions" were initially engaged in an "immanent critique" of "really existing socialism" which had strong moral undertones.[16] They were proposing a "lyrical model of socialism",[17] or a "socialism with human face".[18] The necessity of economic transformation and

15 J. Szacki, *Liberalizm po komunizmie* (Liberalism after Communism), Krakow Znak, 1995.

16 S. Lukes, "Introduction" in: V. Havel, *op. cit*, n. 14., p. 14.

17 J. Strzelecki, *Socjalizmu model liryczny* (A Lyrical Model of Socialism) Warsaw, wyd. Cztelnik, 1989.

18 The exception here is the Polish peasants, who successfully struggled for property and the protection of property rights during the whole period of communist rule in Poland. The history of this struggle is also a history of the struggle for constitutional guarantees of the

establishment of the efficient, free economy came suddenly and rather unexpectedly. Therefore, even if in all post-communist constitutions the provisions proclaiming introduction of free market and protection of property rights were eventually enshrined on the agenda of former democratic dissidents, for the participants of the later round tables, and the first framers of the new constitutions, civil liberties and social welfare rights held a predominant position. In this, the framers of the constitution were supported, in Poland, not only by their electorates, but also by the Catholic Church, with its stress on the concept of human dignity, social solidarity, compassion, the protection of social welfare as a duty of government, as well as the protection of the family and of human life from the moment of conception.

Hence, in Central and Eastern Europe, the characteristic foundation of classical constitutionalism, and of civil rights - the protection of private property and freedom of enterprise - could be rooted only in the purely "theoretical interests" of those who acknowledged the importance of free economy for the formation of free society, and in the interests of the emerging but very small classes of new entrepreneurs, including here also the former communist party *nomenclatura* who turned to individual economic activity.

Apart from economic interests, the new actors' political interests were also questionable. Suspicion of politics as manipulation and instrumentalisation, of the concept of a political "system" as a technocratic organisation of oppression was, and still is, quite openly declared, and empirically proved by the very low participation in democratic elections. Besides, another relevant fact concerning the formation of the new constitutional orders is visible in the lack of interest in the new constitutions. In 1997, in the constitutional referendum in Poland, a country with considerable constitutional tradition, only 45% of citizens participated, and the constitution was accepted by less than 50% of them. In Hungary, the former Chief Counsellor to the President of the Hungarian Constitutional Court has posed the question whether Hungary, or any other (post-communist) society, urgently needs a new constitution.[19] In the Czech Republic, the debate concerning the second chamber of the Parliament did not raise visible public emotions. To this one may add the strikingly low prestige

stability, inviolability, and equality of private ownership of farmland that resulted in the changes of private law (the change of private law that legitimated status quo ownership by granting and recording the deeds of those who had obtained their land through informal trade), of the Civil Code in 1982, and the Polish constitution, 1983. All those changes were aimed at protection of the ownership of farmland, granting stability and equality of rights to owners of private farms. However, the nationalistic motivations, the symbolic value of the farm land as a piece of "fatherland" seem to play here at least as great a role as the protection of property rights.

19 G. Halmai, *Does Hungary (or Any Country) Urgenly Need a New Constitution?*, unpublished paper, 1993.

of the legislature, indicated by public opinion polls. In this, post-communist polities are not so very different from the contemporary theoreticians, proponents of the "new reflexivity" and anti-political politics, as foundations of the late political order.[20]

In 1998, after some experience with the process of building a new constitutional order, it is useful to recall that in the debate preceding the 1989 revolution, the "system" was often equated with the "state". The full title of the quoted collection of essays of the Czechoslovak dissidents, was *The Power of the Powerless. Citizens Against the State in Central-Eastern Europe*.[21] In Poland, suspicion against the state goes hand in hand with the general suspicion towards state law. For nearly two hundred years Poles had been living in the hostile states and under the hostile laws. The "system" and "state law" used to be juxtaposed with the spontaneous self-organisation and self-regulation of society composed of differentiated social groups. Needless to say, such ideas of citizens opposed to the state is not necessarily compatible with the establishment of robust constitutionalism.

This leads to a question about the characteristics of the main ideas involved in the transformation and the conceptual and axiological foundations of post-classical constitutionalism in Central and Eastern Europe. The striking feature of the making of the modern constitutional order, obvious in post-communist countries, is the lack of a clear concept of a "higher" law, like natural law, on which classical constitutionalism was based. Instead of the natural law doctrine, which would place the inviolable principles of a "higher law" above the "man-made" positive order, the construction of the post-communist constitutional order has been supported by the *Rechtsstaat* principle, interpreted in a positivistic sense. This includes also the concept of human rights, interpreted as part of the existing international legal order (international covenants and treaties), having, therefore, the Austinian characteristics of the sovereign's commands, this time from a supra-national sovereign.

Efforts to promote natural law doctrine as a foundation of post-communist constitutionalism, were undertaken in Poland predominantly by representatives of the Catholic Church and a few constitutional lawyers and politicians, mostly from the right wing of the political spectrum. They have been met with strong opposition, and not only of a theoretical nature. Viewed from a sociological perspective, it is, rather, a question of the authority of interpretation of the open-ended and general principles of a "higher law". For instance, the authority for the interpretation of principles of human dignity or the protection of human life, the principle of protection of property rights, of freedom of

20 U. Beck, *loc. cit.*, n. 11, *supra*.
21 *Supra*, n. 14.

expression (and the definition of pornography for instance) causes great social and political tensions and disagreements. The opposition to basing the new constitutions on some natural law principles correlates then with the growing anti-authoritarianism, but also with the growing social differentiation and disagreement about fundamental values on which the new social order should rest.

Here, one may refer to Max Weber's theory of modern society and concept of disenchantment and to modern sociological system theories. According to the latter, modern social systems lack the charismatic centre in the form of core values, as well as that specialised partial system which would "represent the society within society".[22] In traditional society, such a central place was occupied by politics or religion, and by the respective social classes of political and religious elites. Religious justification still supported classical constitutionalism, based on natural law, even if in a very general and abstract fashion, as expressed in the American Constitution and in the French *Declaration of the Rights of Man and Citizen*. In a pluralistic differentiated and democratic society, the question is one of the interpretative authority of politicians or, in the case of Central and Eastern Europe, of the members of the intelligentsia, who did indeed once embody democratic and national values and functioned as "the representation of society within society". The lack of a natural law-founded interpretation of rights results in the proceduralisation of the constitutional order, and in the growing importance of constitutional adjudication. The growing importance of the constitutional adjudication for the emerging constitutional order led to the coining of the phrase "invisible constitution". The notion of an "invisible constitution" acquired an analytical meaning in viewing the post-communist constitutional order as composed of guidelines and principles emerging from the verdicts and decisions of constitutional courts and tribunals - institutions which traditionally protected the liberal constitution and the rule of law. As it has been observed, in a complex and rapidly changing economic, political and social environment, constitutional courts elaborate case by case principles for the interpretation of constitutions. Often, in novel situations, they constitute precedents, and go beyond particular constitutional provisions, especially, if those provisions come from the old, even though amended, constitutions[23] or if they are not more compatible with challenges brought about by transformation. Therefore, the concept of a constitutional order refers to the procedural character of the constitution as a written document, which is subjected to interpretation in the

22 N. Luhmann, *Politische Theorie im Wohlfahrtsstaat*, Munich, Olzog, 1981.

23 A. Sajo, "Reading the Invisible Constitution: Judicial Review in Hungary", (1995) 15 *Oxford Journal of Legal Studies* 253.

process of adjudication. Thanks to the introduction of a popular legal action or constitutional complaint, procedures for the interpretation of constitutional provisions may be initiated by individual citizens or representative organisations.

All of these characteristic features of post-classical constitutionalism in post-communist Europe (the constitutionality or "lawfulness" of the transformation negotiated at the round table talks by the representatives of "civil society" alongside communist party representatives; the importance of international opinion for countries striving for membership in the European Union; the role of social movements in the struggle for a democratic constitution; the emphasis on universal human and civil rights protected by international covenants; social differentiation and anti-authoritarianism; a positivist approach to international human rights protection; the possibility of civic - individual or collective - constitutional complaint or of the *actio popularis*) point to two important ideas for the post-communist, and also the post-classical constitutional order. In the next section of this paper the role of those powerful ideas, incorporated in the concepts of "civil society" and of "Europe" will be explored.

"Civil Society", "Europe", and the Problem of Constitutional Sovereignty

The concept of civil society, notwithstanding its ideological attractiveness and the recent record, proves to be highly unclear and subjected to many interpretations. It functions within the framework of the very different theories, from John Locke and Adam Ferguson, to Hegel, Marx, and Gramsci, to Alexis de Tocqueville, Edward Shils, and Charles Taylor, to mention but a few. It is often used by particular authors as an idea reflecting their own theoretical and ideological predispositions, as to the free market economy and self-responsible economic agents, the political control exercised by society over the functioning of the government machinery, social bonds, "sociability", or the so-called "third sector" of voluntary organisations. Civil society also reflects the mentalities of particular societies, their traditions, ways of life, and expectations which concern the political, economic and social order. In brief, the concept of civil society changes its content across time and space. According to the idea presented in this paper, the epistemological utility of the concept of civil society consists in its reflexivity. The concept itself reflects the traditions, historical and current experiences of society, for the analysis of which it is used. Its theoretical flaws consist in its internal contradictions and lack of clarity.

Presently, the concept of civil society is also used in connection with the theory of societal constitutionalism. It is claimed that civil society in the modern differentiated democratic state, presents not only networks of institutions and organisations independent of the state[24] but is also composed of social groups who promote their identities. It is a society in which professional associations promote the principles of their professional ethics, in which churches function according to their principles, and ethnic minorities struggle for protection of their separate cultures, values and life-styles. A network of civil associations and organisations, regulated by their own rules, accompanied by the inter-systemic mediating institutions, is either described as replacing traditional institutions of organised polity, i.e. constitutions,[25] or is evaluated as an important component of the existing constitutional order. According to the latter concept, collegial organisations in which actors debate the quality of their life, using deliberative and rational procedures[26] corroborate and discursively legitimise the existing constitutional arrangements. From the latter point of view, civil society may be also evaluated as a depository of social values, rules, and customs, of which the "unwritten social contract" consists. In the words of a great philosopher of law, customs developed by society may be viewed as:

> ... a branch of constitutional law, largely and properly developed outside the framework of our unwritten constitutions. It is constitutional law in that it involves the allocation among various institutions of our society (i.e. churches, social clubism, labor unions, trade associations, etc.) of legal power, that is, the authority to enact rules and to reach decisions that will be regarded as properly binding on those affected by them.[27]

The contribution of civil society (understood as being composed of voluntary civic associations, professional associations, trades unions) to the emerging constitutional order, is clearly observable in Poland. The emerging order reflects not only values, rules of professionals ethics, and vested interests emerging as a result of economic transformation, but also reflects the changes in the self-conceptualisation of civil society itself, and the disappearance of the initial "social contract". The first of two cases, which illustrate the entwinement of the regulation of civil with the constitutional order, refers to

24 C. Taylor, *Multiculturalism and "The politics of recognition"*, Princeton, N.J: Princeton University Press, 1992, p. 54.

25 U. Beck, *loc. cit.*, n. 11 *supra*,; D. Sciulli, *op. cit.*, *supra*, n. 12.

26 D. Sciulli, *ibid.*, D. Frankford, "The Critical Potential of the Common Law Tradition", (1993) 94 *Columbia Law Review*, 1076.

27 L. Fuller, *The Morality of Law*, New Haven: Yale University Press, 1964.

morality, the second to economic transformation.

The constitutional debate in Poland was initially predominantly focused on moral matters, among which the issues of the right to life and abortion came to the fore. These became the politically "hottest" issues. At the time of the overthrow of the communist system, abortion was widely permitted in Poland. The 1956 Abortion Act permitted abortions on the basis of both medical and social reasons. After 1989 numerous attempts to restrict abortion were made, most importantly by physicians, who in their newly proclaimed ethical code of medical profession prohibited abortion, as contrary to the Hippocratic Oath. The Ministry of Health, referring directly to this ethical code, adopted regulation permitting a physician to refuse to perform or to assist in an abortion. The Polish Constitutional Tribunal upheld the regulation, on the grounds that a physician's right to refuse could be derived from the Constitution – the freedom of conscience clause of the Constitution of 1952 (at that time still binding).[28] For our purposes, the importance of the decision lies in the reference to the physicians ethical code. Hence, the effect of the Constitutional Tribunal's decision was that the code became a *sui generis* secondary source of constitutional law.

The law regulating abortion was changed twice in the meantime, and abortion, as well as women, became a political target and an object of political manipulation. Moreover, the abortion issue deeply divided public opinion in Poland and became the subject of a political game. The first change took place in 1992, when a new restrictive law was passed, principally banning abortion for social reasons. That law was changed in 1994, after the victory of the former communists, who made the question of abortion an important issue in their campaign. The new law, even more liberal than pre-1992 legislation, was very soon challenged by the "Solidarnosc" Trade Union and Christian parties, and a group of senators referred the constitutionality of the new law to the Constitutional Tribunal. Independently of this reference, a "refusal movement" was broadly supported. Hospital staff, physicians and nurses alike, refused to perform and assist in abortions, even in such cases which were clearly legal and necessary from a medical point of view. There has been no research on that movement, and there are no data on, for example. the internal power games in hospitals, but the movement was broadly supported, if otherwise illegal. Finally, the Polish Constitutional Tribunal in 1997 held the liberal abortion law of 1994 unconstitutional. The Tribunal did not refer to the ethical code of physicians this time, but affirmed the value of life from conception as a constitutional value, and its protection as a constitutional obligation.[29] In

28 Abortion Physicians Case 1991, Decision U 8/90 of January 15, 1991 (OTK 1991, 134-141).
29 *Rzeczpospolita*, June 19, 1997.

effect, the question emerges concerning the binding force of the liberal law of 1994.

These Constitutional Tribunal decisions cause some doubts about the interpretation of the *Rechtsstaat* principle, declared in Article 1 of the old, amended Constitution of 1952, and Article 2 of the new Constitution of 1997. Independently then from the ethical self-conceptualisation of the Physicians' Association, and the popular concept of life protection, the constantly changing law and the verdicts of Constitutional Tribunal awake concern about the protection of the principle of legal certainty and stability, about the trust in law as the foundation of constitutionalism, and about the protection of individual rights. Needless to say, the verdicts are not generally accepted and their content provokes considerable social protest.

The second important example of the impact of civil society associations, trade unions, on the emerging constitutional order in Poland, presents economic transformation and privatisation processes initiated in Poland in 1990. The problem here is posed by primary rights, i.e. the rights to participate in the privatisation process, as an important process which initiates the new division of wealth and power. The Polish privatisation law of July 13, 1990, on the Privatisation of State-Owned Enterprises, had an open character, and it envisioned a variety of ways in which privatisation could be achieved. However, the statute made privatisation dependent on the suggestion or the approval of the employees of the enterprise. Additionally, in its first version, it granted the employees of the privatised enterprise a right to 15% of the whole stock for a preferential price (one third of the nominal price).

The first privatisation law was considerably amended as a result of negotiations between trade unions, employers associations, and representatives of the state, within the framework of the so-called Tripartite Commission, composed of the representatives of those three groups. With reference to the concept of a civil society constitution in the form of agreements (the Gdansk Agreement of 1980 and the Round Table Agreement of 1989), the Commission, issued in 1993 the Pact on the State-Owned Enterprise Under Transformation. The Pact formulated principles which involved changes in the law, including labour law, the law on the employers associations, and the privatisation law. In accordance with the principles of this Pact, the privatisation law was amended. In its new version it granted the employees even more privileges than before, in form of the right to 20% of the whole stock of the privatised enterprise, free of charge. The Pact represents then another example of an extra-constitutional source of law. Embedded in the long tradition of pacts and negotiations, and, supported by the idea that Gdansk Agreement of 1981 and the Round Table Agreement of 1989 served as a source of constitutional law,[30] regulations derived from the Pact on State-Owned Enterprise Under Transformation have a stabilised legitimation.

On the other hand, the effect of the Pact and the amended privatisation law is that the quasi-constitutional order has developed, as result of extra-parliamentary negotiations, which violates the principle of democratic legislation. Moreover, the constitutional principles of equality and equal protection have also been violated. The primary rights in the form of privileged participation in the privatisation process are granted on a very unclear basis to those Polish citizens, who happen to work in the privatised companies, while others are excluded from the process.

With reference to these examples, one has to emphasise the important process of social differentiation, and also the differentiation in the self-understanding of the civil society, which has a reciprocal influence on the emerging constitutional order. It is the regional, cultural, generational, but also economic and ethical differentiation of a society, which once was united by the common enemy ("the system") and whose living conditions were more or less the same. Currently, the once undifferentiated "civil society" which struggled for universal civil and human rights, represents very different ideas on the interpretation of the protection given by those rights. As has been demonstrated, the process of social differentiation leads to the emergence of, not only overlapping, but also conflicting and contradictory ideas, and resulting regulations. In situations, in which the protection of individual rights is weak, and liberal constitutionalism is also weak, influential and powerful social groups exercise an influence on the interpretation of constitutional principles and the structure of the emerging constitutional order.

In consequence, the emerging post-1989 constitutional orders share with the "civil society" its internal ontological and epistemological ambiguities and contradictions, as well as the ambiguities and contradictions which result from the changes in "civil society" itself. These changes include not only its differentiation, but also the lack of liberal traditions of the protection of individual rights, as well as disrespect for state-law, linked to the concept of civil society as in opposition to the state.

The new constitutional orders emerge in a world, whose characteristic feature is posed by globalisation, international integration and, particularly in Europe, European integration. Here one can refer to the ambitions of the new democracies to be integrated into the European Union, because those societies were "always" a part of "Europe". This is of great interest to the societies of Central Europe, in contrast with their weak interest in their constitutions.

30 J. Nowacki and Z. Tobor, *Wstep do prawoznawstwa*, (Introduction to jurisprudence) Katowice, Uniwersytetu Slaskiego, 1995.

Popular support for the idea of European unification, as well as membership for their own countries of the European Union is considerable, albeit based on a rather weak knowledge about Europe itself (in Poland such a general but abstract support was expressed by 85% of citizens). This European engagement takes a very active practical form, what is illustrated by number of complaints directed by Polish citizens or their private associations to the European Commission (1600 in Poland during four years). There are also to be heard very critical opinions of European integration. However, the emergence and importance of supra-national entities, such as the European Union points to the important feature of the idea of post-classical constitutionalism: the diminishing importance of the state, and of the national constitution. Therefore, as classical constitutionalism emerged as the crowning achievement of the formation of the modern nation-state at the end of the twentieth century the formation of supra-national and international institutions influenced internal constitutional orders.

The European Union, or even more generally, the idea of "Europe", has a three-fold importance for the developing internal constitutional orders: cognitive-emotional, political, and legal. "Europe" is then an important frame of reference and source of cognitive ideas and even myths, which help "newcomers" to define their position and rights. "Europe" provides the political language with the necessary concepts and ideas, as well as functioning as a frame of reference and basis for evaluating the national internal state of affairs. Until now, however, it has been a "Europe" of social security, a "Welfare State" Europe. Only to a lesser extent is a "Europe" of the free movement of goods, capital, and persons which, in the consciousness of Central Europeans, especially in the consciousness of the members of "civil society", functions as a source of concepts and self-definitions. Thus, the idea of "Europe" until now seems to promote social-security focused concepts of rights and the constitutional order in the new democracies.[31]

The thesis on the cognitive importance of the European Union, as a frame of reference, but also as the source of concepts and ideas which inform constitutional rhetoric, has also been formulated with respect to the functioning of constitutional adjudication in the new democracies, and directly with reference to their justices interpretative activity. A Hungarian sociologist quotes the Chief Justice of the Hungarian Constitutional Court, according to whom "all European Constitutional Courts are part of the development of a

31 G. Skąpska, "From Rights to Myths: Transformation in Post-Communist Europe", in A. Sajo (ed), *Western Rights? Post-Communist Application,* supra, n. 3.

common constitutional language, or at least its grammar".[32] A Justice of the Polish Constitutional Tribunal puts the problem more directly and bluntly, as to the more precise concept of "Europe". In the debate on the concept of human dignity, newly introduced into the Polish Constitution, the Justice pointed out that, first, introduction of the concept of Europe links the Polish constitutional order with the German constitutional order, being the closest geographically. So for Poland, the introduction of the principle of human dignity into the constitutional order will serve as an important "bridge to Europe". Secondly, because of that link, Polish constitutional adjudication might directly use arguments already debated in the German Federal Constitutional Court in similar cases on the human dignity clause, and further strengthen cultural and cognitive links with "Europe".[33]

The political importance of the European unification for the limits on the sovereign decision-making of the member states is quite obvious. Political scientists speak here about the emergence of post-national Europe, with a centralised decision-making structure in the form of the European Commission. They observe that the limits on national sovereignty could be painful for Central Europeans, deprived of it as they have been for many decades.[34] The same authors also stress the limits of democratic sovereignty, the limits of the democratically elected legislature, that result from the membership in the European union.

Such a development is of importance to the emerging constitutional orders. It is believed that the central pillar of constitutionalism is the sovereignty of the national Parliament. In turn, having a constitution also contributes to the national sovereignty. However, according to one British constitutional lawyer, such a view characterises the passing phenomena of the past few centuries. Currently a fresh look at sovereign statehood and the constitution is needed, in the context of the of the formation of the European Union, and of the divided sovereignty of the Union, its Members States, but also regions within the Member States.[35] Finally, as for the legal effects of "Europe" on national constitutional orders, the most important principle which should be stressed is that Member States are obliged to harmonise their laws with those of the European Union, and, in case of a lack of such harmony, European law shall

32 K. Fuzlet, "The Invisible Constitution. An Inquiry through Sociology of Knowledge into Hungarian Constitutional Adjudication", paper presented at the 1996 Joint Meeting of the Law and Society Association and the Research Committee on the Sociology of Law, Glasgow, United Kingdom.

33 L Garlicki in the debate on human dignity, organised by the International Centre for the Development of Democracy, Krakow, 5 December 1995.

34 R. Bellamy & D. Castiglione, *op. cit., supra,* n 9.

35 N. MacCormick, "Beyond the Sovereign State", (1993) 56 *Modern Law Review* 1.

be applied directly.

Post-Classical Constitutionalism

In the framing of new constitutions we observe the overlap of two epochs of constitutionalism, the classical, and the "post-classical". The latter is an epoch in which partial, or regional constitutions develop within a broader framework of a national constitution (as for instance in the case of Spain and the Constitution of Basque Country) and an epoch characterised by the growing importance of international and transnational law, but also by the growing importance of internal legal regulations: local laws, regulations of professional organisations, churches, corporations. Constitutions in modern societies function within a framework created by supra-national regulations, which pose serious limits on the classical principles of constitutional order (such as sovereignty and democratic legitimacy), but also within a framework created by local laws, governmental regulations, pacts and agreements concluded between the powerful social groups, ethical charters, statutes and regulations, described as "reflexive constitutionalism",[36] and also within a framework created by constitutional adjudication.

The notion of post-classical constitutionalism is very important for those societies, which after the overthrow of their authoritarian, or totalitarian, regimes found themselves with a lack of guiding principles and social differentiation. They are questioning and redefining the principal values and concepts of rights, and cannot refer to established and proven constitutions.[37]

The emerging structure of the new constitutional orders is complex, overlapping, multicentred, multileveled, and not transparent. According to the analysis of such a structure proposed by system theory, modern systems, including a legal system, develop as non-hierarchical, and non-authoritarian entities of high complexity, entities without a centre, and composed of many units which operate on a more equal level, and they cross-cut each other. Those entities (systems) enter into mutual relations across space and time. In consequence of propositions resulting from such a theory, modern

36 U.Beck, *loc. cit.*, *supra*, n. 10.

37 A good example of a stable and proven constitution which structures the complexity of modern constitutional order is Germany. According to the amended German Basic Law, the principle of subsidiarity may be applied to the German constitutional order only to a limited degree, and the amendments affecting the division of the German Federation into Länder, the participation on principle of the Länder in legislation, and the basic principles laid down in Arts. 1-20 (basic rights and principles of political and economic order) shall be inadmissible.

constitutions form and function in an environment which is highly differentiated, non-hierarchical, and circular, composed of many units (subsystems) Such an environment provides a broad "hermeneutical environment" for the interpretation of constitutional provisions. It imposes limits on the fundamental provisions of classical constitutionalism, such as the sovereignty of the nation and the principle of the supreme legislative power of the democratic parliament.

This complex and contingent structure demands some mediating institution, and one cannot help but think here of constitutional adjudication. This brings us to the important feature of post-classical constitutionalism, provided by constitutional adjudication as a mediating institution between differentiated, incompatible and opaque overlapping orders, between "civil society" and "Europe", as sources of constitutional principles and concepts, made on a day-to-day basis, in the process of mediation between those orders and their conflicting demands. Currently, those principles are called "invisible constitutions" and as such, they function instead, or next, to the existing documents. The importance of constitutional adjudication is founded on the fact, that constitutions regulate human affairs, and protect human rights. They are not only "disembedded" and abstract structures, but important tools of human, especially political action, conflict resolution, and protection. The importance of constitutional adjudication consist in its task of elaborating the meaning of concepts and constitutional principles in the complex modern reality, in this way providing citizens, the addressees of constitutional provisions, with important cognitive tools.

12 Women's Rights and the Rule of Law in Poland

MALGORZATA FUSZARA

Introduction

In most instances communist propaganda was not particularly successful in Poland. It is easy to find examples of its ineffectiveness. It is also easy to uncover it. However, in one area this propaganda turned out to be surpassingly effective - it built up a myth of equal opportunity for women and men in our country. Even worse, by primitive examples of equality (the famous slogans and posters showing women on tractors), it helped to compromise the idea of equality of the sexes. Strange changes of meanings and discrediting of certain concepts by communist propaganda also caused many issues to be shamefully overlooked in public debate. One of these is the issue of equality before the law. In this chapter I shall deal with only one of its aspects - the equality of women and men in Poland. Was the principle of equality between women and men really applicable in Central and Eastern European nations during the so-called communist era, or was it one of the myths. Is this principle being achieved since the overthrow of communism? What are the currently perceivable threats to the principle of equality and lack of discrimination? Can a democratic nation of law be built if the principle of equality of the sexes is infringed or if it is undermined by being questioned? These are only a few of the questions deserving investigation.

It seems that the first of those questions has already been answered. Important publications, dealing with issues of unequal opportunity between women and men in Eastern Europe during the communist era, have appeared in the last few years, dealing in some cases with inequality of rights resulting from specific legal regulation.[1] The communist system

1 Ellen Sofie Baalsrud (ed) *Free and Equal? Female Voices from Central and Eastern Europe*, Norwegian Equal Status Council, No 2, September 1992; N. Funk & M. Müller (ed), *Gender, Politics and Post-Communism*, London, Routledge, 1993; A. Titkow & D. Hentyk (ed) *Co to znacny byc kobieta w Polsce?* (What does it mean to be a woman in

professed the principle of equality between women and men, which was even contained in the Polish Constitution, although the wording, typically, made reference to the situation for men as the model. "Women .... have rights equal to men...".[2] The Constitution, in addition to the general protection of women, also contained more detailed principles of equality, for example at work and in connection with pregnancy. However, the principle of equality coexisted simultaneously with "lists of work prohibited to women", which by its name shows that it was a long way from the idea of equality for all citizens regardless of their sex, and giving women truly free choices in the scope of employment. During the transformation of the system in Poland the principle of equality was breached with the official division of job offers into offers for women and offers for men. Initially, one hoped that the new system, together with creation of new opportunities, freedoms, and citizen rights would also lead to lessening the differences in opportunities between women and men. However, the observation of G. Satori was quickly confirmed when he wrote that "freedom in and of itself does not lead to equal opportunity, this illusion of liberalism has to be discarded. Contemporary democracy thus searches for a collection of 'just equality', which does not show up automatically after freedom".[3]

Equality before 1989

Before we turn to recent efforts in the search for "just equality" and proposals for legal regulation which would help to achieve them, we should turn our attention to a few examples from the past. These show the way in which the principle of equality of men and women contained in the Polish Constitution coexisted with lower level regulations, which sometimes openly discriminated against women. One of the most characteristic examples concerned regulations defining admission limits to medical schools.

In 1985 the Minister of Health and Social Welfare issued a rule, according to which in the framework of a limited number of vacancies, places were assigned 50% to women and 50% to men. A case was initiated

Poland?) Warsaw, IFIS PAN, 1995; C. Kaplan, D. Keats & J. W. Scott, *Politics, Environments, Translators: Feminist International Politics*, London, Routledge, 1997.

2 Constitution of the Republic of Poland of 1952, art. 78.

3 Giovanni Sartori, *The Theory of Democracy Revisited*, citation from the Polish translation *Tear Demokracji*, Warsaw 1994, p. 421.

by a woman who alleged that, despite obtaining high marks in the entrance examination, she was not admitted to study medicine, since she did not fit within the 50% allocation designated for women. Some men, who had obtained lower marks than this woman, were admitted in the same year to the same department, since they fell within the 50% quota of places allocated to men. In 1987, the case was sent to the Constitutional Tribunal by the Chief Justice of the Supreme Administrative Court. The Minister of Health and Social Welfare, defending the quota for men at the Medical School, stated that four criteria justified the basis of such a division:

First, certain medical specialities (mainly surgery) require particular psycho-physical characteristics which men possess - thus it is necessary to train a suitable number of male physicians. Secondly, certain specialities (such as radiology and nuclear medicine) are not recommended for women due to their childbearing function. Thirdly, the medical profession required doctors who could give round-the-clock care for the sick. Thus women, due to their maternal and family roles have a limited ability to undertake night duty. Fourthly, an appropriate number of male physicians is necessary to meet the needs of mobilisation for possible war situations.[4] Thus, in his justification, the Minister of Health completely overlooked the principle of equality between women and men. He pointed to the need, in his opinion justified, to introduce quotas, permitting the admission to medical schools of more men than would win places on the basis of marks obtained in the entrance examination.

In principle these arguments were not the subject of evaluation by the Constitutional Tribunal. It was called upon to adjudicate on the constitutionality of legislation and to consider whether subordinate legislation was consistent with the law under which it was made. After cross-examining witnesses (physicians and, in particular, surgeons) the Tribunal pointed out the unsustainability of these arguments. There are many women in surgery and there are modern methods which do not require sheer physical strength. Specialisations are decided after six years of medical studies, so that it was inappropriate to make selections much earlier when students were admitted to study. Referring to the protection of women, especially during pregnancy and motherhood, the Tribunal stated that this protection is provided for in all professions. Appropriate controls were found in regulations of social and insurance law, while they were completely lacking in regulations concerning acceptance to university

4 Constitutional Tribunal, March 3, 1987.

studies. As regards round-the-clock care and night duty, this could also apply to work in other professions, as well as in professions associated with the health care. Indeed, such duties were performed by nurses and auxiliary staff, the vast majority of who were women. Thus limiting the entry of women to medical studies cannot be justified on this basis. Finally, the last argument was held to be unsustainable, since, to a large extent, military academies meet the needs of the armed forces, in which recruitment and limits are subordinated to the needs of defence. The Tribunal also pointed out that women, obviously in this case physicians, could be called to serve in the military if the need arose.

However, since we are interested in the relationship between the rights of women and law-based nation, a review of the legal arguments given by the Constitutional Tribunal is the most interesting. To summarise, the Tribunal indicated three kinds of defects in the decree. First, the Minister exceeded the limits of his authority defined by the Act on Higher Education. This Act proclaimed that the "determining criteria for admission to a course of study is the substantive evaluation of a candidate's skills". However, the Act provided that the appropriate minister may define "other conditions besides initial examinations, considering fate or environmental differences in preparation by candidates which could influence a decision to admit someone for studies" (art. 84 para. 5). In the opinion of the Tribunal the instruction to this regulation clearly states, that, apart from initial examination results, only 'fate and environmental' differences can be taken into consideration. It is not, however, permissible for them to include differences due to sex. The Minister of Health and Social Welfare thus exceeded the authority conferred on him by the Act.

Secondly, the Tribunal made reference to the universally accepted principle in constitutional law, that the rights of the citizens may not be restricted by anything less that primary legislation. Exceptions to primary rights and civil liberties were only permissible if they are authorised by the Constitution and implemented by a legislative Act. This was not permissible in this case, since the Constitution did not provide for any exceptions to the principle of equality. The Tribunal also referred to certain regulations (e.g. on maternity leave, alimony for single mothers) and concluded that such regulations

> ... comprise a way of expanding and strengthening the status and role of women, thus expressing the tendency to consider the principle of equality in practice. The legislative intention is not restrictive, but on the contrary is to expand the guarantee of achieving the principle of equality. Against this,

> considering the legislation to-date, analysing the *ratio legis* that the legislature is continually directed by, it should be stated that, all activities which result in the limitation of equality of the sexes are unacceptable.[5]

Thirdly, the Tribunal made reference to the fact of Poland's ratification of a range of international pacts containing the principle of equality between women and men. Those mentioned were the *International Covenant on Civil and Political Rights*, the *International Covenant on Economic, Social and Cultural Rights* and the *U.N. Convention on the Elimination of All Forms of Discrimination against Women*. The regulation issued by the Minister of Health was deemed to be contrary to the provisions of these international instruments.

These arguments show that the Constitutional Tribunal recognised the correct approach to be self-evident in cases of alleged inequality between men and women, according to the basic principles of the Polish legal system, and indispensable in a law-based nation. These principles include the principle that the Constitution should be obeyed; that a hierarchy of norms should be observed, whereby lower level norms should not conflict with higher level norms. Fundamental is the principle of equality from which flows specific, concrete rights which must be guaranteed by systematic rules and practices, including provisions relating to parenthood. There must be mechanisms to ensure that equal rights are protected in reality. International instruments, ratified by Poland, should be respected. Can it then be said, as is often heard, that, in the area of equality between women and men, Polish law has satisfied all these requirements and standards, while the question of the existence of inequality only applies to the enforcement of the law? Unfortunately, it is not as simple as that.

The 1952 Constitution contained a range of provisions concerning, in part, citizen rights and freedoms, including a provision concerning the equality of women and men. However, it did not contain any complaints mechanism in the event its rules or principles being infringed. Thus, it was necessary to wait until specialised bodies were established, such as the Constitutional Tribunal and the Citizens' Rights Ombudsman to provide a mechanism to protect rights. Only then could we say that Poland had started to meet some of the standards of a nation subject to law. The problem of inequality between women and men could be seen in a classic case. It was possible in practice to violate the constitutional principle of equality with

5 *Ibid.*

impunity, as long as people affected have a way of enforcing the equal rights to which the law entitles them.

The creation within the Polish legal system of bodies, to assist aggrieved persons to assert their constitutional rights or to establish that regulations conflict with higher legal norms, was crucial in determining whether Poles live in a state subject to law. We can ascertain this by analysing compliance with the constitutional principle of the equality of the sexes. Until these bodies were introduced, whatever the Constitution said, it was not possible to challenge a regulation that conflicted with it. At the time of writing, the Constitutional Tribunal cannot intervene even in clear cases if the regulations pre-date its creation.

This occurred, for example, where the Ombudsman challenged the law regulating social insurance benefits in the event of sickness and maternity. According to this regulation, only the mother was entitled to this benefit. The father could only claim it if the mother did not reside at home or was incapacitated by sickness or pregnancy.[6] In 1991 the Ombudsperson attempted to challenge this regulation, referring to the constitutional equality principle and the *Convention on the Elimination of All Forms of Discrimination against Women*. However, in 1992 the Tribunal ruled that it could not consider applications relating to legal provisions published before the law of 1992 amending the Constitution had come into force.[7] At the same time, the Tribunal and the General Prosecutor acknowledged that the Ombudsperson's challenge was "clearly justified". The Tribunal passed the complaint to the Sejm, but the regulation was only changed in 1996.[8]

Similar regulations concerned, for example, leave to care for a child up to fourteen years old. Whereas "[female] employees" were entitled to leave, "[male] employees" were only entitled where they were the sole carer. This regulation was changed together with a change in the Labour Code in 1997. However, it cannot be said that the current law completely satisfies the

6 On the benefit system see M. Fuszara, "Does the Law Protect Women in Poland?" in M. Maclean & J.Kurczewski, (eds) *Families, Law and Politics*, Oxford, Clarendon Press, 1994; B. Laciak, Family Benefits and Social Policy in Poland" in M. Maclean & J. Kurczewski (ed), *ibid.* B. Laciak, "The Family in Social Policy of the Day of Transformation: Decentralisation and Scarcity" in J. Kurczewski & M. Maclean (eds), *Family Law and Family Policy in the New Europe*, Aldershot, Dartmouth, 1997.

7 Tadeusz Zieliński, "Pozycja kobietyw rodsinie i w zyciu politcznym" (Status of Women in Family and Political Life) in *Kobiety w zyciu publicznym* (Women in Public Life), Warsaw, 1995.

8 On the judicial system and the role of the General Prosecutor, see J. Kurczewski, *The Resurrection of Rights in Poland*, Oxford, Clarendon Press, 1993.

principle of equal treatment of women and men. In Poland, as in many other countries, legal provisions are usually worded in what are called gender-neutral forms (though this is often grammatically masculine). In this case they are worded in the feminine gender, followed by the provision that they apply equally to men.

The regulations referred to here, which awarded certain forms of leave or benefits to women only, limited the rights of citizens from at least two viewpoints. From the viewpoint of women, as a result of such solutions they were treated as a completely distinct group on the basis of sex and so were treated worse, since it was not necessary for them to show up for work and women are entitled to benefits, which employers regarded as more costly. For a woman who does not plan to have children, or has children who are already adults or healthy, these distinctions are much less important than the fact that she belongs to the category of "woman". In certain circumstances this categorisation may result in her being laid off from work. This is an example of creating worse opportunities for women in the labour market, because only women have the right to care for a sick child. From the viewpoint of the family and the individual rights of parents, it is for them and not Parliament to decide which parent should take care of a sick child.

The area of professional work and pay probably comprises the most distinctive area, in which it is easy to find examples both of open and hidden discrimination, inconsistent with the constitutional principle of sexual equality. The Ombudsperson has taken action in relation to access to employment. In 1993 he asked the Minister of Labour to define principles for the conduct of employment agencies, so that they would openly adhere to the principle of equal treatment, in particular prohibiting the expression of a preference for applicants of one sex in a job advertisement. It is worth noting that, before 1992, regulations required employers and employment agencies to split advertisements into those for women and those for men.[9] It was therefore easy to see that most of the job advertisements were directed exclusively at men.[10] After 1992 there was no requirement to apply such a division, but there was also no prohibition against specifying the sex of the intended employee. In response to an intervention by the Ombudsperson, the Minister of Labour stated that the division had an informational and statistical nature. Thus defining the sex of job applicants "should not be

9 *Ibid.*
10 *Ibid.*

taken as a factor preferring a certain sex". How it is possible to specify the sex of the intended employee without this being an expression of a preference for a person of that sex is a great mystery understood only by the Ministry of Labour.

Another, more controversial example of unequal treatment concerns the already-mentioned "listing of work prohibited to women". This recently amended list contains both a list of work prohibited to women at particular times associated with pregnancy and childbirth and a list of work prohibited to women "generally". It should be remembered that for many years this type of regulation was presented as conferring "privileges" on women, who could not be employed in positions and on work harmful to health. Overlooking the fact that it was a question of the health of women, and of their offspring, limiting a potential employee's ability to choose work was presented as a privilege, granted for her own good and in her own interest. A simple solution, requiring everyone to be notified of the possible threats to health associated with particular work and leaving the decision to the individual, was not even proposed, let alone implemented.

The lack of such information and the lack of freedom of choice is not surprising in a totalitarian state, which normally limits its citizens' access to information, especially if it could lead to choices other than those expected by the authorities. However, it is hard to understand such treatment of citizens in a democratic society. It also has to be remembered that in a totalitarian nation there was an additional reason for creating such controls, defined as privileges, and regarded as discrimination in free-market states. In communist countries, not only was there a right to work, but, in reality, there was a duty to work, which in some periods was more or less openly expressed in legal regulations. In accordance with the nature of a totalitarian state, an employee might sometimes be forced to undertake work, including work harmful to health. The prohibitions on women performing certain work, the prohibition on night work in industry or on assigning mothers with small children to work outside the workplace, meant, in practice, that due to the child-bearing and rearing roles of women, they could not be forced to undertake such work nor to work in conditions that were particularly harmful to health. The significance of such prohibitions and limitations completely changed in a free market economy and with heavy competition in the labour market. Under these conditions, such regulations and limitations automatically worsen women's opportunities in the labour market purely on account of their sex, regardless of whether or not they are mothers of small children. What had been devised as a privilege could serve as such because the entire economic system was pathological. When the system changed, not only did it lose its character as a privilege, but it became a flagrant expression of a paternalistic attitude towards women, whom the authorities or the system had "to protect" instead of leaving them a free choice, and a simple discrimination in the labour market, limiting opportunities for choice and access to certain work.

Various legal regulations (in the form of subordinate legislation) have turned out to contain sexually discriminatory rules. Characteristic are various additional benefits granted to the wives of workers, but not to husbands. Complaints have been lodged with the Ombudsperson in such cases. One example is a case resulting from the Council of Ministers Ordinance dating from 1986, concerning "Polish Post, Telegraph and Telephone"("*Poczta Polska, Telegraf i Telefon*").[11] Under the ordinance, an employee's wife was granted a fifty per cent reduction in rail fares, whereas an employee's husband only benefited from the concession if he was unable to work and was kept exclusively by his wife. The Ombudsperson applied to the Constitutional Tribunal for a declaration that the Ordinance was not in conformity with the Constitution because it constituted sexual discrimination. The Ombudsperson asserted that the Ordinance discriminated against men, who, as husbands were denied privileges granted to the employees' wives, and against women, as in practice women workers received fewer benefits from the employer than men (e.g. the lack of additional services for the family members). As the Ombudsperson stated, such a rail fare reduction was widely understood as providing "services" as payment for work, which must fulfil the requirement of gender equality. Besides the Spokesman claimed that this sort of regulation conflicted not only with the Constitution, but also with international conventions and treaties ratified by Poland. The Constitutional Tribunal did not have to deal with the case. Before it came to be considered, the Ordinance had been changed. The right to fifty per cent reduction in rail fares was granted to the employee's partner only when he or she was kept exclusively by the employee (regardless of sex). It is worth observing then that the change amounts to "downwards equalisation", with wives being brought down to the level of husbands rather than raising the level for husbands of workers to that previously enjoyed by wives.

11 Constitutional Tribunal, July 19, 1991.

Another specially controversial problem is the pensionable age of men and women. For a long time the lower pensionable age of women in Poland, 60 for women as opposed to 65 for men, was perceived as a kind of privilege for women burdened with double duties, professional and domestic work for family and household. Such a regulation, especially in times of high unemployment, when it is very hard for the pensioners to find additional work, was perceived as discrimination in the job market by many women. A regulation, which, until then, had been a privilege for those women who wanted to use it, turned into a denial of the right to work for women who wanted to continue to do so. Women belonging to groups which were well-equipped to deal with legal regulations noticed the danger very early on. That is why in some branches of the professions, especially in law, the pensionable age of women and men was equalised. Thus the Common Courts' System Rule preserves the privilege of the lower pensionable age for women, but clearly as a privilege, while applying the same age qualification for compulsory retirement, sixty five, for judges of both sexes. Equivalent changes have been introduced to the rules relating to the Public Prosecutor's Office. Other sectors of employment not connected with law have had to wait much longer for the introduction of such non-discriminatory law, and in some branches it has still not been achieved.

Another example of a case involving discrimination against women was the Higher Education Act of 1990,[12] according to which the employment of an academic member of staff (other than a professor) was terminated at the end of the academic year in which the teacher reached pensionable age. Sixty-year-old women were denied the right to continue working, a right which the men retained for a further five years. The right to an earlier pension thus turned into a duty to cease work. The Ombudsperson agreed that the rule violated the constitutional protection of equality of rights, regardless of gender. The Constitutional Tribunal and Sejm shared that view and a satisfactory solution has been reached by changing the regulation. This is not the only group in which a woman's "privilege" became a discriminatory removal of the right to work. A similar case concerned female employees in the Polish' Academy of Sciences (*Polska Akademia Nauk*), where the Ombudsperson applied to the Ministry of Education to propose to the Sejm a formal amendment to the law.

Less fortunate were female employees in other jobs. One case of a woman, employee of the Polish Committee of Normalisation, Measure and

12 Art. 95 ust 2 pkt 1.

Quality, became well known. She did not accept being pensioned off at the age of sixty, while male colleagues of the same age or older could not be compelled to retire. Her case, widely publicised, was applicable to probably all retirement provisions. The Ombudsperson refused to intervene in this case, stating that the Public Offices' Employees' Rule was "not arbitrary and did not have the nature of a command", because the rules laid down that, after reaching pensionable age, the employment relationship *might* be dissolved, but did not *require* the termination of the employment contract.[13] Female employees in high schools and colleges might be said to be fortunate. In this case the relevant legal provision stated that employment was automatically terminated on reaching pensionable age. This the Ombudsperson recognised as inconsistent with the principle of equality, while the provision allowing the employer to terminate the contract without the employee's agreement, even against the employee's will, was not perceived as a violation of the principle. The Ombudsperson's refusal to intervene is surprising, especially in the light of the fact that he himself complained to the Ministry of Labour about the practice of automatic dismissal, finding it to constitute unequal treatment of men and women in access to employment.[14] This failure to take action in the case of a woman, whom the employer chose to pension off five years earlier than her male colleagues, is a clear demonstration that covert and indirect discrimination, where the rules are not expressly discriminatory but allow discrimination, is still an alien concept to Polish lawyers.

Unfortunately, the Supreme Court has confirmed this evaluation in its judgment in this case. The First President of the Supreme Court lodged an extraordinary appeal against a final decision of *Naczelny Sad Administracyjny* (the High Administrative Court). The First President of the Supreme Court claimed that the High Administrative Court should have referred to the Constitutional Tribunal a point of law concerning the consistency of the Civil Servants' Regulation with the Constitution, especially in the light of the proceedings in the Constitutional Tribunal in the analogous case of female employees in high schools and colleges. The First President stated that the employer was aware that the employee was capable of and wanted to continue to perform her duties. The President of the *Glówny Urzad Mia* (the Main Measure Office) admitted that, at the same time, two men had not been dismissed in spite of reaching the

13 Letter from the Office of the Spokesman for Civil Rights, Feb 9, 1993 (unpublished).
14 T. Zieliński, *op. cit.*, pp. 22-23.

pensionable age for men of 65 and were still employed. This can be described as a textbook example of discrimination - a comparison of the situation of women and men in the same place of work, at the same time, revealed that women were treated less favourably.

In spite of this the Supreme Court dismissed the extraordinary appeal against the High Administrative Court's final decision. The Supreme Court's reasoning, that the Administrative Court did not have a duty but a right to apply to the Constitutional Tribunal on a point of law, is understandable. However, it is difficult to understand the Supreme Court's reasons justifying the conclusion that discrimination had not taken place. On the one hand the Supreme Court supported the employer's right to terminate the employment of a person who had reached pensionable age, without any "additional restrictions and duties" relating to that right and even without giving any additional reasons. On the other hand, the Court broadly justified such a practice- in spite of the Constitutional principle of gender equality - as not amounting to discrimination against women, even though women, who wish to continue working, were pensioned off 5 years earlier than men. The Court stated that the earlier pensionable age was a privilege for women, in spite of the fact that "in an individual case it may be perceived as an instance of discrimination". The Court asserted the astounding proposition that "the problem refers to certain 'costs' being borne by individuals privileged in law - the negative consequences of a privilege". "Granting a privileged legal status without any negative consequences may be regarded as an instance of discrimination against the rest, who do not come within the terms of the privilege".[15] It is difficult to understand how a provision, which, according to the Supreme Court's statement, has negative consequences when applied to individuals, can be defined as a privilege. The essence of the complainant's privilege, when she bears only the "costs" and negative consequences of a "privilege" (the impossibility of continuing working and a lower pension as a consequence of a shorter period of employment), will remain a secret known only to the judges in the case.

Many examples such as these provide convincing evidence that we still have enormous difficulties in understanding problems of discrimination. Complaints made by women, not only to the Ombudsperson, but also to different women's non-governmental organisations, demonstrate that, for many individuals and institutions, it is not obvious that discrimination is

15 Judgment of Supreme Court, May 14, 1996, p. 12.

forbidden, despite the clear provision in the Constitution. In many cases the particular problem is the lack of opportunity for individuals to vindicate their rights, in others it is the particularly complicated and arduous process involved (a complaint to the Ombudsperson, his decision to apply to the Constitutional Tribunal with a question on a point of law, the need for the Sejm to respond to the Tribunal's judgment). The seriousness of these cases and several years of experience show how difficult the complaints procedure is in those cases. In some cases, women complaining about the earlier pensionable age have reached the age of sixty five so that for them the decision has become pointless. This is enough to demonstrate the need for a complex solution to the problem.

It is for these reasons that a legislative initiative was taken in the form of a draft bill, "concerning the equal status of women and men", was introduced in the Sejm. The Bill had a rather long history. It was introduced twice - first in autumn, 1996 with the backing of 160 members of the Sejm, then on 6 February 1997, when it was signed by 120 members (the entire lower chamber consisting of 460 members). Special difficulties related to the fact that in contrast with many bills, this one was not introduced by the Sejm's Presidium. In this case the woman member introducing the Bill suggested adding the Bill to the Sejm's agenda. This was approved and the first reading took place. All the Parliamentary groups supported the proposal to refer the Bill to three commissions for further examination - the Commission of Justice and Human Rights, the Commission of Social Policy and to the Legislative Commission. The Bill had extensive support when it was introduced, as evidenced by the large number of signatures in support and the lack of any motion to reject it at the first reading. Nevertheless, some speeches in parliamentary debates suggest that members of the Sejm were not very familiar with anti-discrimination laws in other countries. Doubts were expressed as to whether this kind of regulation existed elsewhere or whether it complied with European law. Some members admitted that women "in some spheres, especially those of professional life, are naturally elbowed aside into number two position, though not marginalised", but thought that equality should be achieved by "normal social practice". The Bill was referred to the three commissions for further examination but there was little chance that work on it could begin before this Sejm's term ended. It was referred in the middle of June 1997 and the Parliamentary elections were held in the middle of the following September. The first move towards the passing of the law on the equal status of women and men has been made but it remains to be seen if the next step will be taken.

A proposal to introduce such legislation in Poland had been made several years before.[16] A law was proposed, specifying the spheres of life in which discrimination might take place, encompassing all possible forms of discrimination and, in particular, creating cheap and simple procedures for vindicating rights, with extensive resort to mediation, could produce a "revolution" in legal consciousness and bring the realisation of sex equality nearer. It is assumed that an anti-discrimination law would refer to the equal status of the sexes and forbid discrimination against both women and men. The definition of discrimination should include overt, direct discrimination and indirect discrimination. The law would encompass all spheres of life and include a list of rights protected. The broadest and most detailed provisions of the proposals relate to the sphere of employment, a reflection of its nature and that this was the most frequent source of complaints. One of the most crucial parts of the Bill concerns the creation of bodies to oversee the implementation and observance of the anti-discrimination provisions and of procedures for the enforcement of rights. Most of the comments on the Bill in debates and by the Government concerned these problems

The most controversial part of the Bill was that ensuring adequate representation for both sexes on public bodies, appointed, elected or nominated by the state authorities. Neither sex should comprise less than forty per cent of the membership of such bodies. The Bill allowed four years for this to be achieved. In many discussions, in which I participated personally, this proposal was attacked. It was the only provision which in a sense automatically made room for women in positions involving power and money. It should be pointed out that there are at present many public bodies which have no women members. *Krajowa Rada Radiofonii i Telewizji* (KRRiT – the National Council for Radio and Television Broadcasting), for example, consists entirely of men.

Public opinion research on the legislative proposals has been conducted by *Centrum Badania Opinii Spolecznej* (the Centre of Public Opinion

16 Malgorzata Fuszara & Eleonora Zielińska, "Progi i bariery czyli o potrzebie ustawy o rownym stausie kobiet i mezczyzn" in *Kobiety: Dawne i nowe role* (Women : Old and New Roles) Warsaw, Centrum Europejskie Uniwersytetu Warsawskiego. Osrodek informacji i Dokumentacji Rady Europy, 1994.

Research).[17] The results of the research are interesting in showing some quite far-reaching incoherence in the opinions expressed. The most general question was whether the action should be taken to increase female participation in public life. The largest group of respondents (44%) supported action on the grounds that women have fewer opportunities to participate in public life. The second most numerous group of respondents opposed such action, while supporting female participation in public life (33%). 11% of respondents opposed such action because they opposed female participation in public life. 12% replied that it was "hard to say". There was a big difference between men and women. 54% of women and 33% of men supported action to increase female participation in public life. The next question referred to enacting a separate law on sexual equality in addition to the Constitutional provision. 25% of respondents strongly supported such a law while 62% thought that the Constitutional provision was sufficient (the rest chose the answer "hard to say"). Here too there was a significant difference between women and men, with 30% of women and 20% of men supporting a separate law.

The most controversial item in the Bill provides that the representation on public bodes of either sex should not be lower than 40% of the membership. This proposal produced the greatest incoherence in the proposals. 25% of women and 17% of men declared support for such a provision. This can be seen by juxtaposing the answers to whether such a provision should be introduced with the opinions about the consequences of introducing such a provision. A substantial majority of individuals declared themselves opposed to "quotas" (68% of men and 59% of women). However, the largest percentage of respondents (42%) expressed the view that a provision on quotas would be a fair way of reducing discrimination against women in public life. Only 20% of respondents regarded such a provision as unjustly privileging women. A high percentage of respondents had no definite opinion (38% did not express a view, 9% chose the answer "hard to say"). There were predictable differences between men and women. 51% of the women and 33% of the men expressed the view that a law on quotas would be a fair way of reducing discrimination against women. More men thought such a law would give unfair privileges to women (men - 26%, women - 14%). These figures show some incoherence

17 "Udzial kobiet w zyciu publicznym - prawne gwarancje rownosci plci" (Women's participation in public life- Legal Regulation on Gender Equality), Research conducted by the Social Opinion Research Centre, January 17-21, 1997, on a representative sample of 1101 adult Poles.

in views on combating discrimination. Many people react with instinctive hostility to the expressions "equalisation of opportunity" or "quota systems", yet, considering the figures, some of the same people expressed the view that a quota system would be a fair way of achieving equalisation and combating existing discrimination.

In the now classic text "Women as a minority group", Helen Hacker dealt with a special use of "minority group" in relation to women. She used Louise Writh's definition of a minority, according to which one can describe a section of the population as a minority group only when it is discriminated against because of certain characteristics. Hacker thought, or rather supposed, in the face of the lack of research relating to the subjective element of that definition, that since women have the "status of a minority group" then they are a minority group. According to her there was no doubt that women had the "status of minority group". In her opinion, however, there was a lack of any subjective element within the group, meaning a belief in the existence of discrimination and taking action to combat it.

It is impossible to rehearse the immense amount of data showing the reality of discrimination in Poland. There is extensive material showing inequality in employment, greater and increasing unemployment among women, differences in wages, very low female participation in the public life, low percentage of women in managerial positions, traditional images of female and male roles depicted in school books. Above, I introduced some problems resulting from various legal provision and the way in which the discriminatory way in which law was applied against women. In fact it would be difficult nowadays in Poland to defend the thesis that the subjective element does not exist, that women are not conscious of being discriminated against.

Research has shown that women in Poland are conscious of discrimination, especially in the job market. The majority of women think that women have less chance of finding a job (62%), obtaining higher wages (60%), being promoted to the managerial positions (52%). The largest groups of female respondents thought that women had less chance of pursuing a professional career (44%), and of successfully managing their own firms (38%). Only in one case did the largest number of respondents state that women possess "greater opportunities" - 48% thought that women had a greater chance than men of losing their jobs. A perception of inequality of the sexes is clearer the more-educated the respondent - 58% of female respondents of primary school and professional school education, 65% of college education and 82% of higher education were convinced that they had a worse chance of finding a job. Asked about the reasons for discrimination, 55% of women pointed to the greater burden of family responsibilities placed on women. The percentage of women pointing to direct discrimination by the employer has been on the increases (from 20% in 1993 to 26% in 1996). A substantial majority of women (71%) were convinced that women in paid employment enjoy greater social esteem than others. A very tiny percentage of women (2%) believe that house wives who are not in paid employment enjoy social esteem. The above quoted data definitely leaves no room for any doubt that the majority of women are convinced that women have fewer opportunities in various spheres of life, e.g. in employment and a significant percentage connect that with discrimination against women. Many of them think that some action should be taken to combat this and to establish equality of opportunity between women and men.

Poland is not alone. "Unfinished democracy"[18] is a concise phrase, describing the situation in many countries, where female representation in public life is still very low and it is not possible to talk about democratic mechanisms for providing access to power in the absence of men and women having equal opportunities to occupy positions of power and authority. "Grateful Slave" is the title of a book describing the problem of inequality of opportunity in the countries of Western Europe. The title refers to women's failure to object to inequality. Research in recent years, conducted in many countries, including Poland, proves that women do not accept the present state of affairs. Perhaps the opposition does not take a particularly spectacular form, but it is of special interest for the lawyer concerned with the rule of law. Numerous attempts are being made to change the law. A frequent response to these attempts is to appeal to that false myth of the equality of women and men in Poland, referred to at the beginning of this chapter. The opponents of change, faced with clear evidences of inequality of opportunity, would rather admit that the law is observed in a discriminatory way, and quite often defend their position by stating that legal provisions are not themselves discriminatory. Nevertheless, for some time now, there has been a divergence in practice from positive law. It is obvious that an empty provision on paper does not guarantee the existence of a state under law, even when a rule has been

18 Haavio-Mannila Elina & C. Badcock. (ed.) *Unfinished Democracy: Women in Nordic Politics*, Oxford, Pergamon Press, 1985.

passed in the proper manner by an appropriate institution.[19] It is crucial that there are genuine opportunities for citizens themselves to defend their rights against violation. It is vital that Constitutional provisions referring to equality of the sexes are obeyed and considered as obligatory for everyone and that there is an accessible procedure for citizens to complain about the violation of their rights. It is time to recognise that Poland, like other countries with communist regimes for years, is not in a special position as regards sexual equality when compared with Western Europe or North America. Some issues for which women had to fight other countries (e.g. the application of the law of rape to married couples) had been dealt with earlier in Poland. Other issues, like the problem of low female representation in the public life, Poland shares with many Western European and American countries, and we look to the Scandinavian example. Inequality in wages is shared with many other countries. There are also some areas, like female participation in science, in which the situation of women in Poland is much better than in western countries.[20]

One can generally state that the problems of women in different European countries are shared by Polish women. For a lawyer interested in the rights of women and in the State under law what would be of particular importance is the action being taken and the changes in the law bringing Poland closer to real equality between men and women. In this context a series of interesting initiatives are worth noting. The new Constitution does not refer to man as the model for woman and drafted in a more "equal" form, providing that "women and men" possess equal rights.[21] The Labour Code has recently been amended to include an anti-discrimination clause which provides that "employees possess equal rights by reason of performing the same duties in the same manner" and refers particularly to the equal treatment of men and women in work.[22] However it is not an ideal provision as there is no reference to the indirect discrimination, but it may be considered to be a definite move towards the introduction of anti-discrimination rules. The Bill on the equal status of men and women was published and received its first reading. It is to be hoped that Poland is making, admittedly slow, progress towards the point where it will be

19 Jacek Kurczewski, "Rządy Prawa" ("Rule of Law") in *Res Publica*, No 3, 1989.

20 Malgorzata Fuszara, "Women in Polish Academe", in S. Stiver Lie, L. Malik and D. Harris (eds), *The Gender Gap in Higher Education, World Yearbook of Education*, London, Kogan Page, 1994.

21 Art. 33,Constitution of the Republic of Poland.

22 Art. 11, Labour Code Amendment of 1996.

obvious to everybody that nobody may be discriminated against, but more than that, we shall achieve real equality of opportunity for citizens regardless of sex.

In reflecting on democracy and justice well-known authors, analysing the principle of equality, stress that the tendency towards equality is an expression of the view that "undeserved inequality requires compensation".[23] "In justice understood as fairness people agree to share their fate; making projects of institutions they undertake some efforts of making profits for themselves of natural, social cases and circumstances only then when it serves the common welfare".[24] It seems likely that the application of these principles of justice, widely accepted by theoreticians of democracy, may bring us closer to the time when, in the pursuit of the common welfare - of both women and men - we begin to approach in many domains, not only declaratory or theoretical equality, but also the real equality of all individuals, regardless of sex, when the law will express and secure the protection of women and men and when discrimination will be a thing of the past.

23 John Rawls, *A Theory of Justice*, Cambridge, Mass., Harvard University Press, 1971.
24 *Ibid.*

13 The Judiciary's Struggle towards the Rule of Law in Poland

AGATA FIJALKOWSKI

Introduction

Milan Kundera once wrote that "[t]he people of Central Europe ... cannot be separated from European history, they cannot exist outside it; but they represent the wrong side of history: they are victims and outsiders".[1] The opportunity to return to the so-called "right side of history" occurred in 1989 with the collapse of Communist rule throughout Central and Eastern Europe. The Polish government, along with other post-communist[2] governments, has re-embarked on the proper path towards democracy and the rule of law, after having been steered off this natural path after the Second World War with the establishment of communist rule.[3]

Communism, for Poles, represented something that was "unnatural", "abnormal" and "unpredictable".[4] In 1989 the Polish Government declared its commitment to establishing the rule of law (*państwo prawa*). This meant the adoption of an interim constitution in 1992[5] to serve as a temporary provisional document before a new constitution was drafted.[6] The interim document included provisions for the separation of powers and guarantees

1 M. Kundera, "The Tragedy of Central Europe", in G. Stokes (ed.), *From Stalinism to Pluralism: a Documentary History of Eastern Europe since 1945*, Oxford, Oxford University Press, 1991, p. 221.

2 J, Szacki, *Liberalism after Communism*, Budapest, CEP Press, 1995, for and interesting discussion of the realities and public perceptions of the development of liberalism in post-communist states.

3 Communist rule was imposed on Poland against the will and political preferences of the Polish People.

4 See M. Łoś, "Property Rights, Markets and Historical Justice: Legislative Discourses in Poland", Working Paper 9302C, Department of Criminology, University of Ottawa, December 1993; V. Havel, "The Post-Communist Nightmare", *The New York Review of Books*, 27 May 1993, pp. 8-10.

5 The "Little Constitution", according to Art. 77 of which, the 1952 Constitution was no longer in force, with the exception of certain provisions.

6 The Constitution of 1997 approved by referendum in October 1997.

of judicial independence.[7] Alongside the interim Constitution, a number of changes were made to the 1952 Constitution,[8] albeit in haste, in order to replace communist slogans and to facilitate the transformation to a market economy. Since then Poles have experienced many revelations and disappointments in their desire to create a rule of law state.

> We have done everything required, and first and foremost we have changed the first article of the constitution, replacing the words "socialist state" with the words "state of law" and into the bargain changing the name of the state. What else can be done? Since the constitution has been changed, it is clear as day that from henceforth the Polish state is a state of law.[9]

Although the appropriate instruments are in place, the development of the rule of law state undoubtedly will take time. The creation of an effective, legitimate state and an efficient administration of justice will depend largely on the ability to overcome the former practices of judicial officials. In order for Poland to become a rule of law state, much depends on the country's experience of liberalism and democracy.[10] Furthermore, it will not be achieved without an effective judiciary. The tasks which at present face the judiciary in the courts at all levels are of paramount importance: to act as a separate arm of government, as a guardian of the civil liberties that are guaranteed by the constitution.

In the rule of law tradition government is legally constituted, the three branches of government respect the law, and citizens and minorities are protected from government excess and abuse. The rule of law requires predictability, generality and equality. It means that government may not coerce individuals except in the enforcement of the law, and it places a limitation on all governmental powers, including legislative powers.[11] It follows that the rule of law does not refer to law in the same sense as laws

7 Art. 1, Constitutional Law of 17 October 1992. This document essentially outlined the powers of the President and the Sejm (Parliament). It made no further mention of the role of the judiciary.

8 The 1052 Constitution was a Stalinist document, based on the 1936 Soviet Constitution, one of Stalin's most audacious pieces of doublespeak.

9 E. Letowska and J. Letowski, *Poland: towards the Rule of Law*, Warsaw, SCHOLAR, 1996, p. 10.

10 Szacki recalls the work of Ludwik Krzywicki, a nineteenth century Polish sociologist who wrote about the way that a country's history affects the creation of new ideas and whether they provide a solution to the tasks faced by society, and whether they are accepted as a solution. See L. Krzywicki, *Studia Socjologiczne*, Warsaw, PIW, 1951, p. 141.

11 F.A. Hayek, *The Constitution of Liberty*, London, Routledge & Kegan Paul, 1960.

passed by the legislator. Constitutional provisions may limit the infringements of the rule of law, but ultimately, the legislator may abolish the law that he has made.

> The rule of law is therefore not a rule of the law, but a rule concerning what the law ought to be, a meta-legal doctrine or political ideal. It will be effective as long as the legislator feels bound by it. In a democracy this means that it will not prevail unless it forms a part of the moral tradition of the community, a common ideal shared and unquestioningly accepted by the majority.[12]

This chapter addresses the notion of judicial independence. I am concerned about the implementation and application of policies which guarantee judicial independence, and how these reforms are interpreted by the legislator and judge. I see three main barriers for judges in their struggle for independence: first, the absence of the will of the legislator to create a strong judiciary; secondly, the inexperience of the judiciary in protecting constitutional rights and liberties, deciding for the defendant rather than the State; thirdly, the practices which are a threat to the rule of law in Hayek's meta-legal doctrine - totalitarian law forced people to behave outside the law and certain practices have remained which may harm the process of implementing the rule of law.

General Background

Poland re-emerged as an independent nation in 1918. Under the leadership of Josef Piłsudski, the military leader who enjoyed wide popularity, the transitory government set about the task of forming a new government. In 1919, a new Sejm was convened, and soon after the "Little Constitution" was adopted, an interim document which remained in force until the new Constitution was drafted. The undertaking was daunting, Poland having been under the rule of the Russian, Prussian and Austrian Empires for over a century, and different regions had different social, political and legal systems. Poland was also multicultural, being composed of several nationalities and ethnic groups (Jews, Ukrainians, Belorussians and Germans). The new Government needed to address different cultural

12 *Ibid.*, p. 206.

standards in different regions.[13] On March 17, 1921, the new Constitution was adopted, restoring the Republic of Poland as a democratic state.

Modelled on the French Constitution and closely the 1791 Constitution, power was given to the *Sejm*, meaning that the executive and judiciary were dependent on the legislature, which resulted in tensions.[14] In 1926 Piłsudski, who felt that a strong *Sejm* had resulted in government corruption and political lethargy, staged a *coup d'état*. He consolidated his power which made for a strong executive and an authoritarian style of government. The constitutional guarantees of judicial independence[15] were replaced in the new 1935 constitution by provisions granting the executive the right to appoint and dismiss judges.[16] Prior to these reforms, the judiciary was subjected to political pressure by the Executive, in particular after the *Brzesc Affair*,[17] when in an effort to introduce certain legal reforms, it suspended judicial immunity and dismissed many judges who were considered to be opponents of the Government.[18]

Piłsudski's death in 1935 offered the opportunity to implement much-needed constitutional reforms. A compromise was needed to provide a bridge between the deeply divided *Sejm* and the Executive, but the opportunity was cut short by the outbreak of the Second World War. In 1939 the country was annexed by German and Soviet occupiers. German law and institutions were imposed in the occupied territories, known as the *Generalgouvernement*, while the eastern territories were incorporated into the Soviet Union. During the war, countless lives were lost, among which

13 The Codification Commission tackled the codification of five different legal systems .As well as Russian, Prussian, Austrian were the French, introduced by Napoleon in the Grand Duchy of Warsaw in 1807, and the Hungarian, in force in a small area of southern Poland. See A. Zamoyski, *The Polish Way: A Thousand Year History the Poles and their Culture*, London, John Murray, 1987; N. Davies, *God's Playground: A History of Poland*, vol. II, Oxford, Clarendon Press, 1981; M. Brzezinski, "Constitutional Heritage and Renewal: the Case of Poland", (1991) 77 Virginia Law Review, 49.

14 See M. Brzezinski, "Constitutional Heritage and Renewal: the Case of Poland", *loc. cit.*, pp. 72-78.

15 Constitution of 1921, Art. 2.

16 Constitution of 1935, Arts. 12, 13 & 65. Piłsudski, in an attempt to strengthen, above all, the presidential powers, had a new constitution drafted to reflect these changes. See "Piłsudski in Power", in R.F. Leslie (ed.), *The History of Poland since 1863*, Cambridge, Cambridge University Press, 1980, 159.

17 In 1930 there was a clash between Piłsudski and his political opponents in the *Sejm*. One of the political groups, the Centrolew called for Piłsudski's resignation. Arrests of the party's leaders followed and continued throughout the 1930 parliamentary elections. The prisoners were detained in the Brzesc fortress. This event, which showed the regime's brutality, shocked the public. See *ibid.*, pp. 171-175.

18 *Ibid.* p. 179.

were most of the best legal minds of the Polish pre-war period, usually targeted by the German and Soviet authorities.[19]

Poland was "liberated" by the Red Army in 1945. Prior to this the provisional Polish government, the PKWN,[20] which operated in the Soviet annexed Polish territories, was already forging a new Polish state in accordance with communist aspirations. It worked closely with Moscow to create the Polish satellite envisioned by Stalin. In relation to the judiciary, the *Resort Sprawiedliwosci*, (Department of Justice of the PKWN), led by Leon Chajn, ensured that only politically reliable judicial officials were recruited in the future administration of justice in the Polish People's Republic.[21] In short the provisional government's aims were threefold: to legitimise the quasi-judicial functions of he secret police, to control citizens' activities and to assume control over private property.[22]

After the "organised" elections in 1945, the Communists assumed power.[23] The Polish People's Republic was officially established in 1952, with the passage of the 1952 Soviet-style constitution, modelled on the 1936 Stalinist Constitution which embodied the main ideas of Soviet legal theory.[24] The Constitution declared that Poland was a "people's democracy", which meant that the interests of the working class were represented by the Communist Party. The Council of State, as the primary executive organ of government, was granted full legislative power. In keeping with Lenin's theory of a centralised bureaucracy, the Communist Party exercised a monopoly of power. No instruments of judicial review were created. Equally, while the document espoused traditional civil

19 This is not the place to discuss the German and Soviet policies to eliminate the Polish intelligentsia.

20 *Polski Komitet Wyzwolenia Narodowego* (Polish Committee of National Liberation).

21 On the policies of the PKWN, which led to the near elimination of the Polish pre-war judiciary, see A. Rzeplinski, *Sadownictwo w Polsce Ludowej: miedzy dyspozycynoscia a niezawisłościa* (*The Judiciary in the Polish People's Republic: Between Subservience and Independence*), Warsaw, Pokolenie, 1989; M. Turlejska (pseudonym Lukasz Socha), *te pokoliene zalobami czame ... Skazani na smierc i ich sedziowie 1944-1954* (*The Black Mourning of this Generation: Those who were sentenced to death and their judges,1944-1954*), 2nd ed., Warsaw, Nowa, 1986; A Litynski, "Obraz sadownictwa karnego perszej dekady Polski Luwodej. Uwagis na marginesie ksiazek Andrzeja Rzepliskiego I Marii Turlejskiej" (A Description of the Criminal Court in the First Decade of the People's Republic. Commentaries on the books of Andzej Rzeplinski and Maria Tutlejska"), (1991) 1-2 *Czasopismo Prawno-Historyczbe*, 153.

22 See A. Rzeplinski, *op. cit., supra*, pp. 17-39, for an excellent synopsis of the purpose underlying the legal measures passed by the PKWN.

23 The results of the referendum election were falsified.

24 As propounded by Andrei Vishinsky, Stalin's leading jurist.

liberties, it provided no instruments for their enforcement. The reason for this was simple: the interest of governing and governed were identical.

The socialist legal system imposed in Poland was highly bureaucratised to ensure complete control over all decision-making. Lenin himself, in an effort to gain control over society, envisioned socialist legality as the uniform application of commands, and revived the institution of the *Prokuratora,* which recalled the model created by Peter the Great, to review judicial decisions to ensure that they conformed with the law. What this meant, in essence, was that court decisions were not immune from review, and that extraordinary review was established as a feature of socialist law. In Poland, the judiciary, bar and police were restructured within a hierarchical structure under the watchful eye of the Communist Party.

The second significant feature of socialist law was the predominance of public law over private law. Public interest translated into state interest, i.e. the Communist Party interest. All Polish judges were trained according to this framework, and received legal indoctrination in Marxist-Leninist theory, and every effort was made to remove, and to prevent the appointment of, politically unreliable judges. No area of law was immune and the administration of justice was reduced to an instrument of political power.[25] This general pattern continued until 1989.

The Round Table Talks

The Sub-Table for Legal and Court Reform (Podzespol do Spraw Reformy Prawa i Sadow), which was created as part of the celebrated Round Table Talks (Porozumienia Okragiego Stolu) of 1989 between the representatives of the opposition Solidarity trade union and representatives of the Communist Government, was first and foremost concerned with the immediate implementation of guarantees for judicial independence and the independence of the courts. The main points of the Sub-Table's agenda were: restrictions on the removal of judges and the creation of an independent constitutional body which would review judicial nominations and appointments.[26] At the same time, equally important goals concerned

25 This is not to say that all Polish judges were compromised and served the regime faithfully. The point is the pressure which judges experienced. Some judges, especially those from the criminal and labour law divisions found a way out of the draconian laws, applied in the mid-1980s to Solidarity members for activities in the banned trade union.

26 "Sprawozdanie z posiedzen podzespolu do spraw reformy prawa i sadow" (Stenographs from the meetings of the Sub-Table for Legal and Court Reform") *Porusumienia Okrageigo Stolu*, Warsaw, m1989, pp. 59-69.

ending the abuses to be found in legislation relating to, and the practice of, the administration of justice to facilitate the transition to democracy.[27]

The creation of the National Council of the Judiciary (*Krajowa Rada Sadownictwa*) symbolised an important step towards guaranteeing judicial independence. This body, whose primary aim is "to guard judicial independence and the independence of the courts",[28] consists of twenty six members from the legislative, executive and judicial branches of government.[29] The Council considers nominations submitted by the general assemblies of the relevant courts.[30] Final appointment (and dismissal) is by the President of the Republic. The Minister of Justice's powers have intentionally been curtailed, although he is allowed to express his opinion on the judicial candidates. Judges are appointed to serve until retirement at the age of 65, extendible to the age of 70 with the Council's approval. Under the previous regime, judges were appointed by the Minister of Justice and, according to the dictates of ideology, judges were chosen to serve the "will of the people" and constituted part of the state's coercive apparatus. Supreme Court judges were appointed by the Council of State to five year terms. At present, the Supreme Court has a special position in the judiciary.[31] It is organised independently of the Ministry of Justice with its own separate budget. Judges are appointed and removed by the *Sejm* on the motion of the President.

While the Council represents an important step towards the establishment of the rule of law, in terms of judicial independence, its powers are seriously limited. The law dictates that the Council relies on the President's "Chancellory Office" for its resources and physical location.[32]

27 Within the area of criminal law, for example, it was important to abolish draconian criminal provisions found in the Criminal Code, such as those concerning economic crimes (the majority of Chapter XXX of the Criminal Code) and to reform the Code of Criminal Procedure, to address, for example, absence of complaints and appeals against police detention. Another significant reform, which still is a topic of debate, is compensation for abuses of past authorities.

28 Art. 1(2), Law of 20 December, 1989 on the National Council of the Judiciary.

29 Under art. 4 of the law of 20 December 1989, the National Council of the Judiciary consists of the First President of the Supreme Court, the President of the Military Division of the Supreme Court, the President of the Chief Administrative Court, the Minister of Justice, and by election, fifteen judges from the lower courts, four members of parliament, two senators and one person appointed by the President of the Republic. The Chair of the Council is chosen from among the members.

30 Gatherings of all the judges from a division (criminal, civil, family, labour and social policy, military, the common courts).

31 Art. 64(3) of the Law on the National Council of the Judiciary prohibits judges from membership of political parties or from involvement in any political activities.

32 *Ibid.*, art. 11.

This may mislead people into thinking that the Council is actually part of the executive rather than the autonomous body that it is. During its existence it has been asked to advise on legislative texts and other matters concerning the judiciary, but has had difficulty in portraying itself as a "real voice" for the judiciary, due to the ambiguity about its capacity and competence.[33]

Despite the strong restrictions on removing a judge from office, the guarantee of the constitutional separation of powers and the creation of the National Council of the Judiciary, the Polish judiciary continues to face problems of legitimacy about its position alongside the legislature and the executive.[34] For a brief period between 1990 and 1991 the President and Parliament heard judicial reservations about the administration of justice. Their main complaints concerned the lack of resources and low pay. Shortly thereafter salaries were increased, producing a surge of judicial applicants. The judiciary experienced a temporary "blossoming" and regaining of their legitimacy, albeit short-lived. The judges did not actually receive the salary increase and many resorted to taking the Treasury to court[35] and compromised themselves during the former regime.

An even more significant barrier for judges in their quest for legitimacy is the controversial matter of those judges who had politically compromised themselves during the former regime. It must be noted that the Polish judiciary did not undergo formal verification in the transition from communism.[36] The first post-communist-led government, under the leadership of Tadeusz Mazowiecki, adopted the 'thick line' approach, which meant the separation of the past from the future, and chose to reform the communist state rather than to destroy it completely.[37] The Deputy Minister of Justice, Adam Srzembosz, under enormous pressure, maintained that Polish judges fought very hard to maintain their integrity, and the judiciary would naturally cleanse itself of those judges who were

33 See J. Wojcechowski, "Dzis i Jutro Krajowej Rady Sadownictwa" ("Today and Tomorrow the National Council of the Judiciary") *Rzeczpospolita*, 14 Feb. 1994, p. 12; A. Zielinski "O statusie prawnym Krajowej Rady Sadownictwa", *Panstwo i Prawo*, 1993, pp. 84-88.

34 The drafters of the Little Constitution of 1992 were more concerned with the distribution of power between legislature and executive.

35 See R. Gilewicz, "Skandal placowy w sadownictwie" (The wage scandal in the courts) *Rzeczpospolita*, 25 March, 1993, p. 11.

36 The Supreme Court underwent an informal verification with a new court selected after the final five year term expired.

37 See M. Łoś, "In the shadow of Totalitarian Law: Law-Making in Post-Communist Poland", in A. Podgórecki and V. Olgiati, *Totalitarian and Post-Totalitarian Law*, Aldershot, Dartmouth Press, 1996, p.275.

politically subservient.[38] When this did not happen, the Ministry of Justice was severely criticised for its approach.

The matter came to a head in 1994 with the passage of a legal provision which allowed the President of the Republic, on the motion of the National Council of the Judiciary, to dismiss a judge if he departed from "principles of judicial independence".[39] This provision was ambiguous in its wording and created a split between the judiciary and groups supporting judicial verification. Judges perceived the new provision as a threat to their independence, claiming that it created an atmosphere of uncertainty, undermining then stability of the office. Supporters of such a measure criticised the ambiguity of the provision and questioned how it would work in practice. The provision was challenged by the Ombudsman[40] and, after being heard by the constitutional Tribunal, the Law was annulled by the Sejm in 1994.[41]

Poland may have missed an opportunity in not carrying out judicial verification. The fact that the Supreme Court was newly elected in 1991 probably did not seem significant because it was not publicised widely. Many of the disgraced judges migrated to the lower courts with which the public is more likely to have direct contact than with the higher courts. The number of judges who were politically subservient to the Communist Party is supposed to be low, but the fact that they were allowed to remain tainted the judiciary and the courts in the public eye. This is another serious obstacle towards creating the rule of law, for if the public expresses a strong distrust of the judges, the entire process of democratisation is jeopardised.

The Call for Judge-Made Law

Since 1989 there has been an increased demand for "judge-made law", despite the fact that this notion usually refers to common law systems that follow judicial precedent, rather than the civil law tradition which Poland follows. Polish judges have begun the formidable task of interpreting the law and making law, intentionally or unintentionally, in a new legal

38 A. Srzembisz, "O wymierzajacych sprawiedliwiej", *Tygodnik Solidaronsc*, 22 September 1989, p.3.

39 Art. 59, Law of February 5, 1993 on Changes to the Law on the Structure of the Ordinary Courts, the Procuracy, the Supreme Court, the Constitutional tribunal, the National Council of the Judiciary and the Creation of Appellate Courts.

40 On the Ombudsman see Kurczewski, *supra*

41 See I Walencik, "Kes niezawisłości", *Rzeczpospolita*, 7 September, 1993, pp 1, 9.

climate.[42] There is a greater reliance on the courts to settle disputes which have arisen during the transformation. Some of these disputes deal with "settling matters" from the past, i.e. searching for social justice for the victims of political abuses.

The judiciary at present is caught in a struggle which involves the legislature in attempting to continue the practices of the former regime and to use the law as an instrument, while simultaneously making decisions which contradict the public demand for justice. For example, in 1993, President Wałęsa proceeded to dismiss the Chairman of the Radio and Television Council and to appoint his own candidate despite the fact that the law was unclear as to the dismissal of members of the Council.[43] The matter went before the Constitutional Tribunal. We can therefore identify a continuity between the new and old regimes' use of the courts as part of the state apparatus.[44] In this case, behind the ambiguity of the legal provision which needed to be clarified was a struggle between the legislative and executive organs about the scope of their power.

Kolarska-Bobinska observes the tension between the need for legal reform and efficiency which is heightened during this period of transition.[45] The introduction of new legislation to effect the legal changes necessary to facilitate the transition to a market economy has proved to be a slow process. This has created the dangerous tendency to act outside or above the law to achieve efficiency.[46] The notion that the law is fully flexible does not disappear, reinforcing the former socialist notion that the law is an unpredictable and malleable instrument.

If this notion of law is not dispelled, then the practice of evading the law may spill over into the rapidly growing area of commercial transactions and business ethics. One place where this is evidenced is in the Bankruptcy Court. The judges of the Warsaw Bankruptcy Court, for example, have observed that nearly 90 per cent of cases are suspicious. Nevertheless, the judges are powerless in their effort to combat illegal business practices

42 According to Letowski, Polish courts make law, but do not admit it because they are either not aware of it or because they do not want to publicise it. See E Letowska and J. Letowski, *Poland*, *op. cit.* n. 9 *supra,* pp. 117-131.

43 See Law of 29 December 1992 on Radio Broadcasting and television.

44 Letowski describes the process where courts and their decisions have been "discovered" by politicians as a weapon in their political struggle. Perhaps we can view this phenomenon as a "*re*discovery".

45 L. Kolarska-Bobinska, "The Role of the State: Contradictions in the Transitions to Democracy" in D. Greenberg, S.N. Katz et al. (eds) *Constitutionalism and Democracy: Transitions in the Contemporary World*, Oxford, Oxford University Press, 1993.

46 Thus power shifts from the legislature to the executive, providing another example of the tension between the two branches of government, *ibid.*

because they lack the necessary legal remedies and, due to inexperience and unwillingness, cases are not actively prosecuted.[47] It is common practice, for example, for debtors to violate time limits laid down in the bankruptcy law and to withhold relevant information. Remedies available from the courts have proved ineffectual.[48]

Intuitive Law and Meta-Level Rule of Law

The notion of "social marginalisation" is one that is relevant to post-communist Poland. It is the way that a given social system is accepted by its population only at a symbolic level, while the basic currents of social life move outside it.[49] Poland is in a precarious situation. The combination of "dirty togetherness",[50] increasing white collar crime and organised crime arising from general social apathy and frustration have created a society which can be described as "displaced", which are neither "out" nor "in".[51] Research has demonstrated that Polish society is not entirely demoralised, as people are able to distinguish good from bad. Under communism, people were under continuous demoralising pressures and demonstrated a high level of tolerance of recognised forms of social and criminal behaviour.[52]

According to Petrazycki, if a certain pattern of behaviour is accepted in a given society, and it regulates certain social processes, then it shapes the core of social life.[53] If we take the "living law" or intuitive law", for example, which is the law which exists between people and affects their

47 "Suspicious cases" refers to those cases where there is evidence that the bankruptcy was intentional, and the debtor has taken advantage of the grace period before the court hearing to transfer assets or to delay handing over the accounting records.

48 Such as arts. 2-9, Law of 21 October 1994 on the Protection of commercial transactions and Changes in Certain Provisions of the Criminal Code, whereby any legal person who knowingly and intentionally conducts illegal business activities at the cost of the State Treasury commits a criminal offence.

49 J. Kwasniewski, *Society and Deviance in Communist Poland: Attitudes towards Social Control*, Berg, Leamington Spa, 1984.

50 This refers to the breakdown of traditional social structures, where relationships take on a unique structure of networks and influence the social system in which they exist: A. Podgórecki and M Łoś (eds.) *Multidimensional Society*, London, Routledge and Kegan Paul, 1979, pp. 202-203.

51 See A. Podgórecki, "Polish Communist and Post-Communist *Nomenklaturas*", in A.Podgórecki and V. Olgiati (eds.) *op. cit., supra,* n. 37.

52 J. Kwasniewski, *op. cit., supra,* n 48.

53 L. Petrayzcki, *O nauce, prawie i moralnosci. Pisma wzbrane*, Warsaw, Panswowe Wzdawnictwo Naukowe, 1985.

behaviour, as opposed to official law, which is the law found in books,[54] we can identify the various roles that law plays in different social situations in the process of socialisation. In a totalitarian regime, however, intuitive law takes on a more significant meaning. Mutual agreements which involve the evasion of law remain hidden from the official law and may be a significant obstacle to the efficient operation of the official legal system.

Emerging business practices, as those seen in the bankruptcy court, provide but one example of hidden "living law", operating outside the official law, which is in many ways, along with the courts, mistrusted as is the process of democratisation. Official law should be a tool of reconstruction. The courts should ensure that planned social changes are implemented during the transformation to democracy. Once the law sets out the appropriate conditioned for free market development, it can provide the impetus for the successful development of democracy and initiation of the process of "detotalitarianisation".[55]

54 *Ibid.*, pp. 267-281.
55 A. Podgórecki, "Conclusions" in *Totalitarian and Post-Totalitarian Law*, *supra*, n. 50.

PART V

RUSSIA

14 Politics versus the Rule of Law in the Work of the Russian Constitutional Court

BILL BOWRING

Introduction

The history of the Russian Constitutional Court, has been exceptionally turbulent. The Court has enjoyed two quite distinct incarnations, and has a pre-history. The first time around, it was born with the dissolution of the Soviet Union at the end of 1991, and, in its first incarnation, was a political actor of the first importance, under the controversial leadership of its Chairman, Judge Valerii Zorkin. It spent a disproportionate amount of time in 1992 adjudicating what might have been the "Russian Nuremburg", but turned out to be a classic political compromise, the trial of the Communist Party of the Soviet Union. That first period ended in suspension in September 1993, as the executive's tanks shelled the legislature.

The new Constitution of December 1993, although intended to represent an apotheosis of the rule of law and transition to democracy, remained without its "third power" for a full eighteen months, until March 1995. The Court's only significant activity during its period of inactivity, apart from the drafting of a new, significantly restricted law regulating its competence and procedure, was the attempted suspension of two of its own members, including former Chairman Zorkin. Even following its rebirth, with a new Chairman, Vladimir Tumanov, a Yeltsin supporter, the Court could not escape political controversy, in July 1995 ruling that President Yeltsin's December 1994 decrees on "disarming illegal armed formations in Chechnya" were "fully consistent with the constitution". The Court was also engaged in adjudicating a range of highly controversial issues, including the volatile relations between the Russian Federation and its subject republics and regions.

The Court, particularly in its first incarnation, has often been criticised for being too much involved in politics, despite the strong prohibitions contained in its constitutive laws. At the time of writing the first draft of this Chapter, another judge, Judge Viktor Luchin, was threatened with suspension of expulsion because of his outspoken criticisms[1] of presidential rule by decree.[2] This criticism is in part based upon the perception that the court has failed to pay sufficient attention to its important task of protecting fundamental human rights. Fundamentally, has the court crossed impermissible borders; has it transgressed? If so, where is that border located?

This chapter will examine the interplay between law and politics in the work of the Court, and will ask whether it is feasible or indeed conceivable that the Court should seek to remain in some sense above politics.

Why are Constitutional Courts Important, and Why Should They Not be Involved in Politics?

Powerful empirical evidence of the perceived importance of constitutional courts exists in the sheer number of states which now possess them. These now number at least 78; their constitutional courts possess a wide variety of powers. The Table of Powers of the constitutional courts prepared by the Slovenian Constitutional Court in 1996[3] shows that few constitutional courts have powers as wide as the present Russian Constitutional Court. Most courts have *a posteriori* (repressive) powers in relation to statutes, but the Russian Court also has powers of "preventive review" both of statutes and of international treaties, as well as "repressive" review of statutes, presidential acts, and rules and acts of subjects of the federation; concrete review at the request of regular courts; interpretation of the Constitution; the resolution of jurisdictional disputes; human rights protection; and impeachment of the President.

There are, broadly speaking, two main substantive reasons given for the importance of constitutional courts. The first is that judicial review is an essential component of the rule of law, the "difference between freedom and authoritarianism ... the difference between order and chaos ... the collective confidence and the inherent conscience of a free people" in the

1 V. O. Luchin, *'Ukaznoye Pravo' v Rossii ('Law by Decree' in Russia)* Moscow, KhGTs 'Veles', 1996.

2 A. Korkeakivi, "A Modern Day Czar? Presidential Power and Human Rights in the Russian Federation" (1995) 2 *Journal of Constitutional Law in Eastern and Central Europe* 76.

3 These have been very helpfully summarised in tabular fashion by the Slovenian Constitutional Court, and the results can be found on the World Wide Web at http://www.sigov.si/us/map/powers/powers.html.

words of an American professor.[4] A leading Russian commentator puts it this way: "One of the central places in these reforms [in Russia] is occupied by the tasks of founding and bringing to life the principle of separation of powers, and of creating a democratic rule of law state. These tasks may only be performed, as world experience has shown, by the creation of real and effective systems of constitutional control".[5] The Latin American scholar Brewer-Carias, discussing the problem of the legitimacy of judicial power within the Austrian or European model of judicial review, concluded that "in a representative and democratic regime, the power attributed to judges to control the deviations of the legislative body and the infringements by the representative body of fundamental rights is absolutely democratic and legitimate".[6] Cappelletti, addressing the "mighty problem" of constitutional judicial review, pointed out, in the cases of Germany, Italy and Austria, that "possibly for the first time in human history, judges of different countries, faced by significant and controversial problems involving social, moral, political and religious issues have boldly decided that it is their duty to search in the penumbrae of the constitutions for value judgments and guide-lines about such issues".[7] Finally, Finer, Bogdanor and Rudden, bringing together for comparative purposes the constitutions of France, Germany, and Russia, amongst others, asked whether constitutions matter, and suggested that "it is possible that the new constitution of Russia may come to have some genuine impact on, and even control, of, the political life of that country ... even if the reader doubts the reality or durability of the Russian constitution ... the text was put to a popular vote, is hard to amend, and does, at the very lowest level of political understanding, identify the main legal authorities within the Federation and lay down the framework within which they are supposed to operate".[8]

4 J.B. Attanasio, 1994 "The Russian Constitutional Court and the State of Russian Constitutionalism" (1994) 38 *St Louis University Law Review* 889.

5 Y.L. Shulzhenko, *Konstitutsionnii Kontrol v Rossii (Constitutional Control in Russia)* Moscow, Institute of State and Law, 1995.

6 This, he says, is characterised by the fact that constitutional justice has been attributed to a constitutional body organised outside the ordinary courts, and not integrated within the general structure of the judiciary. A. Brewer-Carias, *Judicial Review in Comparative Law* Cambridge, Cambridge Universtiy Press, 1989, p. 117.

7 M. Cappelletti, *The Judicial Process in Comparative Perspective* (Oxford, Clarendon Press, 1991), p. 162.

8 S.E. Finer, *Comparing Constitutions* Oxford, Clarendon Press, 1995, p.3.

The second reason often given is that constitutional control is the means by which the primacy of international law over domestic law, enshrined in almost all of the constitutions of the new post-Soviet states, can be given effect.[9] Article 15.4 of the Russian Constitution of December 1993 provides that: "Universally agreed principles and norms as well as international agreements of the Russian Federation shall constitute part of its legal system. If an international agreement of the Russian Federation establishes rules which differ from those stipulated by law, then the rules of the international agreement shall apply",[10] while Article 17 provides that human rights are recognised and guaranteed, "pursuant to the generally recognised principles and norms of international law". While one leading commentator asks whether the new Court, "when confronted with a concrete case, will interpret Article 17 as granting priority to universal human rights standards, irrespective of their treaty or customary origin",[11] the Russian Constitutional Court and its predecessor, the Committee on Constitutional Supervision[12] have already done much, through their case-law, to concretise these principles.[13]

That is, the rule of law now has a dual significance. First, within a state, government is to be conducted according to settled and transparent rules and procedures, and is to be accountable for breaches of those rules. Second, in the context of the international community, those rules and procedures must be compatible with universally accepted standards, and in particular those relating to the protection of fundamental human rights and freedoms. In the case of Russia, both these aspects represents a dramatic break from the practice of the Soviet period, and for both of them the Constitutional Court will be the only effective means of resolving disputes.

The Legitimacy of Constitutional Courts

A constitutional court must therefore play a key role in ensuring the accountability of government to constitutional norms and international

9 V.S. Vereshchetin, "New Constitutions and the Old Problem of the Relationship between International Law and National Law" (1996) 7 *European Journal of International Law* 29, p. 29.

10 Constitution of the Russian Federation, Article 15.4.

11 V.S. Vereshchetin, *loc. cit.*, n. 9 *supra*. p. 37.

12 H. Hausmaniger, "From the Soviet Committee of Constitutional Supervision to the Russian Constitutional Court" (1992) 25 *Cornell International Law Journal* 305.

13 G. Danilenko, "The New Russian Constitution and International Law" (1994) 88 *American Journal of International Law* p.460.

standards. What, however, is the source of its legitimacy as against the democratically elected parliament and president? This is an especially important issue in Russia, where President Yeltsin dissolved parliament and suspended the Constitutional Court on the justification of his own superior democratic mandate.

The question of legitimacy remains controversial even in a constitutional democracy as well-established as Germany, whose Constitution has been referred to as "the mother and father of constitutions".[14] A controversial example is the Court's decision that the constitutional complaints of three former members of the German Democratic Republic's National Defence Council, and that of a border guard, should be rejected, despite their attempt to rely on grounds of justification contained in the GDR's law. The Court held that in the case of a human rights violation so serious that it was opposed to the legal perceptions of internationally protected human rights, positive law must give way to justice. Thus, Article 103(2) of the *Grundgesetz*, prohibiting retroactive criminal effect, would not apply.[15]

The President of the German Constitutional Court has noted that almost all important political disputes end up in the hands of the Court, and acknowledges that because of the open and vague nature of constitutional provisions, the Court is bound to have a "law-making" role in interpreting these norms, one which exceeds the powers of ordinary courts. Nevertheless, she argues, despite this involvement in politics, the Court remains a legal body, which decides questions on the basis of a legal text, the constitution. She is impatient with critics who call for "judicial self-restraint", particularly since they do not define the supposed border between law and politics. She accepts that judges will be affected by their own moral and political convictions when deciding cases, but emphasises the fact that the Court's jurisdiction is "negative": it only acts when the legislature has failed to act or has acted incorrectly.

14 J. Limbach, "Das Bundesverfassungsgericht als politischer Machtfaktor (The Federal Constitutional Court as a Source of Political Power)" (1996) 12 *Humboldt Forum Recht* A summary in English of this Article by David Thorneloe may be found at http://www.jura.uni-sb.de/english/Publications/limb.html.

15 Order of 26 October 1996 - 2 BvR 1851/94, 2 BvR 1853/94, 2 BvR 1875/94 and 2 BvR 1852/94; Karlsruhe, 12 November 1996; an English summary by David Thorneloe is to be found at: http://www.jura.uni-sb.de/Entscheidungen/abstracts/wall.html.

Constitutional Courts in Post-Soviet Europe

It is noteworthy but not surprising that almost all of the post-Communist states of east and central Europe as well as the former USSR have created constitutional courts as part of their new constitutional orders. One commentator refers to this as "a major laboratory of constitutional works".[16] In Poland, the creation of the Constitutional Tribunal (*Trybunal Konstytucyjny*) in 1985, and the granting of the power of judicial review to it in 1986, played an important role in Poland's transition to democracy.[17] Since the adoption of Poland's new Constitution on 17 October 1992,[18] the Tribunal has become still more activist. Bulgaria adopted the first new constitution on 12 July 1991,[19] with a Western European-style Constitutional Court, whose 12 judges were elected one third each by the President, the National Assembly, and a joint meeting of Supreme Court of Appeals justices and the Supreme Administrative Court. These judges have come into repeated conflict with the Socialist Party government, for example over the issue of property ownership.

Romania promulgated its new Constitution on 8 December 1991, and established a Constitutional Court on 16 May 1992. This followed the French model of political rather than strictly judicial review, and is based on the Conseil Constitutionnel.[20] The Hungarian Constitutional Court, working within the new Constitution adopted on 24 August 1990, has been called the strongest in the world.[21] In Belarus, the Constitutional Court created by the new Constitution of 15 March 1994 has already come into such sharp conflict with the controversial President Lukashenko that, on 4 December 1996, following the referendum of 24 November, a number of judges resigned. On 4 March 1997 a new Constitutional Court of 11 judges, six of whom are the President's appointees, and only four of whom had served on the previous court, was sworn in.

16 R. Ludwikowski, "Constitution Making in the Countries of Former Soviet Dominance: Current Development" (1993) 23 *Georgia Journal of International and Comparative Law* 155, p. 158.

17 M. Brzezinski and L. Garlicki, "Judicial Review in Post-Communist Poland: The Emergence of a Rechtsstaat?" (1995) 31 *Stanford Journal of International Law* 13.

18 This small constitution replaced only 7 chapters of the 1952 Polish Constitution, dealing with the division of powers and local government; other provisions of the 1952 Constitution remained in force.

19 R. Ludwikowski, *loc. cit., supra*, n. 16, p. 195.

20 *Ibid.* p. 204.

21 E. Klingsberg, "Judicial Review and Hungary's Transition from Communism to Democracy: The Constitutional Court, the Continuity of Law, and the Redefinition of Property Rights" (1992) *Brigham Young University Law Rev.* 41.

Russia's new Constitution, adopted by referendum on 12 December 1993, contains not only the provision set out above, but a wide range of human rights provisions and guarantees. However, it cannot pretend to stand above politics. As Judge Vladlen Vereshchetin, the Russian judge on the International Court of Justice puts it: "In Russia, [the constitution-drafting process] was directly influenced by the political struggle between the President and the Legislature, and, accordingly, between the major political forces standing behind them. The adoption of the constitution was used as a major weapon in this struggle".[22]

The Pre-history of the Court: the Committee for Constitutional Supervision

The Committee for Constitutional Supervision of the USSR (CCS) was one of the first flowers of perestroika, the concretisation of Gorbachev's recognition of the role of international human rights standards. He proposed its creation in June 1988 at the 19th CPSU Conference,[23] but its 19 members were not elected until 26 April 1990, pursuant to the *Law on Constitutional Supervision in the USSR*, adopted in 1989.[24] It continued its existence through the August 1991 "putsch", were able to draw upon the *Declaration of Human* Rights which the USSR adopted in September 1991,[25] and with its last gasp commented upon the Minsk Declaration of 8 December 1991[26] by the Presidents of Russia, Belarus and Ukraine that the USSR "as an entity in international law and a geopolitical reality has ceased to exist". According to the CCS, this declaration was "without legal force".[27] However, on 23 December 1991 it recognised that the USSR had ceased to exist, and dissolved itself.[28]

22 V.S. Vereshchetin, *loc. cit.*, n. 9 *supra*. p. 32.
23 Mikhail Gorbachev, On Progress in Implementing the Decisions of the 27th CPSU Congress and the Tasks of Promoting Perestroika Moscow, 1988.
24 *Izvestiya*, 26 December 1989.
25 VSND SSSR, 1991, No.37, Art.1083.
26 *Izvestiya* Dec 9, 1991.
27 *Constitutional Committee Denies that USSR has Ceased to Exist*, BBC Summary of World Broadcasts, Dec 13 1991 (TASS, Dec 11 1991).
28 *Soviet Constitutional Compliance Committee to Disband* Xinhua General Overseas News service, Dec 23, 1991.

Although a number of scholars have commented upon the work of the CCS,[29] its activities were hardly known even to the Russian public. However, it considered a number of important cases, out of a total of 29. Its vice-chairman, B. M. Lazarev described its work as "an attempt to bind the highest powers by the law, and to strengthen protection for the rights and freedoms of the individual".[30] For example, on 20 April 1990, in an unprecedented censure of a Soviet leader, it ruled that President Gorbachev had violated the 1978 Constitution when he sought to regulate demonstrations within the Garden Ring in Moscow.[31] Even more far-reaching was its decision, on 29 November 1990, that all unpublished USSR regulations affecting rights, freedoms and duties of citizens violated international human rights norms and would lose their force unless published within three months.[32] It put the USSR ahead of the UK and US when, on 4 April 1991, it requested the USSR Supreme Soviet to ratify the Optional Protocol to the International Covenant on Civil and Political Rights (ICCPR), thus giving all those within the jurisdiction the right to complain to the UN's Human Rights Committee.[33] This was done on 5 July 1991. However, by no means all decisions of the CCS were carried out. For example, on 11 October 1991, in one of its last decisions, the CCS decided that the typically Soviet system of *propiski*, residence permits, clearly violated the rights to freedom of movement and to choose a place of residence in one's own country, enshrined in the USSR Declaration of Human Rights, the UN's Universal Declaration of Human Rights, and international treaties binding on the USSR.[34] This ruling has been openly flouted, particularly in Moscow, to this day, despite the Mark 3 Constitutional Court's decision of 12 March 1996 ruling that exorbitant registration fees violated the Constitution.[35]

29 H. Hausmaniger, "The Committee of Constitutional Supervision of the USSR" (1990) 23 *Cornell International Law Journal* 287; H. Hausmaniger, "From the Soviet Committee of Constitutional Supervision to the Russian Constitutional Court" *loc. cit., supra* n. 12; A. Blankenagel, "Local Self-Government vs. State Administration: The Udmurtia Decision" (Winter 1997) *East European Constitutional Review* 50; Y. L. Shulzhenko, *op. cit.*, *supra*, n. 5.

30 B.M. Lazarev, "Komitet Konstitutsionnovo Nadzora SSSR" (1992) 5 *Gosudarstvo i Pravo* 21.

31 VSND SSSR, 1990, No.39, Art 774.

32 VSND SSSR, 1990, No.50, Art 1080.

33 VSND SSSR, 1991, No.17, Art 502.

34 SND SSSR, 1991, No.46, Art 1307.

35 Outline in Konstitutsionnoye Pravo: Vostochnoevropeiskoye Obozreniye (Constitutional Law: East European Survey) (1996) No.2 (15), 76.

Nonetheless, the jurisprudence of the CCS covered all the important issues. Blankenagel noted that the cases decided by the CCS fell into three categories. First, conflicts between the centre and the regions, decided in favour of the centre; second, conflicts between the legislative and executive, decided in favour of the legislature; and third, conflicts between the citizen and the state, decided in favour of the citizen. The applicant almost always won. He recognised that the CCS was oriented towards civil liberties and the rule of law, as well as constitutional order, and reserved most of his criticism for the weakness of the CCS' jurisprudence, which drew in "scatter-shot" fashion on a wide range of international and domestic sources, without any sense of hierarchy. [36] Hausmaniger approved what he saw as the CCS' cautious approach, but in his view its decisions "leave the reader with the impression that the Committee timidly preferred to act as an advisor to and lobbyist for the legislative and executive branches of government rather than as a forceful representative of an equal third power".[37]

Writing more recently, and drawing upon Russian scholarship,[38] Shulzhenko concludes[39] that the CCS was unsuccessful in protecting the country's basic law. He gives eight reasons. First, there was a real "war of laws" in the turbulent situation of the country. Second, the legal system of the USSR was destabilised, rendering many questions of relations between the USSR and the subjects of the Union undecided. Third, there were too many state organs capable of exercising constitutional control. Fourth, there were frequent changes during this period in the system of organs of constitutional control. Fifth, the CCS had no power to repeal acts which violated the Constitution, save those which violated fundamental human rights. Sixth, the law governing the work of the CCS was very unclear. Seventh, there was no effective means of executing the CCS' decisions. Eighth, there was no co-ordination between the work of the CCS and its counterparts in the Union republics.

36 A. Blankenagel, "Towards Constitutionalism in Russia" (Summer, 1992) *East European Constitutional Review* 25, p. 26.

37 H. Hausmaniger, "From the Soviet Committee of Constitutional Supervision to the Russian Constitutional Court" *loc. cit.*, *supra*, n. 12.

38 B. N. Topornin, 1992 *Konstitutsionnniy kontrol: idei i problemi realizatsii (Constitutional control: ideas and problems of realisation)* in *Konstitutsionniy stroi Rossii (The Constitutional System of Russia)* Moscow, 1992; Y.L. Shulzhenko; *Konstitutsionniy sud Rossii (The Russian Constitutional Court)* in *Konstitutsionniy stroi Rossii (The Constitutional System of Russia)*, Moscow, 1992.

39 Y. L. Shulzhenko, *Konstitutsionnii Kontrol v Rossii*, *supra*, n. 5.

The Russian Constitutional Court: First Incarnation

The dissolution of the USSR gave birth to Russia as an independent state. By a law of 25 December 1991,[40] it changed its name to Russian Federation (Russia). However, legislative basis for the Constitutional Court predated these events. On 12 July 1991 Boris Yeltsin, who was elected President of the Russian Socialist Federation of Soviet Republics (RSFSR) on 12 June 1991, signed the *Law of the RSFSR on the Constitutional Court of the RSFSR*. However, the election of judges (there were to be 15, elected by the Congress of Peoples Deputies on the recommendation of the President)[41] did not take place until 29 October 1991, while the CCS was still in existence.

It should not be forgotten that the Russian Constitutional Court has not been the only Constitutional Court in the Russian Federation.[42] From 1991 to 1993 a number of such courts were established, in Dagestan in 1991,[43] in Tatarstan in 1992,[44] and in the autumn of 1993 in Bashkortotstan, Kabardino-Balkarii, the Mordovian SSR, and the Republic of Sakha Yakutiya.[45]

The 13 elected judges met for the first time on 26 December 1991, just a few days after the dissolution of the CCS, and stressed, in a public statement, that they intended to defend the constitutional system and oppose any threat of dictatorship from any source.[46] They continued their work, in the context of increasing constitutional turmoil, until 7 October 1993, when President Yeltsin signed the notorious Decree No.1612,[47] in which he accused the Court of flagrant violations of its duties and suspended its decision-making powers until the adoption of a new Constitution.[48]

40 VSNDVS RF 1992 No.12 Art 62.

41 As provided in Article 165 of the 1978 RSFSR Constitution. These appointments were made by the Decree "On the Appointment of RSFSR Constitutional Court Judges", VSND RSFSR, 1991, No.44, Art.1450.

42 See N. A. Mikhaleva, "Constitutional Reforms in the Republics of the Russian Federation" (1996) *Russian Politics and Law* 66.

43 *Law on the Constitutional Court of the DSSR*, Dagestan Pravda 23 January 1992.

44 *Law on the Constitutional Court of the Republic of Tatarstan*, Izvestiya Tatarstan, 23 January 1993.

45 Shulzhenko, *Konstitutsionnii Kontrol v Rossii*, *supra*, n. 5, p. 111.

46 Constitutional Court Press Service, *Sovetskaya Rossiya* 27 December 1991.

47 Presidential Decree No.1612 *On the Constitutional Court of the Russian Federation*, *Rossiskaya Gazeta* 9 October 1993.

48 See M. Lien, "Red Star Trek: Seeking a Role for Constitutional Law in Soviet Disunion" (1994) 30 *Stanford Journal of International Law* 41.

Most commentators are inclined to lay most or all responsibility for the Court's demise with the Judges themselves, particularly with their activist Chairman, Valerii Zorkin.[49] It is often forgotten that Zorkin played an extraordinary role for a period.[50] At the height of his perceived importance, the March 1993 issue of the journal *Stolitsa* pictured Zorkin on its front cover, a laurel wreath over his head, and the headline "Triumph of the Peacemaker?". This followed Zorkin's role in mediating between legislature and executive at the VII Congress of Peoples Deputies, the "Zorkin Arbitration" of 9-10 December 1992. The article by Mikhail Sokolov was entitled "Timeo Romanos et Dona Ferentes", a reference to the prize of $5,000 which Zorkin received from the "Rome Movement" (the Committee for National Accord). Sokolov commented that even Zorkin's supporters agreed that the game begun by the Chairman of the Court was complex and dangerous, that he had thrown caution to the winds, and that the Court's legitimacy, already in doubt, could be destroyed.[51]

Herbert Hausmaniger considers that "excessive political involvement outside the Court's core function of judicial review ... did not add to the Court's legal authority and prestige".[52] He suggests that, perhaps, a more constructive effort on the part of the Court would have helped to avoid Yeltsin's action in dissolving Parliament.[53] Elspeth Reid, similarly, concludes that "in its increasing involvement in political controversy, the Court, and most conspicuously its Chairman, made choices which gradually allied it with one side in the constitutional conflict".[54] She notes the warnings by Russian academics,[55] describing constitutional justice as

49 Judge Zorkin was born in 1943, graduated from Moscow State University in 1964, and taught jurisprudence there until 1980. He then became Professor in the Department of Constitutional Law and Theory of the State at the Academy of the Interior Ministry of the USSR.

50 Robert Sharlet, "Chief Justice as Judicial Politician" (Spring 1993) *East European Constitutional Review* 32.

51 M. Sokolov, "Timeo Romanos et Dona Ferentes" (1993) *Stolitsa* No.3, 9.

52 H. Hausmaniger, "Towards a 'New' Russian Constitutional Court" (1995) 28 *Cornell International Law Journal* 349 p. 363.

53 Hausmaniger says that while in Moscow in April 1993, he asked judges and scholars whether they thought that the Court had been prematurely established in an underdeveloped Russian political system. The question was not understood! *Ibid*., p. 365.

54 Elspeth Reid, "The Russian Federation Constitutional Court, October 1991 - October 1993" (1995) 32 *Coexistence* 277,.p. 297.

55 G. Gadzhiev and V. Kryazhkov, "Konstitutsionnaya yustitsiya v Rossiiskoi Federatsii: stanovlenie i problemi" (Constitutional Justice in the Russian Federation: status and problems) (1993) *Gosudarstvo i Pravo* 3, p. 4.

transforming itself into "a weapon in the hands of ambitious politicians, and as "an instrument to destroy Russia's constitutional order".

Shulzhenko comments that particularly in 1993 the Court began to display negative tendencies. In conditions of bitter struggle between the legislative and executive branches, the Court "was to a greater and greater extent drawn into political conflict". This was made possible "in many respects by the active political work of the Chairman of the Court and a number of its members, by their participation in political actions, all of which constituted a grave breach of the demands of the *Law on the Constitutional Court*".[56] He points to "one-sided political decisions", especially that of their *zaklyucheniye* of 21 September 1993 on President Yeltsin's Decree No.1400 *On Phased (Step by Step) Constitutional Reform in the Russian Federation*, and his "Appeal to the Citizens of Russia" of the same date, which they said served as grounds for his impeachment. Shulzhenko concludes that: "In the event, the Constitutional Court played a negative role, and aided and abetted the tragic development of events at the beginning of October 1993."[57]

Are these criticisms justified, or did the Court in fact play an important role in deepening and preserving constitutionalism in Russia? One answer is to be found in the fact that the Court was not abolished in October 1993, and that Judge Zorkin and his colleagues remain judges of the Court to this day. President Yeltsin could no doubt have consigned the Court to the same fate as the Congress of People's Deputies, the Supreme Soviet, and the 1978 Russian Soviet Federal Socialist Republic [RSFSR] Constitution. That is, the Court must have acquired some substantial legitimacy.

I will turn shortly to the most controversial of the Court's cases, the "Trial of the CPSU". But it is worth noting that, despite labouring under a poorly drafted law,[58] requiring, for example, the taking of decisions in plenary meetings, deciding all cases after oral public hearings, and abstention from dealing with other cases as long as an ongoing case continued, the Court was quite productive. It adopted more than 30 acts, including 24 judgments (*postanovleniya*).

It started controversially, when a group of deputies challenged President Yeltsin's Decree creating a new super-ministry combining the Ministry of

56 Y. L. Shulzhenko, *Konstitutsionnii Kontrol v Rossii*, *op. cit.*, *supra*, n. 5, p. 127.

57 *Ibid.*, p. 128.

58 *Law on the Constitutional Court of the RSFSR* VSND RSFSR, No.30, Art 1017, enacted on 6 May 1991. This created, for example, five nonjudicial functions to the Court: the finding (*zaklyucheniye*, Art 74), the representation (*predstavleniye*, Art 55), participation in sessions of other organs of state (Art.26), the legislative initiative (Art.9), and the message (*poslaniye*, Art.54), as well as requiring annual reports to the legislature.

the Interior and the security services. On 14 January 1992 the Court held unanimously, on the basis of the separation of powers, since only the legislature could establish ministries, that the Decree violated the Constitution.[59] On 17 January Yeltsin rescinded his Decree, but the official *Rossiskaya Gazeta*, which was obliged to publish the Court's decision, did so in such a way as to suggest that the Decree remained in force. On 4 February 1992 the Court rebuked and fined the newspaper.[60]

Later cases included judicial review of a number of normative acts, for example by the Supreme Soviet on copyright,[61] by the Congress on freedom of speech,[62] three decisions by the Republic of Tatarstan in adopting its constitution, and on a referendum on its state status,[63] by the Republic of Mordova in adopting its constitution and by the Russian President in implementing central authority in Mordova. In six important cases the Court defended the rights of ordinary citizens, for example the case on dismissal by reason of attaining pensionable age, where the Court applied international instruments including the *International Covenant on Economic, Social and Cultural Rights* and ILO Conventions in order to find the existing Labour Code unconstitutional,[64] as well as other employment cases and cases on housing rights. Indeed, Judge Ernest Ametistov has pointed out that some half of the cases considered by the Court during that period concerned individual applications by citizens complaining of violation of their social (labour, housing, etc) rights. In almost every case the individual won.[65] As Shulzhenko points out,[66] these cases concerned the most burning issues of the time, including the separation of powers, the distribution of competence between the Federation and its subjects, the rights of those subjects, the operation of wholly new mechanisms such as referenda, the status of political parties and social organisations, privatisation, and the right to work. The sessions

59 VSND RSFSR, 1992, No.6 Art 247.
60 VSND RSFSR, 1992, No.13 Art 670.
61 VSND RSFSR, 1992, No.21, Art 1141.
62 VSND RSFSR, 1993, No.30, Art 1182.
63 VSND RSFSR, 1992, No.13 Art 671.
64 VSND RSFSR, 1992, No.13, Art 669.
65 E. Ametistov, "Zashita Sotsialnix Prav Cheloveka v Konstitutsionnom Sude Rossiskoi Federatsii: Pervi Itogi i Dalneishie Perspektivi" (The Defence of Social Human Rights by the Constitutional Court of the Russian Federation: First Conclusions and Further Perspectives" (1995) *Vestnik Konstitutsionnovo Suda RF (Bulletin of the Constitutional Court of the RF)* 13.
66 Y. L. Shulzhenko, *Konstitutsionnii Kontrol v Rossii, op. cit., supra,* n. 5, p. 123.

of the Constitutional Court "became the place of the struggle of different political forces".

However, the most notorious case, and one which blocked the Court's activity for more than six months, from 25 May to 30 November 1992, was the Case of the Communist Party. The judges themselves have continued to argue about the case, which concerned three Decrees of President Yeltsin in August and November 1991, after the "putsch", ordering the cessation of all USSR and Russian CP activity, and the transfer of all Party property to state ownership.[67] A group of Communist deputies sought review of these Decrees, while a counter-petition by supporters of Yeltsin sought a declaration as to the constitutionality of the CPs, on the grounds that their activities had provoked national and ethnic conflicts, and that it was an instrument of coercion by an authoritarian state. The Law on the Constitutional Court did not provide for such a jurisdiction, and this was supplied by a new article 165-1 of the Constitution, adopted in April 1992. As Yuri Feofanov puts it,[68] Russian society expected two mutually contradictory things from the Court. First, a Nuremburg trial, in which de-communization, like de-Nazification, could take place,[69] and second an affirmation of the principles of democracy and law. Despite the fact that the Court heard 46 witnesses and 16 experts in the course of 52 sessions, and the crimes of the CP were abundantly corroborated, the resulting decision was a compromise. The President was entitled to ban the CP's central structures, but not its local organisation. Similarly, he was entitled to seize such party property as had actually belonged to the state; but in all other cases the Constitutional Court had no jurisdiction, and the ordinary courts must decide. The case brought by his supporters failed, on the grounds that the CPSU had ceased to exist altogether, while the statute of the RSFSR CP had not been registered, so that the party vanished without being legitimised within the meaning of the new Article of the Constitution.[70]

67 "On the cessation of the activities of the CP of the RSFSR", "On the property of the CPSU and the CP of the RSFSR", and "On the activities of the CPSU and the CP of the RSFSR", VSND RSFSR, 1991, No.35 Arts 1149 and 1164, and No.45 Art 1537.

68 Y.Feofanov, "The Establishment of the Constitutional Court in Russia and the Communist Party Case" (1993) 19 *Review of Central and Eastern European Law* 623; see also Robert Sharlet, "The Russian Constitutional Court: The First Term" (1993) *Post-Soviet Affairs*, 1.

69 D. Barry, "The Trial of the CPSU and the Principles of Nuremburg" (1996) 22 *Review of Central and Eastern European Law* 255.

70 Y. Feofanov, *loc. cit.*, *supra*, p. 637.

Two judges dissented, Luchin and Ebzeyev, both of whom have since published books.[71] Judge Luchin's dissent, prefiguring his consistent position since then, argued that the Court's decision was based only on political expediency. The President had, he argued, no power to dissolve political organisations by decree, only the Courts could do this. Moreover, Art. 50 of the 1978 Constitution guaranteed freedom of association. The President only enjoyed such powers in conditions of a state of emergency, and had no right to interfere in questions of the ownership of property.

The issue has not disappeared. On 8 August 1996 Judge Ernest Ametistov wrote an article in *Izvestiya* in which he called for steps to be taken to "counter the unconstitutional and unlawful activities of the CPRF". He asserted that it was not a "civilised opposition", because it "grossly violates" the 1992 decision.[72] Indeed, immediately prior to the presidential elections on 6 July 1996, Judge Ametistov went public with a very similar position, together with Judge Tamara Morshchakova, the Court's Vice-Chairman.

This could, therefore, hardly have been a more political case, or political resolution of it. In these circumstances it is laughable that Article 1.3 of the 1991 Law on the Constitutional Court provided that "the Constitutional Court does not examine political questions". As Ovsepian points out, "a correct idea was expressed in an absurd phrase, a phrase that patently contradicted the powers granted to the Court and was, in the end, no more than high-sounding words". This is so precisely because "it would be disingenuous to deny that there is a political element inherent in the organisation and functioning of constitutional judicial review, especially as this is intended to safeguard the Constitution, which is not only a juridical but a politico-legal document".[73] Donald Barry notes that "if the nature of the case was basically politically political rather than legal, it would be extremely difficult for a court to render a decision that was well-grounded in law. Given what it had to work with, it is not surprising that the Court's ruling was seen by commentators from all sides as basically political."[74]

71 V. Luchin, "Chechenskii Vopros: Konstitutsionniy Aspekt" (Chechen Question: Constitutional Aspect) (1995) 10 *Dialog* 19; B. Ebzeyev, *Konstitutsiya, Pravovoye Gosudarstvo, Konstitutsionniy Sud (Constitution, Rule of Law State, Constitutional Court)* Moscow, "Zakon i Pravo", 1997.

72 Constitution Watch, (Fall 1996) *East European Constitutional Review* p.23.

73 Zh. I. Ovsepian, "Constitutional Judicial Review in the Russian Federation. Problems of Depoliticization (A Comparative Analysis)" (1996) *Russian Politics and Law* 46, pp. 51,57.

74 D. Barry, *supra*, n. 69, p. 259.

Blakenagel has now provided the most exhaustive analysis of the activities of the Constitutional Court Mark 1.[75] He concludes that the Court "could not live happily in Russia", not only because of its political activities - and how could it have stayed out of politics? - but also because of its unwillingness to compromise or to apply realism in its conviction that the Constitution must be upheld at all costs. But some of the judges remain unrepentant. For example, Boris Ebzeyev insists that it would be nonsense for the judges to consider a Constitution non-constitutional as a whole.[76] And not only was Yeltsin's action a constitutional coup d'etat; in ruling his actions unconstitutional, the Court was seeking to vindicate the principle that "it is not the state that does a favour to the citizens, but the citizens who delegate power to the state".

The Interregnum

President Yeltsin did not abolish the Court; indeed, the same Decree No.1612 charged the judges with preparing proposals for submission to the future parliament concerning "forms of implementing constitutional justice in the Russian Federation".[77] The judges responded to this request, and also exercised their right of legislative initiative, pursuant to Article 104.1 of the new Constitution. The new law[78] was adopted on 24 June 1994, and came into force on 23 July 1994.[79] However, the President found it very hard to win Federation Council support for his candidates for the additional 6 judges required for the "second" Constitutional Court of 19 members.

It was not until 9 February 1995 that the 19th judge, Marat Baglai, was approved[80] (on 20 February 1997 he was elected the new Chairman of the Court, winning 11 votes from the 19 judges).[81] Russia was therefore lacking a Constitutional Court at the start of the conflict in Chechnya in

75 A. Blankenagel, *"Detstvo, Otrochestvo, Yunost" Rossiskovo Konstitutsionnovo Suda ("The Childhood, Adolescence and Youth" of the Russian Constitutional Court* Moscow, 1996.

76 L. Nikitinsky, "Interview with Boris Ebzeyev, Justice of the Constitutional Court of the Russian Federation" (Winter 1997) *East European Constitutional Review* 83.

77 A. Blankenagel, "The Court Writes its Own Law" (Summer, 1994) *East European Constitutional Review*.

78 Sergei Pashin, author of the first Law of the Constitutional Court, has commented on the new version: "A Second Edition of the Constitutional Court" (Summer/Fall 1994) *East European Constitutional Review* pp.82-85.

79 On the date of its publication in *Rossiskaya Gazeta*.

80 Constitution Watch, Spring 1995 *East European Constitution Review* p.24.

81 *Sevodnya* 21 February 1997.

late 1994, or at the time of President Yeltsin's notorious Decree on Combatting Organised Crime, adopted in June 1994,[82] which gave the police the right to hold suspects without charge for up to 30 days, as well as abolishing banking and commercial confidentiality, and permitting prosecutors to introduce a much wider range of evidence, in violation of the UN's ICCPR and many other human rights instruments. This has been described as "justice delayed".[83]

In addition to drafting its new Law, the Court did engage in some high-profile activity. On 1 December 1993 some 6 of 8 judges only of the possible 13 (Judges Vedernikov and Seleznev were on business trips, Judge Rudkin was in hospital, and Judges Zorkin and Luchin were not present) voted to suspend the powers of Judges Zorkin and Luchin.[84] Judge Ebzeyev has recently published his dissenting opinion, attached to the Protocol of the decision. The decision was based on Article 14.3 of the old Law of the Court, prohibiting judges from being members of or participating in political parties or movements, and Article 18.3, excluding judges with occupations not compatible with their duties. Judge Zorkin was charged with "participation in political movements" and Judge Luchin with participating, as a candidate for the Agrarian Party, in the elections for the State Duma. However, by Article 27, such a decision required a quorum of two thirds of the list of judges. Not only was the decision inquorate, but the charges were never properly substantiated. Both judges were restored to their full powers, in the case of Judge Luchin after he went on hunger strike.

The Russian Constitutional Court: Second Incarnation

On 9 February 1995 the 19th judge was elected and, shortly afterwards, Judge Tumanov, former Rector of the Institute of State and Law was elected Chairman. The new Law of the Constitutional Court[85] contains a

82 Decree No. 1226 on Urgent Matters to Protect the Population from Banditry and Other Manifestations of Organised Crime, *Izvestiya* 15 June 1994. This has now been repealed, thanks largely to pressure from human rights activists, including Sergei Kovalyov.

83 Lawyers Committee for Human Rights, *Justice Delayed. The Russian Constitutional Court and Human Rights* (March 1995).

84 B. Ebzeyev, *supra*, n. 71, p. 140.

85 Federal Constitutional Law "On the Constitutional Court of the Russian Federation", enacted by the State Duma on 24 June 1994, and approved by the Federation Council on 12 July 1994.

number of provisions aimed at "depoliticisation". Article 3 states that the Court "decides exclusively questions of law" (an improvement on the old law, above - this means that the Court decides political questions, but only on the basis of law), and also that it "abstains from establishing and examining the factual circumstances in all cases where this lies within the jurisdiction of other courts or bodies". Moreover, the Court is now prevented from taking the initiative in impeachment proceedings; and whereas a single deputy had standing to apply to the Court, one fifth of the total membership of either house are required to present a constitutional question.

Does this mean that the Court has risen above politics? Within a few months, this was shown not to be the case. On 31 July 1995 the Court delivered its decision on the constitutionality of four presidential Decrees on the conflict in Chechnya,[86] these decrees having been challenged by a group of deputies of the State Duma and the Federation Council. The hearing, which began on 10 July, was extraordinarily bitter. The former Human Rights Ombudsman, Sergei Kovalyov, compounded his unpopularity with all sides when, on 13 July 1995, he appeared as a witness, called by the Communist deputy Anatoliy Lukyanov (former Gorbachev associate, speaker of the Supreme Soviet, and prisoner for a year following the August 1991 *Putsch*), in the Constitutional Court.[87] He argued that the Decrees had led to thousands of deaths and clear violations of human rights, and that this violated Article 15(4) of the Constitution, which provides that: "Generally recognised principles and norms of international law... are a constituent part of [Russia's] legal system." The Court decided, by a majority of 11 out of 19, that the President's decrees on suppression of Chechen resistance were lawful. As if to confirm Kovalyov's worst fears, the Chairman of the Court, Vladimir Tumanov, explained on 1 August 1995 that the real basis for the decision was the *raison d'etat* doctrine that the President has the right to do anything he desires, with no legal limitations, and no accountability to the legislature,

86 These were (1) the Decree of 2 November 1993 on the Military Doctrine of the RF; (2) the Decree of 30 November 1994 on Measures to Restore Constitutional Legality and Law and Order in Chechnya; (3) the Decree of 9 December 1994 on Measures to Stop the Activities of Illegal Armed Formations in Chechnya; and (4) the Government Resolution of 9 December 1994 on Ensuring State Security and Territorial Integrity of the Russian Federation.

87 Laura Belin, OMRI Inc, 22 July 1995.

where he unilaterally determines that the "integrity" of the country is in danger.[88]

The applicants argued that two of the decrees, concerned with the deployment of troops, had violated international treaties to which Russia was a party, as well as Article 15.4 of the 1993 Constitution (see above), according to which both customary and treaty international law are part of the Russian legal system. The Court found that two provisions were unconstitutional: a provision on expulsion from Chechnya, because it violated the human right to freedom of movement; and a provision on restrictions of journalists, because it violated the human right to freedom of expression. In other respects, the President was found to have been acting within his powers, or the courts refrained from exercising judgment. A number of judges, including Judge Luchin, delivered dissenting judgments. Judge Luchin analysed in detail why the deployment of armed forces had no constitutional basis and had led to grave human rights violations.[89]

Despite the controversy, however, it has been argued that the Court should be commended for its strongly internationalist approach, giving pride of place to international law, and, for example, expressly directing the Russian parliament to implement Protocol II to the Geneva Conventions, and stressing that according to the Russian Constitution and to the ICCPR, victims of any violations, crimes or abuses of power should be granted effective remedies and compensation.[90]

The Court, which now acts in two Chambers, has maintained a steady caseload. Recent cases include a decision on 4 April 1996 on the constitutionality of the system of registration in a number of cities; a review on 17 December 1996 of the constitutionality of the 1993 Federal Law on the activities of the tax police;[91] the resolution on 24 December 1996 of a reference from the Russian Supreme Court on a question concerning the Moscow Oblast Duma;[92] the review on 24 January 1997 of a law of the Udmurt Republic;[93] the resolution on 28 January 1997 of a complaint by citizens concerning the Criminal Procedural Code;[94] and a

88 "Constitution Watch: Russia" (1995) 4 *East European Constitutional Review* No.3, p.24.
89 V. Luchin, "Chechenskii Vopros: Konstitutsionniy Aspekt", *loc.cit.*, *supra*, n. 71.
90 P. Gaeta, "The Armed Conflict in Chechnya before the Russian Constitutional Court" (1996) 7 *European Journal of International Law* 563.
91 VSND RF, 1997, No.1, Art 197.
92 VSND RF, 1997, No.2 Art 348.
93 VSND RF, 1997, No.5 Art 708.
94 VSND RF, 1997, No.7 Art 871.

review on 18 February 1997 of the Russian Government's decision on licensing of alcohol.[95]

However, a larger storm is brewing. I have already referred to Judge Luchin's recent book on rule by decree. This was prompted in part by Judge Luchin's dissent in the case, decided in May 1996,[96] on the constitutionality of President Yeltsin's Decree No.1696 of 3 October 1994 "On Measures for Strengthening the Unitary System of Executive Power in the Russian Federation". Judge Luchin points to the extraordinary and unprecedented rise of rule by decree, particularly in the working out of privatisation. This is confirmed by Antti Korkeakivi, who refers to Article 90 of the Constitution, which entitles the President to "issue decrees and directives".[97] During 1994-5, Luchin points out, the President issued 497 normative Decrees, 130 (26%) of which concerned organisational questions, resulting in the "hypertrophic" growth of bureaucracy. Some 176 of these Decrees (36%) concerned questions of economics, social development and culture. According to Luchin, 79 (16%) of these decrees concern the rights of the citizen, and, particularly in the case of the Chechnya decrees, violate them. I have already referred to Decree No:1126 on the Fight Against Organised Crime.

Publication of this book has caused a major storm. Shortly after his election as Chairman of the Court, Marat Baglai held a press-conference at which he said he would clean up the Court. Luchin's book not only calls into question the legitimacy of the decrees themselves, but also the legitimacy of the present Constitution, in view of the very wide powers given to the President. On 25 February 1997 Judge Baglai, who is known to be one of the strongest opponents of judicial outspokenness, told reporters that the judges were studying Judge Luchin's book, and would then decide what to do.[98] In order to suspend or remove Judge Luchin, two thirds of the judges, that is 13 of them, would have to find, pursuant to Article 18 of the Law on the Constitutional Court, that he is guilty, notwithstanding a warning, of continued occupation or activity incompatible with his duties.

95 VSND RF, 1997, No.8, Art 1010.

96 *Rossiskaya Gazeta* 15 May 1996.

97 A. Korkeakivi, "Russia on the Rights Track: Human Rights in the New Constitution" (1994) 1 *Parker School Journal of East European Law*.

98 Maksim Zhukov "Knostitutsionnomu sudye he nravitsya konstitutsiya" (A constitutional judge does not like the Constitution) *Kommersant Daily* 26 February 1997.

Conclusion

Finer, Bogdanor and Rudden note that in terms of textual appearances, the basic powers of the Russian Constitutional Court are not dissimilar to those of the German court. "In terms of political reality, however, it is difficult to see how, after its humiliation by Mikhail Gorbachev's refusal to obey and injunction to appear, and its unconstitutional but effective suspension by Boris Yeltsin, it can readily gain respect."[99] There is no question but that the Court is now working in many respects "normally". However, the really hard problems of presidential power, authoritarianism, and relations between the centre and the regions, are still only on the horizon. The Court will once more be called upon to decide difficult political issues, and will earn its legitimacy by the way it does this. No one doubts the intellectual distinction of the judges. It is to be hoped that they do not suffer the fate of their colleagues in Belarus.

99 Finer et al., *op. cit.*, *supra*, n.8 p. 31.